The Salt Companion to
Mag

THE UNIVERSITY OF
WINCHESTER

The Salt Companion to Maggie O'Sullivan

Salt Publishing

SALT

<small>CAMBRIDGE</small>

PUBLISHED BY SALT PUBLISHING
14a High Street, Fulbourn, Cambridge CB21 5DH United Kingdom

Salt Publishing 2011

Printed and bound in the United Kingdom by Lightning Source, UK

Typeset in Swift 10/12

ISBN 978 1 87685 773 8 paperback

1 3 5 7 9 8 6 4 2

Contents

Introduction

Ken Edwards

I am a veteran of poetry readings – attending them, and, less frequently, giving them or introducing them – but that doesn't mean I always enjoy them that much. They have a social usefulness, of course. At their best they also serve to contextualise the work of a poet I have admired or seek to admire: providing auditory clues as to how to read their work, how it's intended to be paced, what surrounds it in terms of the quality of the aesthetic space or the social context. Then I can go back to reading it on the page.

More rarely, a reading offers direct, visceral pleasure in the sound of language shaped, much as I get from music; and this has more than once been the case for me when listening to Maggie O'Sullivan perform her poetry. I recall, for instance, leaning back on one of those uncomfortable plastic chairs in one of a succession of (usually dreary) London pub rooms that hosted the SubVoicive reading series during the 1980s, listening to Maggie and thinking at one point when I was coming out of a reverie of attention, "Ah, *this* is what poetry is."

No, it doesn't happen very often.

Now, please don't get me wrong. A reader unacquainted with Maggie O'Sullivan's poetry but glancing at a book title or two – *In the House of the Shaman*, for instance – might be led to assume that her performances are affairs of swooping, vatic utterance, overwhelming the audience with mystical power. Nothing could be further from the truth. Her performance style is measured, exact, you might even say controlled. She rarely if ever hesitates or stutters, but there is no rush. She lets the language do the work; the power is already in there. As I wrote on a previous occasion: "In the house of Maggie O'Sullivan the marks on the page and the vibrations of the vocal folds combine into a harmonious whole . . . . Her poetry describes and enacts the multitudinous torrent of the human, animal, vegetable and inanimate worlds, but always from within a still centre of attention and calm."

The scholars assembled for this volume have identified many of the influences on Maggie's work, including the poetries of such as Barry MacSweeney, Basil Bunting and Susan Howe, and the methodologies of Joseph Beuys. But it is worth emphasising that the work was first formed in the context of the poetic experimentation that was going on in London from the 1970s onward, and in particular sound-text writing and performance under the tutelage of Bob Cobbing. Sound *and* text, inextricably bound up together, neither predominating, neither complete on its own.

Cobbing was, of course, a giant as a poet and as an influence. If my memory serves me, I first met Maggie in around 1978 when she attended a day-long workshop given by him as part of a series of Saturday courses I had a hand in organising at Lower Green Farm, Orpington, just outside London. Cobbing did not theorise; he taught by example. I always struggled with the relationship of the visual and the aural in his work: how precisely those abstract patternings functioned as visual scores for aural performance remains something of a dark matter to me. I found no such difficulty in Maggie's work as it developed (the little of her poetry that was published at that time had been much more straightforwardly semantic) – perhaps because she was not and is not actually a sound poet. Nor is she a concrete poet in the classic sense. Rather, she is a lyrical poet with a painter's sensibility. (She is a visual artist too.) Her texts *look* amazing on the page; and they take on new life when spoken.

The few publishing opportunities for out-there poetries at this time meant that many of us poets had to become publishers too, and Bob Cobbing, with his pioneering do-it-yourself Writers Forum press showed us how to do it. The advantage lay in being able to make books that were visually imaginative, doing justice to the materality of the poems. Maggie joined in, making some rather beautiful little books in modest editions under the Magenta imprint over a number of years while she was living in London and in proximity to the entry-level printing facilities at Cobbing's home – this activity only ceasing with her move away from the capital to rural Yorkshire.

When I got around to publishing her in 1984, it was visual work (an extract from *point.blank.range*, in *Reality Studios* 6). When Reality Studios merged with Wendy Mulford's Street Editions to form Reality Street in 1993, Maggie's *In the House of the Shaman* was the second book we published. And for the 2006 re-publication in one volume of nine out-of-print 1980s books, under the title of *Body of Work*, there was only one practical solution to the problem of presentation, which was to scan each of the original pages; the *look* of those pages was so crucial that re-setting was not an option.

That Maggie, along with Geraldine Monk, was one of the few women working in a very male-dominated avant-garde was not something that was particularly remarked on in those early years. That's how it was. However, by the early 1990s things were changing, perhaps more so in the USA than the UK, where the dominance of Language writing among the literary avant-gardes had brought with it greater participation by women poets. The idea of an anthology to explore this new phenomenon had a number of independent gestation points, but when the time came to launch this project it was natural for Reality Street to turn to Maggie to be the editor. As an outstanding practitioner who also had an unrivalled knowledge of advanced work being done by women poets on both sides of the Atlantic, she was ideally placed.

The title, *Out of Everywhere*, was her idea, taken from a remark by an unidentified audience member at a public discussion with Rosmarie Waldrop (transcribed and published in *The Politics of Poetic Form*, Roof Books, 1990). The gist of it was that women doing non-normative poetry were doubly excluded: as avant-gardeists, from the mainstream poetry scene, of course; but also from normative "women's writing" contexts, the burgeoning women's canons of the day. This empathy with marginalisation is something that burns brightly in Maggie O'Sullivan's universe, and is not confined to gender issues. This theme is further pursued in some of the contributions to this volume, for instance in Mandy Bloomfield's and Nicky Marsh's essays.

Out of Everywhere bears the clear imprint of Maggie's sensibility. Following her introductory remarks, where she cites the pioneering work of Gertrude Stein, Mina Loy, HD and Lorine Niedecker, she opens the anthology with a series of visually challenging and impressive text-art works by Susan Howe, Joan Retallack, Tina Darragh, Paula Claire and Diane Ward. As a publisher and writer, I am grateful to Maggie for the educative value of her anthology. One highlight for me was her selection of a number of Canadian poets previously unknown to me. It is safe to say that were it not for this I would probably not have got around to publishing Lisa Robertson subsequently. Overall, the quality of her selection in 1996 is evidenced by the anthology's still being in use as a textbook today.

Voicings and voicelessness, metaphysics (whose complexities Romana Huk explores here), hidden histories, paradox and contradiction, linguistic pleasure, neologisms and nonce-words (check out Peter Middleton), materiality, breath, animal and human consciousness, colour, page design, Dickinsonian punctuation and the politics of form – there is great richness to be found in Maggie O'Sullivan's poetry. For those as yet unacquainted with or new to it, the essays in this present volume form an excellent introduction to it and to its underlying themes. They are, of course, no substitute for the texts themselves or, if you are able to hear her live, the poet's own vocalisations of them (there are online recordings and CDs available); but in their various approaches they begin to do justice to this rather extraordinary and complex poet.

Colliderings: O'Sullivan's Medleyed Verse

Charles Bernstein

Every poem was once a word.

If culture were an accident, then the job of the poet might be to write the report rather than rectify the wrong. If culture were the product of a supreme fiction, then the poet's job might be to find the authors and clue them into things – not as they are but as they appear.

Maggie O'Sullivan begins one of her readings by invoking an "unofficial" word (also the title of one of her books). In this sense, and perhaps paradoxically, O'Sullivan is in a main line of British poets, a line that swerves, with clinamacaronic speed, from Blake to Swinburne, MacDiarmid to Raworth, Carroll to Bergvall, Cowper to Loy, Kwesi Johnson to Bunting, Rossetti to Fisher. In their own way, each of these is an anti-representative poet: one who takes the office of poetry as the creation of spaces between sanctions; outside, that is, received categories.

You can't make a poem unless you are willing to break some verses.

In Roots of Lyric: Primitive Poetry and Modern Poetics, Andrew Welsh makes the distinction between "song melos" (with its externally derived regular meter) and "charm melos" (whose more chaotic sound patterns emerge internally). O'Sullivan's poetry is unmistakably *charm*. In "riverrunning (realizations" (in *Palace of Reptiles*), she put it this way: "A Song Said Otherwise, half sung / half said SINGS"; where "Otherwise" is also a music that is "Edgewise" [*Palace*, p. 59], wise to edges and others and also edgy; othering and auditing rather than authoring.

To half-sing a song is to stutter into poetry and back to music, your back to the music, part incantation, part pleat. "Stammering before speech," O'Sullivan writes in "riverrunning (realizations" [*Palace*, p. 60]: not just *prior to* but *in the face of*. The beat is off mark so as to be on tangent. A stone thrown into a pond (pound, pun) produces rings of concentric circles around the point of entry. The charm is to create a rhythm in the counter-current, via the interference (the event): *the shortest distance between two waves is a sign*. This is what O'Sullivan calls "colliderings" [*Palace*, p. 63].

Compared to the magnificent hieratic credo of Bunting, "Take a chisel to write," O'Sullivan sounds our poetic a-anthem of the *Unofficial Word*:

> BEAT,
> > BELLOW
> > > me Cloth /
> > > > Shakings of chisel/
> > > > > Chounded all pitches – [*Body of Work*, p. 304]

The shaking chisel (trembling, warbling, stuttering, faltering) marks a radical shift not just of aesthetic but ethic. The legitimate aspirations of pitch, not our tent, but our voicings. *Chounded*: a collidering of hounded, bounded, & founded with chow, with chew, what we eat in our mouths, the visceral words of the unofficial world we make by inhabiting.

O'Sullivan, in a 1997 interview, puts it this way: ". . . my work is driven by the spoken, sounded or breathing voice. Particularly I have always been haunted by issues of VOICELESSNESS—inarticulacy—silence—soundlessness—breathlessness—how are soundings or voices that are other-than or invisible or dimmed or marginalized or excluded or without privilege, or locked out, made Unofficial, reduced by ascendant systems of centrality and closure, configured or Sounded or given form & potency; how can I body forth or configure such sounds, such tongues, such languages, such muteness, such multivocality, such error—& this is perhaps why the non-vocal in mark & the non-word in sound or language—make up much of the fabrics & structures of my own compositions." [Brown, p. 90]

On October 27, 1993, O'Sullivan performed "To Our Own Day," from *Kinship with Animals* (Book II of *In the House of the Shaman*) at SUNY-Buffalo (audio file available at PennSound). O'Sullivan called the poem, "my favorite of all the pieces I have ever written." The poem takes O'Sullivan just over 40 seconds to read. I keep listening to it in a loop, dozens of times. Each listening brings something new, something unfamiliar; and the rational part of my ear has a hard time comprehending how this is possible, how such a short verbal utterance could be so acoustically saturated in performance. To be sure, this experience is produced by the performance of the poem and not (not so much) by the poem's text, where fixed comprehension (however illusory) comes sooner.

Each time I listen to "To Our Own Day," I recall best the beginning, the first several words. But once the poem gets underway, I listen anew, almost without recall, the combinations of unexpectable words create a sensation of newly created, permutating sense-making at each listening. I keep thinking I will "get it" (and be finished with it), but I hear different things, make different associations, each time I listen. This is the primary condition of "charm" in Welch's sense.

In the Buffalo performance, the tempo moves from a fairly quick speech tempo (some space after each word) to a more rapid song tempo (almost no space between the words) and then ends with the slightly slower speech tempo. The intonation (pitch) sounds consistent throughout: as a result there is no change in the inflection: each word is receiving a just measure of care. (I mean to relate this to "just intonation" in music, as well as to chant.)

The circular shift in tempo created a top-like effect, quickly gaining speed and slowing down slightly at the end. The words seems to trip on one another, gaining acceleration first through the echo of the accented vowel sounds and then, near the end, by a string of intense alliteration. The effect of word modulating into word is partly the result of the way O'Sullivan extends the vowels: it is as if a continuous stream of mutating vowels was punctuated by a counterflow of consonants; as if the consonants were rocks skimming in the water, surrounded by concentric circles of rippling vowel sounds.

O'Sullivan's words lead by ear. Hers is a propulsively rhythmic verse that refuses regular beat; an always morphing (morphogenic) exemplum of Henri Meschonnic's distinction between the ahistoricity of meter and embodiment of rhythm. But O'Sullivan's is less an embodied poetics than a visceral gesture ("pressed synaptic"): not an idea of the body made concrete but a seismographic incarnation of language as organ-response to the minute, shifting interactive sum of place as tectonic, temporality as temperament, self is as self does.

"Birth Palette" (*Palace of Reptiles*):
In the beginning was the enunciating; words are the residue of a hope.
So often O'Sullivan avers syntax for axial iteration, *word | ord | wo | rd | drow*, as if Adam grooved on applets and sugarcane, always on the eve of being able. Naming, here, is an avocation, kissing cousin of invocation and melody.
This is a poetry not of *me/me/me* but *it/it/it*.
Ecopoetics as echo-poetics.

"Knots, whorls, vortices" – O'Sullivan quotes this phrase from Tom Lowenstein's study of the Inuits [epigraph to "Doubtless" in *Palace of Reptiles*, p. 31]; this trinity is emblematic, not of O'Sullivan's forms but of her *stamp*. Which, in turn, suggests the connection between her project and the intimations of the archaic that infuse her poems: a cross-sectional boring through time, whirling the sedimentary layers into knots. The archaic material pushes up to the surface. Collage and pulverization are at the service of a rhythmic vortex.

O'Sullivan's engagement with Joyce, especially the late work, is both intimate (in-the-sounding) and explicit (in-the-naming). If Joyce's words are like refracting, crystalline black holes, O'Sullivan's are trampolines.

"Plover bodying": in flight; "irre-reversible 'almostness' ": no more irritable striving after permanence (irreversibility), the inevitability of the not-quite, the *now* in *neither*. "MAPPING OF LONGINGS | we never arrive at": *Almost* is itself subject to reverse – there, *not there*; here, *not here*. The inebriation of *fort/da*, the stadium of the "hap-hazard UNCLENCHINGS": Fort DaDa.

There is no rhythm without song and yet song codes the acoustic surfeit that is O'Sullivan's ore. "Iridesce!"

O'Sullivan's visceral vernacular ("carnal thickness"): autochthonous verse, tilling the inter-indigenous brainscape of the Celtic | Northumbrian | Welsh | Gaelic | Scots | Irish | Anglo | Saxon transloco-voco-titillated strabismus. It's not that O'Sullivan writes directly "in" any one of the languages "of these Isles," but that they form a foundational "force field" *out of* which her own distinctive language emerges, as figure set against its grounding.

Native to the soiled, aberrant ("errmost"), aboriginality.
"At this point, *they* merge & ARE."
[*Un-Assuming Personas, Body of Work*, p. 61]

Dialogic extravagance in the articulated, dithrombotic, honeycomb pluriperversity.

"TO BEGIN A JOURNEY, / enunciate."

You say utterance, I say wigged-in, undulating, wanton specificity. Utter defiance as language-particle pattern recognition system. Defiance as deference to the utterly present, actual, indigestible, sputtering imagination of the real as punctuated rivulets of fragrant nothings in the dark dawn (stark spawn) of necessity's encroaching tears.

The medleyed consciousness of these sounds, these languages, is made palpable in O'Sullivan's poems, which lend themselves to recitation, while resisting thematization. Her words spend themselves in performance, turn to gesture, as sounds wound silhouettes and rhythms imbibe ("re-aspirate") incantation.

O'Sullivan cleaves to charm: striating song with the visceral magic of shorn insistence.

Works Cited by Maggie O'Sullivan

"*all origins are lonely*" (London: Veer Books, 2003)

In the House of the Shaman (London: Reality Street, 1993)

"Interview" in Andy Brown, ed., *Binary Myths 2* (Exeter, UK: Stride, 2004)

Palace of Reptiles (Willowdale, Ontario: The Gig, 2003)

Unofficial Word, which is collected in *Body of Work* (Hastings, East Sussex: Reality Street, 2006).

Notes

An earlier version of this essay was first published in *Ecopoetics* 4/5 (2004-2005). The essay was both expanded and excerpted as the introduction to *Body of Work*.

Otherwise uncredited quoted phrases are from "*all origins are lonely*": "pressed synaptic," "Plover bodying," "MAPPING OF LONGINGS / we never arrive at," "haphazard UNCLENCHINGS," "carnal thickness," "errmost," "TO BEGIN A JOURNEY, / enunciate."

In section 19, I quote two phrases of O'Sullivan ("of these Isles" and "force field") from a conversation we had in London in July 2004.

Maggie O'Sullivan's Material Poetics of Salvaging in red shifts and murmur

Mandy Bloomfield

> Particularly I have always been haunted by issues of VOICELESSNESS – inarticulacy – silence – soundlessness – breathlessness – how are soundings or voices that are other-than or invisible or dimmed or marginalised or excluded or without privilege, or locked out, made UNofficial, reduced by ascendant systems of centrality and closure, configured or Sounded or given form & potency: how can I body forth or configure such sounds, such tongues, such languages, such muteness, such multivocality, such error — & this is perhaps why the non-vocal in mark & the non-word in sound or language – make up much of the fabrics & structures of my own compositions.[1]

As these words indicate, Maggie O'Sullivan's poetry has been persistently concerned with marginalisation and silencing, and with lost or suppressed aspects of language and culture. The poet has frequently linked this preoccupation to her Irish ancestry and the diasporic experiences of her parents whose 'oral culture / the struggle for voice despite centuries of repression', she says, 'has a lot to do with my poetics'.[2] An acute awareness of this cultural and familial legacy of diasporic and class-related disempowerment has induced a sensitivity in her poetry to a vast array of suppressed articulations, whose multiplicity she gestures towards here.

As her aspiration to 'body forth' such unacknowledged presences might suggest, O'Sullivan's poetry seeks to give physical 'form & potency' to absence and silence. In a conversation on Charles Bernstein's Studio 111 recording series at Penn Sound, the poet says 'writing is a body-intensive activity . . . the whole body is engaged in the act of writing'.[3] This emphasis on the corporeal dimensions of writing makes for a poetic practice rooted in a sense not only of the bodily activity of the poet, but of the written word made flesh in a very literal sense. In her remarks on issues of voicelessness cited above, the poet tentatively offers the material, corporeal dimensions of the 'non-vocal in mark & the non-word in sound or language' as possible resources for a poetic embodiment of the multiple inarticulacies she wants her work to encompass. Yet notably the 'non-vocal' and 'non-word' are negatively defined entities here, dimensions of language which the poet presents as excluded from categories of voice and linguistic articulacy by their 'non' status. Thus O'Sullivan implicitly frames her pursuit of '-lessness' and muteness via 'non' forms in terms of a series of problems which her work both raises and engages with: how are absence and lack to be 'bodied forth', given presence? How might negatively-defined material poetic dimensions such as the 'non-vocal' and the 'non-word' constitute a kind of presence? In what ways might they give 'form & potency' to silenced and excluded aspects of language and culture?

I would like to investigate such questions by looking at two of O'Sullivan's more recent works, *red shifts* (2001) and *murmur – tasks of mourning* (2004), the latter being currently available online at the poet's website.[4] These works testify to the ways in which her engagement with issues of voicelessness and inarticulacy has in recent years involved an amplified visual emphasis on 'the non-vocal in mark & the non-word in sound or language'. O'Sullivan has long been interested in working with visual materials – both in her writing practice and in her 'large colourful expressionistic assemblages/paintings' which she worked on 'side by side' with her poetry in the 1980s and 90s, and which feature on the covers of *In the House of the Shaman* and *Palace of Reptiles*, for example. But as she explains to Dell Olsen in an interview, her more recent work aims for a synthesis of her poetic and visual work, pursuing a practice 'where potencies, energy fields, traces of actions/activities move in an open, ongoing dissolving/deformance of the verbal/visual/sculptural into one practice of many heuristic pathings.'[5] This shift is evident in works such as *red shifts* and *murmur*, which make extensive use of colour, texture and collage, extending O'Sullivan's previous experiments with the visual and tactile dimensions of her writing and melding her poetic and visual arts practice. The square-format pages of *red shifts* also allude to an intermedia practice, echoing the archetypal 'white cube' of the contemporary art gallery and thus wittily offering the book as a layered, two-dimensional exhibition space.[6] For all the two-dimensionality of the page, the book's concrete reference to the gallery space invokes the 'sculptural' quality to which the poet refers in her description of her recent practice; in so doing, it indicates a pursuit of further dimensions and extended capacities, thus physically embodying the expansive impulse which is also evident in O'Sullivan's tendency to use lengthy lists of often diverse terms when speaking about her poetic practice.

My discussion of the increasingly visual turn of this work in recent years and its role in the poet's pursuit of the material traces of suppressed and 'voiceless' aspects of language and culture will proceed via a close reading of *red shifts*. I would like to suggest that this work's emphasis on the visual dimensions of the poetic page functions as an amplification of O'Sullivan's 'body intensive practice'. Through its corporeal foregrounding of the 'non-vocal' and the 'non-word', O'Sullivan's poetry offers the sensuous materiality of the poetic page as a mode of bodying forth silenced, lost or disavowed aspects of language and culture. This poetry makes an argument for an avowal of what J. M. Bernstein calls 'sensuous meaningfulness, the kind of nondiscursive meaning that material things have, material meaning'.[7] In the latter stages of this essay I will turn to a discussion of *murmur* in order to unpack some of the wider political stakes of this claim for material meaningfulness in O'Sullivan's poetry.

The synaesthetic corporeality of *red shifts*

A notable feature of *red shifts* is its emphasis, from the first, on the page as a visual space. It is often the opening – made up of two distinct but sutured pages – that forms one of the basic working units of the poem. In her essay in this companion, Marjorie Perloff points out that this work formally resembles an artist's book, and indeed, *red shifts* has many artist's book-like qualities.[8] Facing pages are often treated as a single space, as in the poem's initial opening (figure 1), and this alerts readers to the importance of reading and looking across the opening as well as down the page, even when facing pages are not so literally fused as they are here. Indeed, in the poem's initial opening, this 'instruction' for a reading strategy is given almost mimetically by means of two visual 'diagrams' – the undulating black line that meanders down the far left-hand side of the opening, imitating the typical movement of the reading eye, and the red zigzag which moves across the pages and leads, on the far right-hand side, to the rest of the work. In this way, the poem's first pages suggest to its readers a mode of negotiating the work

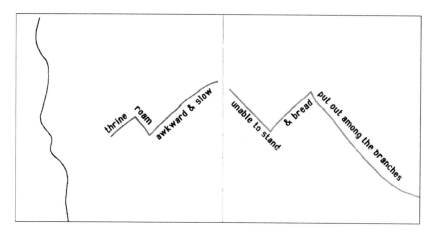

Figure 1. Maggie O'Sullivan, *red shifts* (Buckfastleigh: Etruscan, 2001), first opening (unpaginated). Original in colour.

as a series of spaces which require visual navigation and a multidirectional – and multidimensional – reading practice.

The first opening of *red shifts* also brings to attention and raises questions about relations between the different sensory modes which this poem requires readers to deploy, most prominently those implicated in the negotiation of verbal and visual material. The visual cues on these first pages are highly gestural marks, drawn with marker pens or with a fine brush and ink. Thus the wavy black line and red zigzag claim a direct link with the hand and the body, a genesis in a 'body-intensive' practice.[9] In sharp contrast, the heavily pixellated, blocky appearance of the verbal material on this page points to the mediation of a machine. The starkly differing visual qualities of word and visual mark seems at first to suggest different modes of production for verbal and visual material in this poem and to posit a separation between the written and the drawn. Yet at the same time, the placing of words along the contours of the red zigzag in the first opening of *red shifts* enacts an integration of word and image; the reading of the printed word/phrase/line must unavoidably take the movement and contours of the zigzag into account, whilst the red mark itself is not only a red mark but also a poetic line, a template around which verbal material shapes itself. Furthermore, the visible pixels of the printed words highlight the essentially visual quality of all printed words – the pixel being a unit of visual space – and bestow an optically-perceived textural quality upon each rough-edged individual letter.

By means of the 'non-vocal in mark', then, *red shifts* confronts readers with what Johanna Drucker calls language as 'phenomenological, apprehendable, immanent substance'.[10] Both in its gestural marks and in its more recognisably language-based forms, O'Sullivan's writing insists on 'the capacity of the image, the poem, the word, or the mark to *be*, to exist in its own right on an equal stature with the tangible, dimensional objects of the real world.'[11] Her work makes a claim to the status of physical '*being* rather than *representing*'.[12] In *red shifts*, this physical sense of '*being*' often involves an insistence on the corporeality of the poetic page. The hand-drawn marks, patterns, spills, and washes of often blood-red ink that occur throughout the pages of this poem emphasise a bodily component of inscription by means of these marks' associations with the human or animal body – whether through the gestural quality that claims a proximity to the writing or drawing hand, in their correspondence to corporeal elements such as blood, or their incorporation of visual forms that resemble bones, eyes, scales and feathers. So too, diacritical marks such as dashes and slashes foreground the material presence of print upon the page – writing's own 'bodily' presence – and words printed in a red font frequently link type to the corporeal qualities of the blood-like red ink used throughout the book.

But it is not only visually that O'Sullivan's poem engages its readers with a corporeal dimension of the poetic page. Sound also plays a large part in this process. Garrett Stewart proposes a notion of the 'phono-text' to suggest how 'reading voices'; even silent reading 'proceeds to give voice, or at least to evoke silently such voicing'.[13] Stewart's notion of how 'reading voices'; proceeds from the question '[w]here do we read?' He asserts, '[w]hen we read to ourselves, our ears hear nothing. Where we read, however, we listen.' For him, it is in the *space* of reading, more specifically in the 'somatic locus' of the 'reading body' that sound gets voiced. Where we read the lines 'sh - - - sh - - - sh - - - sh - - - - / hurrish - - -' on the third page of *red shifts*, then, the 'non-word in sound' is voiced in the corporeal substrates of the reading body.

O'Sullivan's *red shifts* foregrounds this sense of the 'where' of reading not only in its many vocal elements, but also in its visual emphasis on the page as space. The 'where' of reading in this poem is located not only in the reading body but rather in an exchange between the space of the page and the 'somatic locus' of the reading body. So in *red shifts*, sound is often inextricably intertwined with visuality. As well as looking at, say, the red zigzag shape of the poem's opening page, we might also listen to it; this shape invokes the rising and falling of intonation or sound, and its hard edges also visually chime with hard consonants such as 'k', 't' and 'b' which litter the verbal material on the page. So here the poem offers the 'non-word in sound or language' as a material component of the work which is entangled with language but which is also not reducible to abstract linguistic functioning.

As my reading of the possible acoustic effects of the red zigzag suggests, from its opening pages *red shifts* induces an exchange between and blurring of optical, textual, oral, and textural qualities. As Dell Olsen perceptively notes, O'Sullivan's recent work suggests a synaes-thetic practice which is 'moving towards an interchange of senses: hear-ing seems to become sight and vice-versa'.[14] Furthermore, the notion of synaesthsia not only suggests ways of describing the sensory exchanges that O'Sullivan's poetry invokes and aspires to induce, it also proposes ways of thinking through the sensory, corporeal underpinnings of language that this poetry insists upon and wants to emphasise. The work of neuroscientists Vilayanur Ramachandran and Edward Hubbard proposes that the condition of synaesthesia – in which, for example, different musical notes evoke particular colours for some people, or certain tactile experiences induce a sensation of taste – is caused by a kind of cross-wiring or 'cross activation' between neighbouring areas of the brain that deal with sensory experience.[15] They go on to suggest that to some extent 'we are all closet synaesthetes', that we all have the capacity for some level of sensory interchange, and that furthermore, synaesthesia may well provide some of the foundations for language.[16] In particular, they argue, '[h]umans have a built-in bias to associate certain sounds with particular visual shapes'. In a test conducted by psychologist Wolfgang Köhler, participants were presented with two shapes, one curvy and amoeba-like and the other sharp and pointy. When asked which is a 'bouba' and which a 'kiki', 98 percent of all respondents named the rounded shape as 'bouba' and the angular shape 'kiki'. Ramachandran and Hubbard remark that '[t]he brain seems to possess preexisting rules for translating what we see and hear into mouth motions that reflect those inputs'.[17] Whilst they hardly claim to offer a fully worked-out theory of language, Ramachandran and Hubbard's studies of synaesthesia do propose ways of understand-ing language not just in terms of the arbitrary conceptual links insisted upon by Saussurian linguistics, but also in terms of sensory, corporeal processes. Such a conception of language is highly consonant with O'Sullivan's poetry, which wants to stimulate or rejuvenate corporeally-rooted linkages between various sensory dimensions and between these sensory dimensions and language. Furthermore, this poet's insistence on 'non-vocal' and 'non-word' elements of language that resist subsumption to abstract and system-based semantic functioning places faith in the corporeal and sensuous aspects of language to provide alternative modes of articulation for voiceless and marginalised presences.

The performative page

From its first opening, then, *red shifts* (figure 1), embodies a corporeal, multidimensional conception of language which exemplifies O'Sullivan's aspiration towards a 'dissolving/deformance of the verbal/visual/sculptural', a splicing and melding of multiple sensory dimensions.[18] But the poem's first opening not only strikes up an interplay and 'dissolving' between printed word and visual mark, between sight and sound, it also constitutes a gestural acting-out; it is a multi-medial *per*formance as O'Sullivan's coinage 'deformance' suggests. As Drucker points out, the foregrounding of visual materiality emphasises the performative capacity of writing:

> a visual performance of a poetic work on a page or canvas, as a projection or sculpture, installation or score... has the qualities of an enactment, of a staged and realized event in which the material means are an integral feature of the work.[19]

In O'Sullivan's poem the visual dimension is a crucial – if not the only – performative dimension of this 'verbal/visual/sculptural' work. But what is it that is being performed in this poem, beyond the fusing of textual, visual, tactile and oral dimensions of experience?

Red shifts evinces the poet's sense of the poetic page as '[a] place of existence, journeying. A sacred space of undiminishment. Of dream. Of ritual. Of magic.'[20] This ritualistic conception of the space of the page is evident from the verbal-visual-tactile performance of the work's first opening, which transforms the page(s) into a ceremonial space, a space where '& bread / put out among the branches' constitutes a form of offering. Furthermore, the poem begins with one of O'Sullivan's characteristic neologisms, 'thrine', which in an act of typographic and acoustic 'dissolving/deformance' suggests simultaneously the word 'thine', an archaic form for 'your' or 'yours', and 'shrine'. Additionally, the 'o' sound from 'roam' bleeds into 'thrine', making it point equally to the word 'throne'. In its proximity to 'shrine' and 'throne', 'thrine' calls to mind without actually designating a site invested with ceremonial significance, and implies that the task of performing its rites may be read as at least partly 'thine', the reader's.[21]

One ritualised act that *red shifts* recurrently performs is the physical struggle to articulate, even to breathe. In the poem's third opening the phrases '**b-r-e-a-t-h-i-n-g——in**' and '**b-r-e-a-t-h-i-n-g——out –**' (*rs*, unpaginated) are fragmented, hyphenated and printed in a diagonally rising-and-falling shape, simultaneously representing and performing a difficult process of breathing by means of inseparable visual and oral components. The hyphens break up the word, and the ascending and descending printing embodies a breath that not only rises and falls but catches; the point of the jagged peak suggests a sharp switch between inhalation and exhalation. At the same time, the printing of these phrases enacts a breaking of sound, fragmenting the phonetic qualities of the word 'breathing' and making audible 'the non-word in sound or language' in the form of a faltering, uneven breath.[22] This verbal-visual enactment of ragged breathing performs a sense of debilitation that infuses *red shifts* and which is evident from the poem's first opening, where the lines '**awkward & slow**' and '**unable to stand**' indicate a struggling and incapacitated body. The poem's following pages enact a recurrently thwarted endeavour to perform a speech act. A speaker's whimper '**cant hold my breath/my breath / sobbing**'(*rs*), points emphatically to an undertaking hindered by grief and by a silencing violence suggested by 'savage / tonguesbled'(*rs*) and the repetition of 'sh - - -'.

In this way, O'Sullivan's poem gives form and substance to a state of inarticulacy, 'bodying forth' an enacted struggle for speech. Furthermore, for this poet, as I mentioned at the outset of this essay, the struggle to speak is rooted in a cultural legacy of marginalisation, displacement, and silencing informed by her own sense of cultural and familial history. The negotiation of voicelessness in *red shifts* partly involves an excavation of this past. Fragments of a diasporic Anglo-Irish history are silted into the poem's performed struggle for articulation. Spellings and neologisms regularly suggest Irish pronunciation as in '**windfella**' or '**AcurrsZ'd**' or '**Whatter Ye Fukkas**'(*rs*), and these are often printed in enlarged and/or emboldened fonts which serve to emphasise, or, in sound terms, 'turn up the volume' of enunciations bearing traces of an Irish inflection.

In addition to these sound-residues, the poem contains narrative fragments of an Irish heritage; 'paddy.took.after.my.grandmother's. | people.' (*rs*) invokes a story of a familial past whose Irishness is signified by the name '**paddy**'(*rs*). Whilst this tiny fragment or beginning of a story gestures towards a sense of generational continuity, the full stop after each word enacts a recurrent interruption which suggests a fracturing of families and links between generations. Meanwhile, '**bellowing the roads** used drive them the 10 or 12 miles'(*rs*) points to a rural way of life revolving around '**bellowing**' livestock, a mode of existence whose pastness is indicated by the word 'used' which works most powerfully here as 'used to'. Meanwhile, the line's syntactical disjointedness and its visual jump from enlarged bold type to a smaller unemboldened font embody a sense of a discontinuity, whilst the line 'break cattle' on the previous page intimates the destruction of livestock and the way of life associated with it. These traces of an Irish rural heritage both indicate the roots of the 'ancestral self' of the poet and, by both linguistic means and material shifts, demonstrate a diasporic sense of severance from a '<u>lost</u>'(*rs*) familial and cultural past.[23]

This loss is imbued with a sense of violence, as phrases such as '<u>**ruptures crossing**</u>' and 'tear of the wind'(*rs*) suggest. Furthermore, the intimation of violence is almost always linked in some way to the act of speaking as in the lines 'hard gutteral | —— ~~threadened~~ ------- ~~threatened~~ to kill'(*rs*). Here, 'hard gutteral', suggesting harsh-sounding 'guttural' speech, appears to be the subject that threatens 'to kill'. And yet there is so much more going on here that both the source and the target of this murderous threat are highly ambiguous. The crossing-through of the word 'threatened' constitutes a symbolic act of violence, declaring an intention to eliminate, to 'kill' the presence of the word. So this crossing-out of 'threatened' both suggests a removal of the threat 'to kill' and implies that the act of killing is no longer merely threatened but actualised. Meanwhile, the word '~~threadened~~' with which this second line begins also bears the marks of an attempted erasure, and the suggestion is that this is connected to the violence of the 'hard gutteral' and the replacing of the 'd' of 'threadened' with a sharper-sounding 't' to make the word 'threatened'. In the process, meaning has also shifted; the neologism 'threadened', whose meaning(s) are unclear and potentially multiple, but which is primarily suggestive of a past act of threading and thus of a sense of continuity and succession, mutates into the word 'threatened' whose more sharply defined meaning

suggests an endangerment of the multiplicity and linkages 'threadened' embodies.

Yet the line that crosses through 'threadened' is not only a mark of
erasure; because it extends backwards (our usual reading habits tell us)
from the beginning of the word, it becomes visually suggestive of a linking thread from some 'before' onto which the letters of 'threadened'
appear to be strung. Furthermore, 'threadened' is not only crossed
out/threaded, some of its letters are also underlined, emphasised; the
letters 'r', 'e', and 'd' are brought to attention in this way and then seemingly engender the word 'reddened' which makes up the next line. This
move is simultaneously a demonstration of the generative power of
even the most uncertain, ambiguous, and partially erased articulations,
and at the same time it intimates a kind of 'bleeding', a 'reddened' stain
issuing from the violence previously intimated. Throughout the process
of reading these intricate verbal-visual interactions, though, the status
of the 'hard gutteral' remains resolutely ambiguous: is this harsh-sound-
ing entity a violent utterance? Is this the source of a murderous threat?
Or is it 'hard' in the sense of 'difficult'? And is the gutteral something
that issues from the 'gutter', from the site of the abject, the expelled,
the marginal? And/or is it something that 'gutters', that sputters waver-
ingly, inarticulately?

The performative pages of *red shifts* recurrently weave together
suggestions and enactments of violence, displacement, physical distress
and inarticulacy informed by patterns of violence, silencing, and suffering shaped by ideological and material configurations of power and
domination. O'Sullivan's poem demonstrates ways in which such lega-
cies are embedded in language itself. Elsewhere, at the close of her
published interview with Andy Brown, the poet quotes the words of
Tom Leonard:

> It's not simply a matter of class register, but the politics of domi-
> nant narrative language as would-be encloser of the world,
> language as coloniser. For this the language has to be presumed
> 'invisible' to its referent. I like to make it visible in different ways.[24]

For O'Sullivan, as for Leonard, language plays a key role in the opera-
tions of power carried out in the name of the 'dominant narrative'. As
potential 'encloser' and 'coloniser', language is part of the construction
and the perpetuation of what she calls 'a restrictive culture' which
marginalises, excludes and silences that which occupies a position
'other than' the dominant privileged one.[25] The notion of language as

'coloniser' of course carries additional historical freight in the context of the Irish history – with its colonial past – which informs O'Sullivan's poetic sensibilities. Like Leonard, O'Sullivan aims in her poetry to critique and counter this process by making language 'visible in different ways'.

By constructing a language entity with visual, corporeal presence which performs a stuttering, struggling inarticulate speech act, then, *red shifts* hopes to make visible processes of marginalisation and silencing embedded in language. But crucially, O'Sullivan's multidimensional writing also wants to expand the capacities of language, contesting its appropriation by and complicity with structures of oppressive power. By putting hitherto untapped physical resources of written/printed/sounded language into play, this poetry aspires to give form to those voices which are 'locked out, made UNofficial, reduced by ascendant systems of centrality and closure'.

Archaeological salvaging

O'Sullivan's poetic resistance to 'a restrictive culture' in *red shifts* involves not only a mining of language, but also an engagement with hitherto unacknowledged possibilities of a wide variety of marginalised cultural materials. For O'Sullivan, the history and culture – both modern and ancient – of what she refers to as the 'Celtic fringes' of the British Isles provides a particularly rich terrain for such an undertaking.[26] Many of the pages of *red shifts* incorporate archaic traces into their verbal and visual compositions, such as the opening depicted in figure 2 which all at once resembles a list of ingredients for a magical spell, enacts a ritualistic performance with the route through the rite marked out by a 'pathway' of red shapes, and embodies an archaeological dig of a ceremonial site with its findings mapped out among visual representations of stone-like shapes.

Elsewhere, *red shifts* borrows and redeploys motifs and symbols from Celtic art and mythology. The zigzags and spirals that recur throughout the poem, for example, are often seen in ancient Celtic art, where they are invested with a wealth of symbolic significance. Often found carved into stone at megalithic and palaeolithic sites such as Newgrange, Knowth and Fourknocks in Ireland and featuring particularly in passage grave sites, these symbolic motifs are associated with the cycles of life and nature, and (spirals particularly) the passage between life,

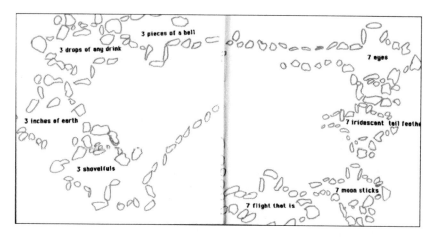

Figure 2. from *red shifts*. Original in colour.

death, and rebirth.[27] Archaeologist Richard Bradford proposes that these carvings might have constituted a 'prehistoric cosmology', a map of the stars in the night sky whose configurations and movements were interwoven with ancient peoples' ways of making sense of their world.[28] These patterns and the lost cultures they reference function in *red shifts* as traces of extinguished ways of life and modes of relating to the world whose unrealised possibilities and potentially transformative powers the poem wants to retrieve.

O'Sullivan's approach to the salvaging and redeployment of such archaic traces owes much to the influence of Kurt Schwitters and Joseph Beuys, which she reflects on in her poem/ statement of poetics 'RIVERRUNNING (REALISATIONS'. She relates how she began in the 1980s to make 'assemblages or visual constructions informed by Schwitters's Merz works made up of discarded materials from everyday life, such as used tickets, food labels, and scraps of newspaper. In his 'superb use of the UN – the NON and the LESS – THE UNRE-GARDED, the found, the cast-offs, the dismembered materials' O'Sullivan finds a parallel for her own 'concern for the retrieval of potentials within material'.[29] Her weaving of salvaged cultural fragments into multimedia collage, amalgamating them with other kinds of references and other kinds of forms in a poem like *red shifts*, then, similarly aims for a such a 'retrieval of potentials', embedded in abject or negatively-defined cultural 'cast-offs'.

This poetics of salvaging is also shaped by the poet's engagement with the work of Beuys, with whom she shares an interest in Celtic mythologies and artefacts, and a shamanistic veneration for the natural world. Indeed, the poet ascribes her move in 1988 from London to Yorkshire, 'from the city to the moorland impress of tongue', to the 'transformative experience' of working on a BBC *Arena* programme on Beuys a couple of years earlier.[30] O'Sullivan's 1993 work *In the House of the Shaman* uses a quotation from him as an epigraph to its second section 'Kinship with Animals': 'To stress the idea of transformation and of substance. This is precisely what the shaman does in order to bring about change and development: his nature is therapeutic.'[31] O'Sullivan's intimation of the untapped energies of 'dismembered materials' echoes Beuys's shamanistic belief in the transformative and 'therapeutic' power of particular materials, such as the felt and lard he recurrently used in his sculptures and installations.

O'Sullivan's poetry brings methods of assemblage, an attention to unacknowledged or 'cast-off' cultural remains, and a faith in the transformative energies secreted in such materials to her poetic excavation of archaic cultural residues. The opening from *red shifts* depicted in figure 3, where fragments gleaned from the remains of a lost Celtic culture are collaged together with other verbal and visual elements, exemplifies a poetic 'retrieval of possibilities' by such means. On the verso page, the zigzags and spirals of Celtic symbolism, drawn and printed in red crayon and black ink, form part of a multimedia collage which also features an enigmatic, partly humanoid form surrounded by rivulets of blood-like ink. Simultaneously fleshy and skeletal, anthropomorphic and animal-like, this strange figure embodies a site of intersection and transition between the living and the dead, the mortal and the otherworldly alluded to by the abstract Celtic forms, as well as a fusing of the human and the animal which echoes animistic elements of ancient pagan belief systems and rituals.

Image and text, occupying separate pages in this composition, are placed in a dynamic dialogic relation that expands the possible meaning effects and sensory effects of this space. 'this red', for example, finds a visual 'reply', in the ink and crayon reds on the opposite page, whilst the red zigzags resonate suggestively with the lines '**draw ing breath's** / broken fanging', forming a 'drawing' of ragged breathing or of jagged fang-like shapes which recalls the 'b-r-e-a-t-h-i-n-g' compositions discussed earlier. Meanwhile, the humanoid-skeletal form resonates with the crossed through word '~~DECOMPOSITIONS~~' which linguistically points to

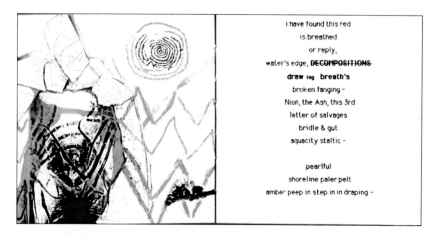

Figure 3. From *red shifts*. Original in colour.

processes of corporeal decay inferred by the visual juxtaposition of plump fleshiness and bone-like forms. Celtic symbolism is invoked once more in the lines 'Nion, the Ash, this 3rd / letter of salvages', which refers to the '3rd / letter' of the ancient Ogham alphabet named Nion, the Celtic name for the ash tree.[32] This reference to 'the Ash' echoes across the opening with a tiny, seemingly photographic, image of a silhouette of a house next to a large tree pasted over the red zigzags. In this opening of *red shifts*, then, a process of interplay between various appropriated fragments and between their different materialities has the effect of invigorating each fragment's significance, sparking off meaningful energies in a series of dialogues between one reference and another, one kind of materiality and another, one mode of articulation and another.

In his essay on O'Sullivan's 'Medleyed Verse' for the present volume, Charles Bernstein describes her work as 'a cross-sectional boring through time, whirling the sedimentary layers into knots. The archaic material pushes up to the surface.'[33] His words point to the 'whirling' energy of this poet's archaeological activities, but also to the ways in which her poems embody a sense both of a depth of time, a 'boring' through 'sedimentary layers', and a spatial 'surface' to which excavated material rises. Indeed, we might interpret this 'surface' quite literally as the surface of the page itself, a space which embodies residues of the 'whirling . . . sedimentary layers' of concretised time. In other words, the surfaces of O'Sullivan's archaeological pages become sites of intersection between a depth of time and spatial surface; they are spaces imbued with specific, materially manifested historical residues in which a core sample of time and the material page meet and become intertwined and energised.

O'Sullivan's intertwining of the spatial 'place' of the page and the temporal 'sedimentary layers' of the archaic in a poem like *red shifts* aims towards an invigoration of the transformative potentials of these materials. If the page is '[a] place of damage, savagery, pain, silence: also a place of salvage, retrieval and recovery', then the archaeological activities of this poetry aspire both to register 'damage' and enact 'retrieval'.[34] In the opening depicted in figure 3, the line 'Nion, the Ash, this 3rd/ letter of salvages' brings attention to precisely these processes in the poem. The designation of Nion as the 'letter of salvages' indicates the strong associations between the ash tree and the power of the sea in Celtic lore; small pieces of ash wood were (and sometimes still are) used as charms against drowning by those going to sea.[35] Yet in O'Sullivan's poem Nion is a 'letter of salvages'. Nion is thus not exactly equated with safe passage over the sea but rather becomes a sign of that which has been shipwrecked and rescued, that which has gone through processes of both 'damage' and 'retrieval'. And indeed, the opening in which this reference to Nion occurs displays an array of 'salvages', including the tiny, fragmented image of the house and tree and the spirals and zigzags: flotsam and jetsam of lost or forgotten or suppressed ways of life.

As O'Sullivan's remarks on Schwitters suggest, it is important that her poem constitutes itself as an assemblage of the discarded, because of the affinity between 'THE UNREGARDED' and the voiceless, 'cast-offs' and the expelled, 'dismembered materials' and silenced presences which share the status of the unacknowledged, the abject, the violently suppressed. The salvaged remains that make up these pages occupy and constitute a kind of borderland, a 'water's edge' or 'shore-line' between past and present, forgetting and recall, and between a depth of time and the space of the page. This marginal site is a dwelling place of the silenced or inarticulate. It is '[a] place of damage, savagery, pain, silence', of 'broken fanging', of 'DECOMPOSITIONS', of loss and threatened oblivion, but it is 'also a place of salvage, retrieval and recovery', where unrealised transformative potentials might be glimpsed in the ebb and flow between savagery and recuperation, between the lost and found, or between the skeletal and the fleshly, the jagged and the rounded, the word and the image, the past world of the archaic fragment and the present moment of the poem.[36]

A readerly engagement with the materialities of the poem's various elements is central to the transformative processes it hopes to enact, and in the back and forth of reading between the visual and verbal sides of this space, or between a skeletal and a fleshy form, or between the photographic and the hand drawn, meanings multiply and also contradict one another. The poem invites its readers to become part of its processes of retrieval, to participate in its rituals of mourning and of recovery, to share the synaesthetic corporeality of its 'existence, journeying' and to follow its 'many heuristic pathings'.[37]

The clearest example of this is in the poem's multiple incarnations of the colour red. Embodied in various ways throughout the poem, red carries different connotations according to its material form and the wider context of the page. In the opening depicted in figure 3, for example, red ink spills form a visual network around the fleshy-skeletal bodily form, suggesting flows of fluids around the body (and the watery verbal imagery on the facing page strengthens this inference). But the crayon red on this page signifies in different ways – the expressive strokes echoing Celtic designs claim a primal and vital link with past cultures, via the drawing hand which participates in a retrieval of these cultural traces. The word 'red' printed in black ink on the facing page differs again; it is a 'red' that is 'found' by an 'i', a 'red' that is 'breathed', thus constituting itself as a medium or meditative space in which breathing perhaps becomes less difficult than elsewhere in the poem, and in which an articulation of selfhood becomes a possibility. And yet the various materialities of these reds are never deterministic; these same spilled, drawn and printed reds might well be read differently, as the homonymic overlap between 'red' and 'read' suggests. The red zigzags could well be read as an angry scrawl, or as representative of a violent and rough set of waves. The important thing to note is that this is a red that, as the title puts it, 'shifts', its possibilities for meaning multiplying, but also sometimes conflicting and contradicting one another with each incarnation in a different physical form and with each reading.

Such indeterminacy gestures towards the teeming possibilities held within the materials of O'Sullivan's pages, the multiplicity of latent potentials embedded in the poem's material strata. Indeed, this work recurrently brings to attention and seeks to address the ways in which an engagement with materiality is a 'lost' or unacknowledged or suppressed element of reading practices more generally. As I have argued throughout this essay, an insistence on the material, corporeal dimensions of writing and reading, a foregrounding of what J. M. Bernstein refers to as 'sensuous meaningfulness' is inextricably bound up with this poetry's resistance to a 'restrictive culture' and its 'retrieval of possibilities'. Furthermore, I want to suggest that in its avowal of 'the kind of nondiscursive meaning that material things have, material meaning', this poetry embodies and proposes a particular kind of materialism.[38] In order to elaborate on O'Sullivan's materialism and the ways it manifests itself in her recent work, I would like to move on to a discussion of her poem *murmur – tasks of mourning*.

Numinous materialism

Comprising a series of highly visual and tactile language and image arrangements, *murmur* continues O'Sullivan's synaesthetic practice of 'many heuristic pathings' pursued in *red shifts*.[39] In its current form as an online poem, *murmur* – seemingly paradoxically – evinces a hand-made, collage aesthetic that foregrounds the visual and textural qualities of its multimedial compositions as the bearers of fecund meaning potentials. Although the electronic medium is generally thought of as a disembodied space, and the screen does not have the literal materiality of the page of a book, the process of scanning in high-quality images of the poem's hand-made pages enables the work to retain and reproduce minute physical particulars. Things like the different qualities and textures of paper used, the creasing caused by gluing collage materials on unstretched paper (see figure 4), or the impasto surface of acrylic paint (figure 5) are retained by the process of scanning, and they are reproduced with rich vibrancy on the computer screen.

Such an insistence on material details is crucial to this work's formal embodiment of multidimensionality. Yet this poem intimates a violence done to materiality, and particularly to the corporeal 'body' of language. Repeated references to a 'BODYTEXT' and to a process of 'savaging salvaging' or a 'savaging salvaging body'(*m*) are woven through the poem. This work presents itself as a suffering body, as the page depicted in figure 4 suggests. Visually resembling a corset, and echoing the shape of a feminine torso, this page simultaneously embodies a rift, a suturing, and a sense of constriction. The 'body' of language on this page is printed on the surface of a fragile tissue paper whose wrinkled and torn appearance both emphasises the materiality of the printed word and results in 'Erasures' and

Figure 4. O'Sullivan, from *murmur* (unpaginated).
Original in colour.

'rupture'(*m*) of verbal material. The two lines of hand-stitched crosses echo this process of erasure or crossing out, and at the same time they emphasise a 'bruty fissuring'(*m*), as the very last line of *murmur* has it. This poem thus constitutes a suffering 'BODYTEXT' which performs '*tasks of mourning*', as its title suggests. Given the physical forms of damage bodied forth here, this work is at least partly in mourning for a loss of potential or an impoverishment of language induced by the disavowal of material meaningfulness in a 'restrictive culture'.[40] I would like to propose that the 'Erasures', restrictions and 'rupture' both linguistically referenced and physically evinced in the torn tissue-text in figure 4 might be read in the light of a suppression of sensuous materiality, a silencing of the meaning potentials of the sensory and the nondiscursive.

J. M. Bernstein traces just such a delegitimation of material meaningfulness through modern Western thought. It is manifest, he argues, in Descartes' famous discussion of a piece of wax, which rejects sensory perception as a valid mode of knowledge and abstracts sensory encounter to mathematical, formulaic rationality.[41] It is also there in Kant's account of judging in his *Critique of Pure Reason* in which 'what belongs to the domain of the *intelligible* stands opposed to what belongs to the domain of the *sensible*.'[42] According to this schema, sensory, intuitive experience can only be meaningful insofar as it is subsumable to rational concepts; thus, according to J. M. Bernstein, sensuous meaningfulness has been delegitimated in modernity as a form of knowing or thinking. Furthermore, he argues,

> [i]t is not too much of a stretch to see the abstraction from particularity and sensory givenness as the abstractive device of modern forms of social reproduction: the subsuming of the use values of particular goods beneath the exchange value of monetary worth, or the domination of intersubjective practices by norms of instrumental reason that yield the rationalization or bureaucratization of our dominant institutions.[43]

The 'rupture' wrought on the sensuousness of the poetic page or 'BODY-TEXT' in O'Sullivan's poem, then, can be read as testimony to the violence of a 'restrictive culture' which subsumes materiality to processes of abstracting, instrumentalisation, and enclosure.[44] Yet at the same time, the flower-like shapes that emerge from the brutalised and sutured corporeal text articulate an aspiration towards recovery and healing, towards a 'salvaging'(m) of delegitimated materiality, even as the torn edges of these shapes carry the enduring physical traces of a process of 'savaging'(m).

O'Sullivan's poetic salvaging of material meaningfulness aims both to critique and counter the 'restrictive culture' of the present. Says the poet in an interview with Charles Bernstein, 'we're living in such a profoundly materialistic world, that [the] magic and beauty, and joy and power that is in language is not appreciated, or not known'.[45] Here, she makes a direct, causal connection between the 'materialistic world' of late twentieth-century consumer capitalism and a diminishment of the capacities of language. In this respect, she echoes a line of thought central to Language writing, which aligns language use under capitalism – especially that of the language arts – with the logic of commodity fetishism. Ron Silliman's key essay 'Disappearance of the Word/ Appearance of the World' argues that '[w]hat happens when a language moves toward and passes into a capitalist stage of development is an anaesthetic transformation of the perceived tangibility of the word, with corresponding increases in its descriptive and narrative capacities'.[46] Words, Silliman avers, have become part of a transactional process under capitalism. Stripped of their 'perceived tangibility', they are made transparent, instrumentalised, and valued only for their referential and discursive values, for the ways in which they can be exchanged for an image of 'the World'. As is well known, writers associated with Language poetics want to resist this logic of instrumentalisation and commodification; as Charles Bernstein and Bruce Andrews put it, '[i]t is our sense that the project of poetry does not involve turning language into a commodity for consumption; instead, it involves repossessing the sign through close attention to, and active participation in, its production.'[47] For O'Sullivan too, transactional uses of language, and a sense of restriction and loss of potential embody and echo an empty materialism of contemporary existence. Her poetry wants to counter 'materialistic' contemporary culture with another kind of materialism: one that acknowledges and employs the physical, visually and acoustically embodied dimensions of language in a 'production' of meaning that critiques the logic of instrumentality and consumption.

However, O'Sullivan's particular form of materialism is not only concerned with forming a critique of the commodity forms of contemporary culture; it is also imbued with a shamanistic sense of the unacknowledged 'magic and beauty, and joy and power' embedded in the sensuousness of language. Speaking to Charles Bernstein, she declares a belief 'in the transformative, alchemical forces that are inherent in languages' naming not only Beuys but also figures such as Jerome Rothenberg as influences on her conception of language's transformative potentials. Rothenberg's work with 'primal poetries', she says, provides ample examples of 'language constructions designed to bring about change', such as healing chants, for example, which demonstrate 'the magic in language, the potency, transformative potential in language'.[48]

This numinous sense of multidimensional language does not quite cohere with the materialist politics which O'Sullivan shares with the aspects of Language poetics that I have just outlined. Hank Lazer points to a discomfort with such a 'spiritual' sensibility:

> While it is common to valorize the importance of such writers as Robert Duncan and Jerome Rothenberg, a closer examination of their poetry and poetics immediately places us within writing traditions that are openly mystical, romantic, and, in the case of Rothenberg, shamanic and magical—all qualities that are disturbing to most innovative contemporary poets, many of whom have developed a poetics more obviously reliant on tenets of cultural materialism and an anti-romantic metaphysics.[49]

Indeed, the 'shamanic and magical' dimensions of poetries such as Duncan's, Rothenberg's and O'Sullivan's fundamentally conflict with the materialist basis of Language writing. The cultural materialism that Lazer points to is essentially a mode of disenchantment that seeks above all to wrest language from the enchantments of the logic of commodity fetishism which, in suppressing the materiality of the word and its processes of meaning-making, enables language to appear to transparently offer access to an easily consumable 'reality' beyond the word. An attribution of 'magical' dimensions and powers to language, no matter how materially embodied, is effectively a re-enchantment of language, albeit a re-enchantment that in poetries like O'Sullivan's wants to offer alternatives to the commodity fetishism of consumer capitalism.

O'Sullivan's poetics melds a sense of the 'magical' properties of multidimensional language with a materialist understanding of contemporary culture and the exchange economies of signification. Besides a repossession of the sign 'through close attention to, and active participation in, its production'[50] her work hopes to rescue its 'magic and beauty, and joy'.[51] O'Sullivan's materialism embraces a gnosis of the unfulfilled and possibly transformative potentials of language's sensory dimensions, of its material meaningfulness. Her poetry aspires to expand upon the usual modes of writing, saying and reading, to extend the senses used to read with and thus to bring about an active engagement not only with the economies of making meaning, but also with numinous, potentially transformative properties of language.

Such an activity is evident in O'Sullivan's extensive use in *murmur* of gestural marks which strongly resemble language but are not recognisable or legible as such. In the page shown in figure 5, for example, a number of roughly hand-drawn boxes filled in with pink crayoned letter-like marks and red impasto paint fill the top two thirds of the page. These boxes recall processes of form filling: processes that epitomise a

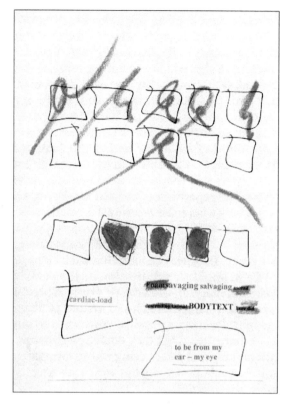

Figure 5. From *murmur.* Original in colour.

bureaucratised social world. But whereas the straight, mechanical lines and restrictive options and enclosures of official forms interpellate the writing subject into a process of cross-examination, of self naming, labelling, self-justification and restrictive categorisation, the hand-drawn quality of O'Sullivan's boxes and the expressive nature of the marks that fill them signal a resistance to such imperatives. The gestural 'signs' of this page certainly contest the notion of 'turning language into a commodity for consumption'; their very illegibility refuses instrumentalisation or translation into any kind of easily-consumed meaning.[52] But *murmur*'s unofficial boxes and glyph-like marks also gesture towards alternative domains and modes of knowledge and meaning making, their very illegibility and gestural power hinting at hitherto unplumbed esoteric dimensions of material writing.

Johanna Drucker, commenting upon the use of 'somatic traces' by visual artists such as Mira Shor and Pierre Alechinsky says that 'The [gestural] trace makes itself in the dynamic pleasure of material making and as such, remains a sign which has not yet reached the threshold of meaning'.[53] Indeed, O'Sullivan's marks evince just such a 'pleasure' of the materials of making and marking signalled by the way these illegible signs ecstatically spill outside of the hand-drawn boxes. And yet this physical spilling-over both suggests that these signs have 'not yet reached the threshold of meaning' and at the same time that they exceed it. Furthermore, O'Sullivan's somatic traces, although illegible, are so much like letters that they seem to belong to a secret language or unfamiliar script. The repetition of certain marks not only upon this page but across others where these gestural formations occur strengthens this suggestion. In this respect, they function as glyphs, which differ from gestural traces in that they implicitly claim to belong to some sort of symbolic langauge. Drucker remarks that such signs 'have meaning not accounted for in linguistic substitution . . . the power of the glyph – whether alchemical, magical, esoteric, or exotic is precisely this resistance to recuperation within the closed system of mere meaning.'[54] O'Sullivan's glyphs describe a physical resistance to any notion of a 'closed system of mere meaning'; they embody a dynamic and ongoing process of mark making and deciphering whose forms seemingly participate in an esoteric symbolic activity but which are never resolvable into closed, graspable 'meaning'.

As Drucker's phraseology helps to emphasise, the resistance to 'mere meaning' embodied in O'Sullivan's somatic marks points to the inadequacy of an equating of legible language with semantics, and an aspiration to move beyond linguistically or discursively-tied processes of meaning making into a 'multidimensional, kinaesthetic, sentient terrain or environment for the body to enter and move through'.[55] This terrain, hopes the poet, might be imbued with the lost 'magic and beauty, and joy and power that is in language'. O'Sullivan's gestural glyphs suggest that such 'magic and beauty, and joy and power' might lie precisely in the sensuousness of the material dimensions of language, in a kind of meaningfulness that contributes in unacknowledged ways to processes of meaning-making at the same time as it resists subsumption to discursively based forms of cognition and interpretation. In her work, is it precisely the sensuous dimensions of language and intuitive modes of experiencing and re-cognising, which are the voiceless aspects of language and of culture, the domain of that which is marginalised and excluded. This poet's excavations of the material page seek to give tangible and meaningful form to 'UNofficial' dimensions of the word and the world with which it is intertwined. In so doing, O'Sullivan's poetic forms call for a re-cognition of multidimensional modes of meaningfulness and materially embedded traces of 'other-than or invisible or dimmed or marginalised or excluded' aspects of language, history and culture.[56]

Notes

[1] Maggie O'Sullivan, 'In conversation with Andy Brown', in *Binary Myths 1&2: Conversations with Poets and Poet-Editors*, ed. by Brown (Exeter: Stride, 2004), pp. 155–160, p. 159.

[2] O'Sullivan, quoted by Jerome Rothenberg and Pierre Joris (eds.), 'Commentary', *Poems for the Millennium*, 2 vols (Berkeley: University of California Press, 1995–98), II (1998), p. 835. I deal with this poet's investigation of this cultural and familial legacy in another essay, '"Dragging at the haemorrhage of uns – ": Maggie O'Sullivan's excavations of Irish history', *Journal of British and Irish Innovative Poetry*, 1. 1 (2009), 11–36.

[3] Maggie O'Sullivan and Charles Bernstein, 'A conversation with O'Sullivan', (sound recording of an interview) Penn Sound Centre for Programs in Contemporary Writing <http://writing.upenn.edu/pennsound/x/OSullivan.html> [accessed 30th June, 2008].

[4] *red shifts* (Buckfastleigh: Etruscan, 2001), hereafter abbreviated to *rs*; and *murmur: tasks of mourning* <http://www.maggieosullivan.co.uk/murmur.html> [accessed June 12th 2007], hereafter abbreviated to *m*. This work is soon to be published in book form by Veer Books. As *red shifts* and *murmur* are unpaginated, I will not give page numbers when quoting from these works. Wherever grammaical correctness permits, I have retained O'Sullivan's use of the lower case in these titles.

[5] O'Sullivan and Dell Olsen, 'Writing / Conversation: an interview by mail November–December, 2003', *How2*, 2.2 (2004) <http://www.asu.edu/pipercwcenter/ how2journal//archive/online_archive/v2_2_2004/current/workbook/writing.htm > [accessed 30th April 2007] (para. 6 of 58).

[6] Indeed, Etruscan books classes this book as an 'exhibition' in its back-matter and on the back cover.

[7] J. M. Bernstein, *Against Voluptuous Bodies: Late Modernism and the Meaning of Painting* (Stanford, California: Stanford University Press, 2006), p. 47.

[8] See Marjorie Perloff's essay, '"The Saturated Language of Red": Maggie O'Sullivan and the Artist's Book', in the present companion.

[9] O'Sullivan and Charles Bernstein, 'A conversation'.

[10] Johanna Drucker, *The Visible Word: Experimental Typography and Modern Art, 1909–23* (Chicago & London: University of Chicago Press, 1994), p. 43.

[11] Drucker, *Visible Word*, p. 49.

¹² Drucker, *Visible Word*, p. 10.

¹³ Garrett Stewart, *Reading Voices: Literature and the Phonotext* (Berkeley: University of California Press, 1990), p. 1.

¹⁴ O'Sullivan and Olsen, (para. 26 of 58).

¹⁵ Vilayanur S. Ramachandran and Edward M. Hubbard, 'Hearing Colors, Tasting Shapes', *Scientific American*, 288. 5 (2003), 42–49, p. 55. <http://psy.ucsd.edu/chip/pdf/SciAm_2003.pdf> [accessed 25 January, 2007].

¹⁶ Ramachandran and Hubbard, p. 58.

¹⁷ Ramachandran and Hubbard, p. 59.

¹⁸ O'Sullivan and Olsen, (para. 6 of 58).

¹⁹ Drucker, 'Visual Performance of the Poetic Text', in *Close Listening: poetry and the performed word*, ed. by Charles Bernstein (Oxford: Oxford University Press, 1998), pp. 131–161, p. 131.

²⁰ O'Sullivan and Olsen, (para. 8 of 58).

²¹ See Perloff's essay in this companion for further insightful readings of this page of *red shifts*, along with many of the other moments I discuss here.

²² O'Sullivan, *Binary Myths 1&2*, p. 159.

²³ O'Sullivan, *Binary Myths 1&2*, p. 156.

²⁴ Tom Leonard, quoted by O'Sullivan, *Binary Myths 1&2*, p. 160.

²⁵ O'Sullivan, *Binary Myths 1&2*, p. 160, 159.

²⁶ Maggie O'Sullivan and Charles Bernstein, 'Interview by Charles Bernstein (1993)' (sound recording) <http://mediamogul.seas.upenn.edu/pennsound/authors/OSullivan/ OSullivan-Maggie_19_intrvw-by-Brnstein_Buffalo_10-27-93.mp3> [accessed 29ᵗʰ August, 2007].

²⁷ See for example George Nash, 'Light at the End of the Tunnel: the way megalithic art was viewed and experienced', in *Art As Metaphor*, ed. by Aron Mazel, George Nash and Clive Waddington (Oxford: Archaeopress, 2007), pp. 123–143 & Michael J. Kelly, *Newgrange: Archaeology, art and legend* (London: Thames and Hudson, 1982), pp. 128–185.

²⁸ Richard Bradley, *The Significance of Monuments: On the shaping of human experience in Neolithic and Bronze Age Europe* (London: Routledge, 1988), p. 108.

²⁹ O'Sullivan, 'RIVERRUNNING (REALISATIONS', Palace of Reptiles (Willowdale, Ontario: The Gig, 2003), pp. 57–70, p. 67.

³⁰ O'Sullivan, 'RIVERRUNNING (REALISATIONS', p. 67. The Arena programme was directed by Caroline Tisdall and made in 1986 just before Beuys's death. It was screened in 1987 (British Film Archive listing at <http://ftvdb.bfi.org.uk/sift/title/136912> [accessed 16ᵗʰ September 2008].

³¹ Joseph Beuys quoted by O'Sullivan, *In the House of the Shaman* (London: Reality Street, 1993), p. 28.

[32] Jane Gifford, *The Celtic Wisdom of Trees: Mysteries, Magic and Medicine* (London: Godsfield Press, 2006), p. 9.

[33] See Bernstein's essay in this companion, p. 2.

[34] O'Sullivan and Olsen, (para. 8 of 58).

[35] Gifford, pp. 9, 29.

[36] O'Sullivan and Olsen, (para. 8 of 58).

[37] O'Sullivan and Olsen, (paras. 9 & 7 of 58).

[38] J. M. Bernstein, p. 47.

[39] O'Sullivan and Olsen, (para. 6 of 58)

[40] O'Sullivan, *Binary Myths 1&2*, p. 160.

[41] J.M. Bernstein, pp. 22, 29.

[42] J.M. Bernstein, p. 5.

[43] J.M. Bernstein, p. 23.

[44] O'Sullivan, *Binary Myths 1&2*, pp. 160, 159.

[45] O'Sullivan and Charles Bernstein, 'Interview by Charles Bernstein (1993)'.

[46] Ron Silliman, 'Disappearance of the Word/ Appearance of the World', in *The L=A=N=G=U=A=G=E Book*, ed. by Bruce Andrews and Charles Bernstein (Carbondale and Edwardsville: Southern Illinois University Press, 1984), pp. 121–132, p. 125.

[47] Bruce Andrews and Charles Bernstein, 'Repossessing the Word', in *The L=A=N=G=U=A=G=E Book*, pp. ix–xi, p. x.

[48] O'Sullivan and Charles Bernstein 'Interview by Charles Bernstein (1993)'.

[49] Hank Lazer, 'The People's Poetry', *The Boston Review*, (2004) <http://www.bostonreview.net/BR29.2/lazer.html> [accessed 18th September 2008] (para. 19 of 70).

[50] Andrews and Charles Bernstein, 'Repossessing the Word', pp. ix–xi, p. x.

[51] O'Sullivan and Charles Bernstein, 'Interview by Charles Bernstein (1993)'.

[52] Andrews and Charles Bernstein 'Repossessing the Word', pp. ix–xi, p. x.

[53] Drucker, 'The Art of the Written Image', *Figuring the Word: Essays on Books, Writing and Visual Poetics* (New York: Granary Books, 1998), pp. 57–75, p. 65.

[54] Drucker, 'Art of the Written Image', p. 69.

[55] O'Sullivan and Olsen, (para 52 of 58).

[56] O'Sullivan, Binary Myths 1&2, p. 159.

Maggie O'Sullivan and the story of metaphysics

Romana Huk

The title of Maggie O'Sullivan's best known collection of poems, *In the House of the Shaman*, has proven something of a red herring for her readers. To be sure, it signs one way toward understanding the position that O'Sullivan takes up in her performative art, as stuttering wanderer between somatic, phenomenal and linguistic realms – a position significantly less vatic, I hope to suggest, than those available in both the spiritual *and* secular mysticisms that underlie numerous forms of twentieth-century avant-garde work.[1] Yet many would, like Andrew Duncan, assume that such references to shamanism link her project with romantic primitivism's (or "neo-paganism's") re-mystified excursions in modern art, and the supposed achievement, through linkage to natural forces, of ecstatic subjectivity that 'seems unaware that any reality exists outside it' – 'Why, this is nothing less than the earth', Duncan continues, 'rising up to engulf us' (267).[2] Though I feel drawn to Duncan's ability to be engulfed by O'Sullivan's work, such assessments simplify its dynamics as well as perpetuate the mystification and conferral of romanticised authority upon poets that others, like Lawrence Upton, rightly qualify: 'Whereas the poet/shaman as an inculcator via the power of words proposes a world which may be *controlled* by language, the poet as student and re-maker of language proposes a world which exists *in* words' (14).

Or in this case, even more precariously, in their 'Derridean deferral', as Aaron Williamson has argued in his incisive review of *In the House of the Shaman*. He claims that she 'adopts [it] as an aesthetic quantity – with its designed maintenance of the suspension of closure along each phonetic extension – rather than as ontological crisis' (88).

Yet he also suggests at the start that the Schwitters-esque art-construction by O'Sullivan on the book's cover, 'An Order of Mammal', is clearly evocative of Christ on the cross, consisting as it does of what looks like a 'smashed breast plate . . . mounted into a Christic attitude' (86). Like many fine artist-critics who have not ignored the theological dimensions of postmodern work, despite the difficulties of reconciling it with the era's much-documented irreverence, Williamson notes but leaves at loggerheads the tension between Derridean and Christological elements in the piece. Asserting that the book's cover art, 'resonant opening marker' that it is, represents 'misremembered heraldry, a pageant relic of the waking time', he converts the sacrificial image of otherness at its centre into one of art's 'achieved immutability', its 'high-gain self- definition' accomplished through 'the rooting of language into its own celebration'. This leads to his assignment of traditional (if eroded) visionary powers to the poet-shaman, concluding that O'Sullivan 'produces and allows for an autonomous energy – a sorceric battery' (89) with, at its 'centre', an 'ouroboros' maintaining 'a humid interiority of language' (88): a primitive, fertile world unto itself, Duncan's earth rising up to engulf us. These conclusions cause him to compromise his Derridean reading as well, which sits uneasily beside the work seen as a reliquary attuned to noble origins.

The 1960s–70's connection of shamanism with the possibility of redeemed post-war consciousness continues, perhaps, to power such readings; one need only remember Mircea Eliade's classic work on the topic, *Shamanism: Archaic Techniques of Ecstasy* (1964), to call to mind the religious rhetoric of fabled, cleansing, romantic "oneness" and return to origins that so profoundly permeated that study:

> Man lived at peace with the animals and understood their speech. . . .
> While preparing for his ecstasy and during it, the shaman abolishes the
> present human condition and, for the time being, recovers the situation
> as it was in the beginning. (99)

But as O'Sullivan puts it in the title of a 2003 work, 'all origins are lonely', suggesting that her desires lead her elsewhere. Though many continuingly romantic models for metaphysical poetics perpetuate such visions of purer origins and potential returns to all-but-Edenic unity, more radical postwar trends in both poetry and religious philosophy have replaced their tendency to effect *unification* of all things – often through metaphor or identification between self and otherness (here, the animals) – with strategies for facing difference, or *non-identity*.

It soon becomes evident in reading O'Sullivan's work that any invocation of Derrida needs updating with his own late-career consideration of how his similar project of facing difference veered into strange relation with theological ones in order to get at the only-seemingly contradictory performance of deferral in her metaphysically-inclined poems/assemblages. Among poets and critics of the avant-garde, related interest in how these poetries have responded to and been shaped by these convergences is developing; O'Sullivan's work, as I hope to demonstrate, becomes singularly relevant and provocative to this conversation.

I want to begin by thinking about O'Sullivan's relation to postmodern linguistic philosophy and what Shira Wolosky calls 'language mysticism' – the maverick revision of metaphysical inquiry conducted by writers like Beckett and Celan which was spawned by mid-twentieth-century crises in thoughts about language, history and subjectivity. Her negotiation of such realms of inquiry is indebted to and yet differs from those American poetic mystical traditions that recent critics have described as explicitly 'romantic' or 'gnostic',[3] and that have been, since mid-century, devoted to sources like Blake, Jung and Zen. Often acknowledging such debts, and similarly engaging in what she calls 'new/ancient forms of imaginings without limits that engage with multi and meta-physical breathing/soundings and fluidities',[4] her work also updates the differently-situated postwar metaphysics of European writers like Beckett and his compatriot Brian Coffey. Though O'Sullivan often references her Irish ancestry in her work, few have considered how she herself fits in that tradition, replete with its twentieth-century deployments of Yeatsian mysticism *and* Beckettian goodbyes to all that. Late in this particular modernist line we find Coffey's long-neglected reconsideration of both, through what Dónal Moriarty describes as his 'somatic rhythms' that reference Yeats's revivalist dedication to Irish song-making in poetry – something that O'Sullivan does too, in addition to encountering and contemplating Celtic "figures" in both landscape and language. Equally well, it seems important to briefly consider one or two of O'Sullivan's predecessors in metaphysical experiment in the U.K. – such as John Riley and even J.H. Prynne, given his (albeit much-ironised) engagement with shamanistic images in his early work – and what they contribute to such conversations, which otherwise tend to be focussed on figures in the American grain.

In addition, then, to working in latter-day, respectful homage to the long line of what Jerome Rothenberg has anthologised as *Technicians of the Sacred* (1985), as well as to more recent poetries of the neo-romantic 'occult' such as that of Duncan,[5] O'Sullivan like Derrida radically *critiques* western metaphysics at the same time that she recognises that even such critique has continued, like Heidegger's 'Poet in a destitute time' (featured in the epigraph to her poem "Garb"), to 'attend, singing, to the trace of the fugitive gods' (1993; 50). Though engaged for years in surpassing Heidegger's own critique of metaphysics, Derrida would in the 1990s admit that '*deconstruction* [too] *is structured like a religion*' (Caputo and Scanlon, 4) – or, as John D. Caputo explains by colourfully mixing discourses, deconstruction too is 'gladdened by the good news of alterity by which we are always and already summoned' (1997, 18). It remains committed, in other words, like the ancient mystics, to the act of negating representation in favour of 'a faith in the *viens*', in what Derrida calls *l'invention de l'autre*, the 'incoming of the other', which inadvertently relegates it to an inherited position of waiting, of continuing *aporia*.

O'Sullivan, on the other hand, by deploying a poetics of embodiment rather than *ascesis* in her performative poetry, and excessive "presence" in language as *presentness* and "error" – the latter a ubiquitous word in her work used, I would argue, in its oldest etymological sense of "wandering" – abandons deconstruction's disavowed but potent desire for transcendence. Instead she enters "the word's" shifting landscape, a movement that she frequently images as *cutting into* the perceived, the immediate and physical, which "bleeds" back; she does so "shamanistically", perhaps, attending to the often violent *body* of language as both her means of being in the world and as her disease. Her directions take her into what David Marriott calls a 'non-apophatic theoasthetics' which pursues otherness *within* the linguistic frame and "body" of the world (64) without recourse to Christian, romantic "natural supernaturalism" (Altieri 100) or Jewish messianism or mysticism (most often associated with Kabbalistic practice discovering hidden patterns in words). O'Sullivan's updated shamanistic interests signal an alternative to both the vatic pronouncements and the waiting games of western cultural Judeo-Christianity through other kinds of what she calls 'metaphysical', 'interrealmic'[6] (2003, 68; 1983, unpaginated), *activity*.

I

Given that any interest in "the primitive" is almost instantly associated with the much larger group of postwar poets in the U.S.

interested in the same, it becomes important to reiterate that O'Sullivan's practice differs significantly from two strains of it: 1) that of, for example, current U.S. poet John Taggart, whose apprehension of "correspondences" and ultimate "unity" happens via traditional means in which 'the process is metaphor'[7]; 2) earlier approaches to transcendent vision through neo-Whitmanesque, neo-Olsonian models of self-explosion via *self-projection* upon a native landscape. One recent study of the latter, Devin Johnston's *Precipitations: Contemporary American Poetry as Occult Practice* (2002), describes the work of post-war poets such as Olson and Duncan and, in their wake, others like Nathaniel Mackey and Susan Howe, as being coeval with mystical processes of both self-dissolution and receptive apprehension – or receipt of sublime 'precipitations' out of the old chaotic sublunary matrices, if ones updated to accommodate post-nuclear age imaginations. But by beginning with Olson's description of 'proprioception' – his suggestion that through it 'projection is discrimination (of the object from the subject) and the unconscious is the universe flowing-in, inside'[8] – Johnston in his book defines a postwar American attraction to occult practices that *begins* with 'a return to physicality' and yet ends with what he names 'immanence, albeit through a transcendence of normative conceptual limits' (18). The self is never dissolved in such processes, only made larger – "all the world".

Though it becomes difficult to assent to all that Johnston argues with regard to the whole group of these poets – particularly his assertions that they are all latter-day Romantics who 'aspire to sublimity' (128), are 'preoccupied with apocalypse' (131), compose through Blakean processes of being 'taken over' and effecting 'dictation' (15) and that they ultimately, and 'with vatic grandeur, . . . attribute to poetry a revelatory capability beyond the limits of society or ideology' (20) – their project of achieving transcendence *does* often seem, as it does in the much of the linguistic theory that inspires postmodernist work, to bear relation to the *mystification* of anti-metaphysics (though most would assume they are bent on demystification *tout court*). Desires for 'take-over' by the "other", and facilitation of 'precipitations' of the real through romantic models of negative capability, do indeed deliver us back to the early mystics' subversions of medieval doctrine through their modellings of consciousness that can empty its "self" of institutionalised representations of divinity to await inspiriting, the 'secret word' about the ultimate unity of all things (Eckhart 46). *Both* ancient and modern-day mysticisms might be said to conduct their processes via *a priori* reasoning about otherness – or what Rosmarie Waldrop has dismissed as the 'God . . . who lays out meanings to start with' (143). Indeed, mystical language might be said to be proleptic of Olson's thoughts above; as John D. Caputo writes, 'The medievals regarded "inanimate" things (without a soul or *anima*) as "contracted" to themselves, while beings possessed of a soul overflow their bodily limits and reach out into ("intend" or "tend into") the world' (2001, 45). Such emptying of selfhood re-sets the stage for neo-romantic visions of oneness and, more consequentially, for re-inscription of poetic performance as a drama of immanence, of return to self.

Somewhere between this and her mentor Beckett's (as well as Derrida's) flirtations with negative theology, Susan Howe uses bridal imagery to suggest that the process of 'strik[ing] through [the mask]' of words literally courts 'death [as] the unspeakable other' in her poetry, whose face seems to her at times interchangeable with the 'bridegroom' whose coming will effect her own unity within infinity. Such frightening desire for negation, 'dangerous' though it may be, leads to a mysterious place that conflates with more positively imagined 'perfect absence'. As Will Montgomery writes, Howe's work 'is always shadowed by an impulse towards an inaccessible space that effaces difference. This yearning for a destructuring outside – "something out of the world – God, or the Word, a supreme Fiction", . . . – might perhaps be described as a form of neo-Romanticism' (99). Such 'unspeakable' apophatic imaginings also coincide very deeply with Derrida's, and their emotional valence coincides too with his fears and longings at the end of 'Structure, Sign and Play'. That early and very famous essay ends by wondering about might be coming to birth, slouching towards Bethlehem, through deconstruction's procedures – something that could, like Howe's 'bridegroom', be either terrifying or enthralling – which in any case is certainly desired by him, if necessarily unimaginable:

> Here there is a sort of question, call it historical, of which we are only glimpsing today the *conception, the formulation, the gestations*, the *labor*. I employ these words, I admit, with a glance toward the business of childbearing – but also with a glance toward those who, in a company from which I do not exclude myself, turn their eyes away in the face of the as yet unnameable which is proclaiming itself and which can do so, as is necessary whenever a birth is in the offing, only under the species of the non-species, in the formless, mute, infant and terrifying form of monstrosity. (1978, 370)

And such desires/fears of the 'unnameable' also correlate with those of Beckett, Howe's predecessor in experiment, whom some have read as being a 'failed mystic', 'an ascetic without beatitude', whose 'negative way' is to strip off the language of the 'Christian man trapped . . . in the temporal world [of semantic logic] and unable therefore to attain his true selfhood'.[9] Yet Wolosky would argue that Beckett's critique of such mystical negation means to ultimately return us to the only world we *can* know: the text, by 'exhibiting . . . the consequences of *devaluing language in the name of what would supposedly surpass it*' (124, my emphasis):

> If silence does promise an end to this flow and this confusion, it does so neither as ideal release nor as redemptive accomplishment. The release it offers proves instead to be a kind of defeat. The narrators may dream of reduction as an avenue to true self-knowledge: 'As if to grow less could help. . . . Hoping to wear out a voice. . . . Or the breath fail better still, I'll be silence, I'll know I'm silence.' But in the end this abolishes the very conditions of knowing: 'No, in the silence you can't know, I'll never know anything.'

> (Wolosky 123; Beckett, *Stories and Texts for Nothing*, 112).

While it is true that Derrida also abjures silence, asserting that he engages with negative theology *only* because it 'perhaps holds to a promise', as he puts it, 'that of the other, which [he] must keep because it commits [him] to speak where negativity ought to absolutely rarefy discourse' (1989, 14), his theories exhibit what he came to call messianic visions delivered by such negativity fostered ubiquitously in postwar philosophy and filtered through his own Jewish background. Perhaps Roy Fishers's perception, offered in the suburbs of his post-war-*Waste Land* poem, 'City', of life continuing more truly through a structurally proliferating *cover-up* of the absent center, a 'polytheism without gods' (Matthias 142), might serve as an apt description of poststructuralism as well, given that it finds ways to posit the same "old God" *as* that irreducible absence: the same in another name, still at the centre (or origin) and still coming for us but only at the end of time.

As well-known postmodern theologian Mark C. Taylor has explored it in his book *Erring: A Postmodern A/theology* (1984), *both* visions of absolute origin *and* absolute end (such as deconstruction's above) propel one back into the Judeo-Christian narrative of history which 'haunts the historical imagination of the west even when it is not directly acknowledged' (153). Its inseparability of plenitude, loss and exile – ancillary to creation, fall and redemption – breeds what Taylor calls the 'unhappy consciousness', a form of experience he connects to the contours of the abstraction 'history' itself:

> With eyes forever cast beyond, the victim of unhappy consciousness lives in memory and hope. . . . Satisfaction, however, proves elusive; it is never present or is *infinitely* delayed. . . . For the unhappy self, the pursuit of satisfaction necessarily becomes an effort to become other than what one is. History, at least in part, grows out of the ceaseless struggle for transcendence, a struggle that every discontented subject anxiously enacts. For this reason, the historical process is inseparably bound to the activity of negation. (151)

In other words, the absent satisfaction, infinitely delayed, structures the present movement of desire towards *it* and away from what *is present*, in the same way that "the signified" structures signification in language use. Derridean deferral, or deconstruction's negative dialectics, hardly dare name the direction in which their desire moves. Encountered is just the bare stage of *Waiting for Godot*, where the lone tree is *only* a symbol – a willow, a gallows, whose leaves make the sound of 'all the dead voices' (40). The Godot or 'Mr Knott' who functions as absence in Beckett's texts galvanises the dispositions of bodies on stage or page through the delivery of his word – that he 'will come tomorrow' (Beckett 58). Characters in such end-games ceaselessly circle an abyssal centre, literally 'becoming a cemetery of performance' as Fisher's 'City' speaker fears it (Matthias 137). They also risk disappearing from acting or action altogether: 'You're sure you saw me', shouts Didi, 'you won't come and tell me tomorrow that you never saw me!' (Beckett 59). Humanity becomes absence made in God's image; forever awaiting *the promised* by deferring *the now*. 'We are stillborn', says Dostoyevsky's underground man at the turn of the modern era, lamenting the delivery over of the immediate experience of 'real individual body and blood' to textual/scriptural prescription; 'for generations past have been begotten, not by living fathers, and that suits us better and better. . . . Soon we shall contrive to be born somehow of an idea' (Dostoyevsky 91). 'Born', indeed, as Derrida would have it (by metaphor) in the long quote above, out of a 'conception' of the other which then enters as a mere photo-*negative* of the sublime repeatedly envisioned within the human history such theory hopes to (but cannot) "move beyond".

II

Recent poetry has often and inadvertently effected the same iteration of such paradigmatic negation (and deferral, or 'waiting') that theory has done. Not acknowledging its embeddedness in metaphysical models, it ends up repeating them – repeating their imagined "ends". And imagining alternatives at this stage of history (or, as Beckett might have it, on this stage of history) is, as deconstruction itself argues, difficult. Does the acknowledgement that the process of deconstructing western theological systems has itself been structured like a religion throw us back, then, into a processual chiasmus literally book-ended by 'hyperessentialities'? Put another way, with experimental writing specifically in mind, is negation of convention really only swigging 'old wine' for inspiration, as Andrew Duncan suggests in his assessment of the early work of O'Sullivan and others engaged in what he terms 'the Conceptual Project' as it took form in London (in the works of poets like Allen Fisher, Robert Sheppard, and cris cheek)?

> The method is one of programmed immaturity: the artist wants permanently to be in a state where the elements of technique are uncertain and full of surprises. It is a state of Utopian optimism, bottled like an old wine, which lets people believe that investigations will really throw up a swarm of exciting and active mysteries. Certainly it relies on a set of founding paradoxes and edges which is used up by exposure and not easily added to. A phrase of the time was 'the Western box', implying that there was a limited mentality belonging to the West, which of course the mind-expanded traveller . . . was outside and above . . . .. The scheme reminds me of creation myths – that curious excitement about imagining the origin of institutions, with its glimpses, although imaginary, of alternative realities. (158–9)

It becomes difficult to know whether the reading demonstrates more clearly than the text the problems it locates there about imagining and desiring origins and endings. In any case, in my own view O'Sullivan's poems are doing something much less grand than this, and at the same time far more relevant, in that they *attempt*, at any rate, difficult as it is, to effect a non-teleologically inflected encounter with their immediate materials, one that Taylor would argue is possible only after the postmodern turn – after, that is, 'history ends and erring begins'.

Riley grappled with something of the same project in his explicitly Christian work, drawing his own distinctions between teleologically-inflected and avant-garde forms of theoaesthetics: 'The difference between power and energy is that the former is teleological, the latter presupposes no end, it posits the endless expression of itself, it poses as the timeless agent of evolution . . ." (447). Riley, like Pound and those theologians who influenced them both (Erigena and Grosseteste among them), wished to abandon reified constructions of the divine in order to newly perceive what Pound called 'a world of moving energies' (Grant 132; Pound 154, 'Cavalcanti'). His long poem written in the 1970s, 'Czargrad', therefore linguistically wavers, errs and wanders in the light and shadow of its sensually perceived energies, contemplating the idea that 'the City' (whose name in his title simultaneously calls up ancient Constantinople and future utopias) 'exists' even now, 'jewelled in time', 'no nearer no further than fifty thousand years ago' (*CW* 166, 65). Interested in more mystically-oriented Eastern Orthodoxy, Riley's poems call themselves 'Apophatic Icon[s]'[10] because they attempt to fuse deconstructive impulses with revised incarnational ones, finding inspirational sources in ancient icons that paradoxically portray the unrepresentable divinity made manifest in the homely materials of the world (gold on wood) – in other words, always already incarnate in the imperfect world. But reinterpreting *both* iconostatic and traditionally mystical imaginations of a 'God' 'high up over the cloud formation'[11], Riley's project is to move towards 'the one manner of knowing : to reach out / as a leaf swivels in sunlight' (162) and the understanding 'that the past the present and the future have no motion' (165). In other words, only living things have motion, *we* (like shamans) move between these spaces hypostasised in our textual imaginations of them. Therefore the poet becomes a worker, a maker, moving between sensual and symbolic realms, reconstructing the signage for what Heidegger, in 'The Origin of the Work of Art', calls 'world' rather than earth, because such making happens between "the real" and the Wittgensteinian, linguistic limits of human knowing.

In Coffey's 1970s poem *Advent*, too, we are 'always in human circumstances / no angels and prone to forget / we can work only from point to point' (41). In other words, the poem contradicts John Taggart's assertion that in the ever-forgetful present one must look to the eternal, Duncanesque 'Word' buried in the "collective unconscious" of language[12] – suggesting instead with his line-end that the forgetful present is the *only* starting point for poetry. In general, European postwar poets in the experimental vein have had less truck with Jung than their U.S. counterparts; even neo-Thomism in the work of particularly

Jacques Maritain, Coffey's teacher in Paris, had more influence on especially Catholics who wished to reconcile belief with modern philosophy. Teaching, as did Thomas Aquinas, that *both* physical and metaphysical knowledge begin with the senses and continue to depend upon them, *never* fully transcending them, Maritain takes an alternative route toward arguing that the poet's 'creative intuition' must become, like Olson's, a matter of 'blood and spirit together'.[13] Neither are stimulated by "capitalised" absolutes or ideals like 'Beauty', or conventional lines of poetry like those of Petrarch to 'Laura false advent idol' – who surfaces briefly in the poem as an unhelpful relic (14) – but rather by 'the passing swan beauty beauty swan', the 'flow going past not nothingness' (15): moment by moment perception, because movement and change, unlike absolutes, are what we *have*. But both Olsonian trawling for origins and teleology self-deconstruct in Coffey's poem, whose very title implodes (meaning as it does both the season of waiting and the actual arrival). And though Christological imagery emerges as Revelation-like vision by the poem's end, offering up a situation of being stretched between past and future that could suggest Christ on a cross as well as the poet and his poem, it becomes reabsorbed in the only current possibility for 'freedom': 'height of power' 'seen' only, 'surely / where friend gives greatest gift', 'saves from bondage' (41–2). Such allegorically sacrificial vision – proleptic of what Derrida and postmodern theologians like Jean-Luc Marion would envision as "the true gift": a model for possible-impossible, god-like intervention in economies of exchange value – combines with paradox offered as a method for overturning the world's hierarchical forms of reason that result in palindromes of self-reproductive narrative: 'Slaves with tyrants beget tyrants with slaves' (41). And yet, though the final line, 'so be it', reasserts the ambiguity of the poem's status and vision with its translation of the Aramaic "amen" – updating, perhaps, Beckett's early statement that 'all poetry . . . is prayer' (1984, 68) – Coffey's transformation of the whole of his dissertation on spiritual history into the most tentative of communications does not obviate its invocation of the end of the story and rescue from impasse.

The struggle to emerge out of the story of metaphysics with its beginning- and end-time – which Coffey is caught up in narrating as *progression* out of 'the day before letters', 'innocent days before conflict' (11) – becomes so easily and ironically "Fall-en" back into the narrative once again. Such images of loss of "primitive" innocence, rife in twentieth-century poetics, suggest the difficulty of the task at hand – or the

accuracy of Derrida's prophecy concerning the impossibility of meaning being fully *present* to consciousness, given that the very idea of
meaning is the idea of a repeatable ideality. Indeed both Riley in his
dreams of bejewelled Jerusalem and Coffey pinioned at the crossroads
of time might be said to join Clov in *Endgame* as he unsuccessfully (and
increasingly verbosely) invokes the end of history through hapless *repetition* of Christ's final words: 'finished, it's finished, nearly finished, it
must be nearly finished' (Beckett 1958, 1).

III

If *not* repetition of the story of western metaphysics, what then? For all
the problems I have with Taylor's thought, his word "erring" becomes
key for me as descriptive of another kind of emerging *activity* within
language. Instead of the usual chronicling of differences from positions of sameness, gathering events and phenomena into the *ur-*
narrative invisibly suturing up the gaps, such activity effects meetings
with the non-identical – i.e., everything outside the self (and many
aspects within). In the twentieth-century it arises somewhere between
the injunctions of a number of those people O'Sullivan has often listed
as influences: Stein, in her particular attraction to verbs and prepositions because, as she puts it in "Poetry and Grammar", "they can be so
mistaken"; Beckett, in his famous and fragile hope of "failing better";
J. H. Prynne, in his reaction against the 'imperious recruitment' of the
copula, which negates singularity – or, in Hegel's words, 'say[s] "this
rose is red"', applying 'an abstract universal [that] does not apply to the
rose alone'; [14] Wittgenstein, with his urging to look upon language
games as *primary* phenomena – '*Look* at it! That's how *it is*! Don't ask
why, but take it as a fact!' – in order to 'wonder at the existence of the
world', as he put it in his 'Lectures on Ethics' in 1929 (86), and 'see the
world as a miracle'. Such suspension of "judgement" exceeds, in recent
practice, the romantic, Coleridgean ability to view all the world as
holy. Perceiving the relation between language and incarnations of
"the real" with critical difference – i.e., the very idea that "the word
be[comes] flesh" – current metaphysical writing might be said to
pursue "all the world" again by attuning itself to what perception
continually blocks despite its constitutive status, what Paul Celan
called 'a *wholly Other*'.[15] Upending orthodox taboos by recovering
ancient practices, such as shamanism, that engage in movement

between phenomenal and linguistic spaces, the latter of which perpetuate temporal/teleological distinctions and visions, is common – if now
practiced with neither panache nor authority, but with a "stutter".
'(EAR MY STUTTER' one of O'Sullivan's lines enjoins us – because hearing can literally mean incarnating *now* (1993, 52); therefore her "noisy"
verse in 'GARB', for example, with its capitalised emphases/errors,
seems pitched to out-shout the smooth-talking heard daily, like the
'FELL NOISE' made 'politically emphatically in parliament today' (51).
Erring is a word Taylor uses with all of its earliest senses intact: meaning both "wandering" and making Wittgen(Steinian) mistakes that
become the (Heideggerian) world and *over*come the everywhere-domi-
nating story of fallen human "being":

> The prospect of *radical* purposelessness emerges with the realization that
> "becoming has no goal and that underneath all becoming there is no
> grand unity" [a line from Nietzsche's *Will to Power*]. This release silences
> the yearning for transcendence by calling into question the exclusive
> opposition between what is and what ought to be. Like origin and conclu-
> sion, the center [sought] to *cure* the open trace by founding the eternal
> play of scripture. If, however, the divine milieu is an acentric . . . totality,
> which neither begins nor ends, then it would seem that nothing
> inscribed within this non-centered whole can be centered or whole. By
> freely affirming the primordiality of lack, the interiority of exteriority,
> [and] the difference of identity, the erring trace overcomes the despair of
> unhappy/lacerated consciousness. When becoming no longer needs to be
> validated by reference to past or future but can be valued at every
> moment, one has broken with the law. Such transgression does not breed
> guilt and sin . . . but is inseparable from grace. (156–57)

Such '*cur[ing]* of the open trace' is profoundly contrary to the kinds of
shamanistic "healing" that a poet like O'Sullivan achieves in her paradoxically erring state of 'grace'.

Her most obvious and important predecessor in considering the
benefits of such erring as well as shamanism as a model for poetic
activity is Prynne, most notably in 'Aristeas, in seven years' (1968) , his
earliest experiment in thinking 'singularly' and 'nomadically' – along
the 'errant world' (22). This celebrated poem is, in Simon Jarvis's brilliant reading, one that breaks with both narrative cognition and narrative form in its attempt to rethink economies of valuation, be they
political, financial or poetic. It takes as its matter Herodotus's report of
the lost poem, the *Arimaspea*, by the 7th-century poet, Aristeas of
Proconessus, who constructed it as an account of his leaving behind

his native island 'to catch up with / . . . the forms of an alien vantage' (17) among the nomadic and semi-nomadic peoples of the Russian steppes. As Jarvis explains, 'The Evenk word *khamat-mi*, "to catch up with", is also used as a technical term within Evenk culture for the shaman's dance performed with the hope of attracting animals and securing success in the hunt' (77). Updated by Prynne, Aristeas's shamanistic 'catching up' with these nomadic peoples is also a matter of 'hunting'; it was in part prompted by financial crisis in his community and the desire to discover where the nomads procured their ornamental gold. (Shamanism is not, in other words, a wholly innocent activity in this poem; nor would it be in O'Sullivan's work to come.) But the other discovery Aristeas makes is that the nomads' 'vantage is singular / as the clan is without centre' (23) – since the mobile larch-pole that holds up the shaman's tent 'represents the central axis of the clan-world' (Jarvis 79). What one encounters as a result is continual difference, the singularities of new situations, rather than the expectation of return, the end of journeys. And, as Prynne imagines it, as Aristeas 'thin[s] out' the self 'who was' (21), he comes to 'proceed quite otherwise than as a chronicler of the displaced from the established place of civic settlement' (Jarvis 77).

Prynne's project connects powerfully with O'Sullivan's, though she illuminates the differences in her approach as well as the title of *In the House of the Shaman* in her writing-in-order-to-reflect-on-her-writing-process called 'riverrunning (realisations for Charles Bernstein':

> . . . In naming my work
> after [Beuys'] I am tributing his work: fluid, changing,
> inviting new material, urging new responses. His urge to
> begin with mistakes, to show frailty . . . is at once
> starfish abdominal nuance   its moorings unsuspected –
> rescued starlight.
>
> *
>
> Jerome Rothenberg and the exemplary work he makes wide
> is a key, too in my workings. A richness of difference:
> Disparity: Difficulties: Dismemberment/Reconstitution:
> Sickness: Contradiction: Improvising upon: INTENT.
> ADJUSTING TEETH / WITHIN WORDS / WOUNDS OF CHANCE /
> CARESSER OF CHAOS LEAPING HABIT –
>
> (2003, 68; all typographical "errors" O'Sullivan's)

The account of an account of an account that Prynne produces in his poem in order to trouble narrative remains within the customary disposition of language as *re*-counting what occurs, or has occurred in ages past, whereas O'Sullivan's work moves toward *being*, presently, the occurrence itself. The poet's positioning in Prynne's poem remains outside what is recounted; in O'Sullivan's, the poet is present not in but *as* the work, 'show[ing] frailty', being 'dismembered' in order to 'reconstitute' subjectivity as *made* provisionally, moment by moment. Such practice is also not a matter of passively receiving occult 'precipitations' as Johnston calls them, or 'align[ing] poetic power with irrational forces' (20), but rather becomes a thinking poetry if a struggling one, receiving nothing aside from impression upon itself by non-identical materials. These are encountered *actively*, through its making 'colliderings' among words and their referents amid their differences (rather than Taggart's 'correspondences') happen, through 'moving m eye out', as she puts it in another passage from the work. The abbreviated pronoun suggests the collapsing of 'my' and 'eye', or the subject's becoming continually colliding perception itself – with the body participating – recovering *not* any romantic or Jungian or Olsonian 'unity of experience as the prime matter for poetry' (Mellors 1998, 68) but rather a 'richness of difference', the *limits* to all such comfortable discoveries of sameness. Therefore for her, 'living word[s]' are already 'arisen' (and 'advent' over) because rather than being involved in accounting or recounting or gathering everything back into the accepted story, 'realising' meaning is here a matter of being moment by moment an anchor out of its depth, in motion:

> Poetry finds my life – Poetry as she has Arisen 'AS SHE
> ARRIVES OUT OF THE FUTURE, WORDS LIVING', moving
> m eye out among the ribbed & swimmish places
> Uncoiled,Endowed among us
> in the arrival of
> remembrancing   responding   realising   journeying
> the moment by
> moment
> anchor out of her
> depth that is
> LANGUAGE
> DANCE
> DREAM
> 'COLLIDERINGS'
>
>   (2003, 'riverrunning . . . .', 63)

Certainly Olsonian and even Emersonian by heritage, such a model drops, however, the subsuming activity of the transcendental "eye". And though the 'SHE' above is seemingly drawn straight out of Duncan's 'Structure of Rime I', where '. . . there is a woman who resembles the sentence. She has a place in memory that moves language' (12), in O'Sullivan's case this figurative force of alterity comes not out of memory but *into it*, manifest as it is in the present 'WORDS LIVING' – rather than the 'sentence', whose paradigm as legacy would hinder the 'uncoiling' of language's meaning-making possibilities in her fluid now-time. Above, the poet simply begins to move to the sensually perceived 'arrival' of what is always already there: the "living word" in which both past and future are collapsed (as are the words 'Uncoiled,Endowed') and always changing, inflected by the now. That word is a living fossil, 'ribbed and swimmish', unfinished, and not valued for its traces of absolute "origin" even if one's own evolution is apparent in its fishy endowments (which are both attributes and gifts for O'Sullivan, who reinterprets the miseries of Derridean deferral and Barthesian slippage as *positive* linkage of past and future in the moment rather than as entrapment; shamanically she moves between them). Her making a *present activity* of nouns (such as "remembrances" made 'remembrancing') and things of activities like hearing (made as we saw into 'EAR[ing]') casts them all into a kind of Steinian verbal "mistaking" and therefore *remaking* of perceptual space. This is because her 'tend sees errant' as she tells us on the next page; and what she has always been attracted to in Duncan's work she lists as 'Mistakes, Da-mage, Duncan's "MISUSE, MISUNDERSTANDING, THE WHOLE SPIRITUALISED UNIVERSE"', making of "damage" something magical and philosophical: mage, magus. Thus while it is true that O'Sullivan's work, like Derrida's, reverances *l'invention de l'autre* – the incoming of the other: the unadmitted and erroneous, here the 'SHE' of language – her sensual collisions between the physical incarnations of words and phenomena, as well as the linguistic memories words hold of constantly "creating the world" and cutting it up in the process, make that incoming more stuttering, imperfect *and therefore more immediate* than anything dreamt of in Derrida's philosophy.

This, then, is O'Sullivan's late-twentieth-century version of what Blake admired in his predecessors like Milton, which O'Sullivan recalls in 'riverrunning': 'subversion: Milton's "UNTWISTING THE CHAINS THAT TIE"' (66). Yet her subversions proceed utterly differently from those of the 'mind-expanded traveller' (a descendant of Blake's 'Mental Traveller'), who moves 'outside and above' in order to glimpse 'alternative realities', as Andrew Duncan put it in my earlier quote. Instead, 'riverrunning's' 'TALK' (its first word; also its genre as delivered in Buffalo and Vancouver) begins with a linguistic deconstruction of all narratives or 'Tell-Tales' that nonetheless asserts: 'DON'T YOU KENNET OR HAVEN'T I TOLD YOU EVERY TELLING HAS A TALING AND THAT'S THE HE AND SHE OF IT' (59). In other words, in her work, the evolution of the new happens through erotic play between 'THE HE AND SHE OF IT', those 'TELLING[s]' and 'TALING[s]', narratives and physically-present speakers remaking each other alongside ever-changing phenomena – including words. Here, colliding the foregoing capitalised representation of narrative with 'A Crack A Rip A Spin' results in,

> In Irish, AMHRAIN: CEOL:
> A Song, A Song Said Otherwise, half-sung/half-said,
> SINGS – Speaking the Self/whom sang/Singing over/ –
> The Irish again – ABAIR AMHRAN – Say us a Song –
> Say, Speak / Words Spoken / Give Us Your
> Tongue It to See – dark blades how sang crows
> Disquieting the auditorium's fabular harmonics –
> Worlds by Words / Telling Alive mirrors to the
> Stream affrighted Speaker and listener – turn by turn
> Between, & the moon late in rising – Live Blood/Its
> Rise with the Other / A Wilder Air Chancing to poetry's
> Music (amplified) Edgewise –
> > Then.Now.There.Here.
>
> > > (59)

In O'Sullivan's work 'Worlds by Words' are actively *remade* by erotically 'Tongu[ing] it' or transforming codified language into the 'half-sung/half-said'. In Irish, the familiar expression *'abair amhrán'*, or 'sing a song', can also be translated 'say a song', as O'Sullivan suggests above both in words and in the upheaval of sound in these lines that produces another kind of sense. It 'disquiet[s]' the auditorium's 'fabular harmonics' – connecting by "mistaking" such 'fabulous' (unbelievable) musical harmonies to the Latin *'fabula'* (a story, tale). Such 'Music (amplified) edgewise' – allowing 'Other[ness]' in – collapses narrative's temporal organisations by 'mirror[ing]' the 'Stream' that 'affrights' *both* 'Speaker' and listeners who rely on such fables of organization and habitually resist the 'Then' (both past and future) flowing, as in her last line above, without spatial separations into the 'Now'.

As Nate Dorward beautifully explicates them in a short review of her recent composite art work, *red shifts*, the many 'Stream[s]' or images of 'flowing water' in O'Sullivan's work often not only 'carry evocative lyrical or descriptive freight: . . . **"buckled raved sheens"**', for example, which delivers the Coffey-esque lower-case beauty of such non-selfpreserving movements. They also connect themselves to the body in phrases like 'aquacity staltic', the latter word of which Dorward explains is 'a rare word meaning "styptic", [which] also suggests "peristalsis," the wave-like muscular motions of the digestive tract'. Though Dorward reads this connection as one that suggests water's 'treacherous hunger for the living', my sense of it is rather different and more positive. In her 'Working Note' to a selection from the book for *HOW2*(1:5, 2001), she tells us that among her 'inspirations' were 'my father's words and the New Grange markings', referring with the latter to the familiar Celtic, flowing whorls that transform the kerb stones at the entrance to this enormous Irish ancient burial site into signs (and enter many of her drawings for *red shifts*). The phrase 'aquacity staltic' seems more importantly connected to several foregoing images of continuing life, not death, including 'Nion, the Ash', a rune used as a charm to *prevent* drowning, as Dorward explains (and one connected to O'Sullivan's 'Shielding Ash of memory' ('– that bread should be –', 30); an Eliotic 'letter of salvages' (the latter word referring to the restoration of, or insurance against, lost property in shipwrecks); and the styptic or blood-staunching definition of the word "staltic" itself. All this suggests to me a longed-for immersion in – and not transcendence of – such de- and recompositional processes, and a radical revision of Eliot's notion that such drowning/dying is life itself. Her work rarely depicts phenomenal matter yearning to absorb the living but rather the reverse; therefore her 'Telling Alive', as she calls it in the quote from 'riverrunning' above, is an 'eating alive' to form utterances encountering the immediate, *through* the body, which is *also* always changing as a result, ingesting the world: a process O'Sullivan constantly links to the continuous (and potentially violent) exchanges between language and otherness, the non-identical. Like Prynne, she does not romanticise the necessary work of the shaman, but rather takes the long view of the world of her work as 'a place of damage, savagery, pain, silence; also a place of salvage, retrieval and recovery. A place of existence, journeying. A sacred space of undiminishment' (O'Sullivan/Olsen, 2). Yet her damaged speaker and broken open lines and words are paradoxically "w(holy)" undiminished, as the quote from 'riverrunning' above explains by splicing 'Live Blood' with 'Its/Rise with the Other', in another Christic echo recalling the resurrection of Christ and the

Christian paradox that self-sacrifice achieves immortality and the life of the whole.

'A LUTE IN THE MIDDLING AIR – interspeciel/interrealmic Joy' is what sounds itself, then, in O'Sullivan's 'lacerated' work,[16] rather than the 'unhappy/lacerated consciousness' Taylor describes above. Yet I find myself uncertain that such 'Joy' is quite what Robert Sheppard calls "exuberance" in her act of writing (5); there is, in it, far too much red and blood in *the cutting into presence* that language effects – 'adjusting teeth / within words' as she puts it in the first quote from 'riverrunning' above. As she makes amply clear in *red shifts*, 'entrancing' into being through linguistic 'erring' (a word that arises in numerous forms throughout the work) also runs the risk of being 'sutured' to 'cure' its wandering 'INEXACT / locutions', of becoming simple mimicry of the appropriative behaviour of what she calls 'the saturated language of red': 'speech['s] / apt-leash of similars', or identificatory and metaphorical logics, which when 'swung' 'cut[s] into' 'the full of a sack . . . / lengthwise'. Applied to human relations such behaviour results in the only text actually coloured bright red in the book – that which describes 'paddy', an Irish boy, perhaps the 'fourth son' alluded to early on, who is here circumscribed by a blood-red line of words and its leash of similars: 'paddy.took.after.my.grandmother's. / people. / paddy took after', always already belatedly. Thus though accompanied at the top of the book's cover by something reminiscent of a red "No Stopping" sign from the U.K.'s *Highway Code* (which might suggest desired, full-on flow for this work's present and sensual traffic of words), the red scar of that suturing runs across the front, back and inside flaps as well as into the drawings of *red shifts*. Its jaggedly-drawn, zig-zagging crayon line, surrounded by more abstract, pencil drawn lines as encasement – which becomes the complicated sign of life-bearing human blood-lines but also linguistic construction formed 'at an angle', unlike any of the other flowing lines and blotted, bleeding elements to be found in the watercolour accompaniments to the text – runs straight over the neck of a fishy live thing "caught" on the back-cover.

In complement to its predicament, we feel the speaking figures in the text – both male and female in this "story", the 'he and she of it' we might say – struggle, rightly or wrongly, to get their heads above water, above the "natural" flow of 'breath[ing] in' and breath[ing] out' that also visually traverses the page. Unlike American "breath" poetics, which involve a one-way expulsion of interior into exterior, a mapping of breath capacity onto poetic line, O'Sullivan's revision of the model takes in air/the world in order to be transformed by *it*, before sending it back out, transforming the world. This becomes her alternative, "post-immanence" definition of "spirit" (which of course means by etymology "breath").[17] But for the speakers at the start of the poem, the goal is to emerge separate, *one*-self, to desperately define 'i my / self. my own ————' against 'errs of animal rising'. They struggle repeatedly to 'hold [their] breath' in fear of dissolution in those fluid relations. Their debut on the book's first page is made by an initial flowing black line drawn perpendicularly to what follows: the first red zig zag, along which biblically-echoing words begin to move with great tentativeness: 'thrine / roam / awkward and slow / unable to stand / & bread / put out among the branches'. The powerful first construction, 'thrine', with its sounds reminiscent of both "thine" and "mine" and, with the next word's vowel annexed, "throne", might suggest at first immanent divinity again, available in the romantic re-achievement of lost original *unity* between self and other, man and nature. But O'Sullivan's model of "natural" relations is based on constructive *difference* – therefore the initiating discrepancy between linguistic and non-verbal "movement" is made clear on these first pages, as these words move up and down 'at an angle', signalling artifice disconnected from nature's initial, flowing line. These pages deliver, in other words, or rather in Taylor's above, O'Sullivan's 'free affirmation of the primordiality of lack', even if her speakers in the poem have yet to demonstrate the same affirmation.

The next page begins 'broke' with awareness of that lack/rupture and of an inability to use 'raised arms' to access the scriptural 'bread' or manna imagined just out of reach. Such disappointments quickly result in violent attempts to protect the self's seemingly fragile, isolate integrity; therefore the word 'DECOMPOSITIONS' appears crossed out in the text, and 'threadened' (in the flow) becomes 'threatened' in a line that crosses out both in order to resolve 'to kill' – while 'cant hold my breath/my breath' is followed by repeated 'sobbing'. Such regret, such 'unhappy/lacerated consciousness' of loss, is signed as *textual* inheritance near the middle of the book, in the two-page spread that compares the line '"sometimes she cries', which occurs in the proper place for text, at the centre of the first page, and the line '& sometimes she is / again"'. The latter occurs beyond the extreme lower right margin of the next page – a positioning that, like the 'hare in field / . . . flaught ist –' at the end of the book, suggests (as does the Scottish word 'flaught', which means a flicker, a flash, a flake) what is *really* in danger of being lost: radically liminal immediacy less captured by the linguistic realm; 'the UN, the found, the disremembered'.

The speakers' subsequent attempts to 'riverrun', to 's[ing] all along the river for practise', leave only 'whispers' from their 'sundered splash' into 'easel wink marine ecstacy', the flow; encounters with otherness in *accounts* such as '7 iridescent tail feathers' ringed by what look like red pebbles – the 'collected pebbles' of 'speech' cited earlier – form, by the book's end, ancient burial chambers. But following these sepulchral pages the 'reach of the peacock's / blistering blistering thresholds' appear to contest any accounting for the unquantifiable, then the 'moor shim' which, in its very delicate accompanying drawing, frames white space as blistering and unreadable as those thresholds, along with fading ink at its margins and the 'blistering' and break-down of speech/speaker as well. '[S]he / scribble contusion . . . / . . . this. / crep. / ant.' – which refers to both the Latin *crepāre*, to break, recalling the first actions in the poem, and "crepance", the injury that one hind foot on a horse will deliver the other due to the wearing of horseshoes. This becomes a pun on the initial questions posed about 'ruptures crossing / hoove lost?' – which also reads: "who've lost?" The response would seem to be that none have, though all have changed in O'Sullivan's 'sacred space of undiminishment' *through* such 'damage', such attention to singularities and excesses beyond perception and recordings, such impinging of otherness upon text and *vice versa*. The small, tentative, living and moving thing made by the writing – 'this. / crep. / ant.' – perhaps even puns on the pronunciation of 'crêpe' as well as 'crept', transforming the 'bread' unreachable on the book's first pages into food for thought and remaking thought on its final ones.[18]

Therefore the world's coming into the poet's ken or linguistic presence (and again, *vice versa*) is often figured not as *necessarily* but as potentially violent collision in the work – as in the encounter between her speaker, flying geese, and 'the wire they'd stuttered into' in her heartbreakingly beautiful poem about, once again, coming into linguistic consciousness in Ireland, 'winter ceremony'. The geese in the poem's epigraph, which reads *caoi chadhan in oidhche fhuair* ('or geese grieving in the cold night'), are taken from an anonymous seventeenth-century Irish poem whose title O'Sullivan translates as 'Ugly Your Uproar at My Side' (*Ní Binn Do Thorann Lem Thaoibh*). As that title might suggest, the liabilities involved in hearing – made more explicit later in *red shifts* with its homophonic connections between the frequently used word 'erred' and 'heard' (particularly in non-aspirating dialects) – are critical in the poem and determine whether otherness survives such 'inter-realmic' collision. Thus the geese enter just after the smallest child of the Irish family, the 'i' of the poem, who has been contemplating the movement and sound of these birds on the lake as well as in the sky, wills language to commingle with them, wills the rise of 'words | of | EVERY' (15), at which point we turn the page to find the birds 'all nearly dead or broken . . . as i unpeeled them from the wire they'd stuttered into – '(16). The following two down-falling vertical lines on the page suggest, as they do throughout the piece, that words cannot give the child the virtual grip it longs for over such attractive phenomena; and yet, as the child brings water, abandoning words and 'humming them back into themselves', 'each-bird- | bird-each-body began to stir from its shine—leaned ruin . . . back into its flighting dwell its gooseness'. The move from repetitively naming and reducing 'each bird | bird' is towards apprehension of 'each body': each with *relations* to 'gooseness' rather than the categorising name 'goose'. This suggests that the child (who indicates a connection with the listening/imitating 'Magpie' – and, by sonic similarity, perhaps with our author 'Maggie', though it remains ungendered) is connected to the poem's opening speech. There, as in *red shifts*, perception involves the noting of

HARES

   going so

    flew/
    nt _____

           (9)

in "fluent" movements – here signalled by the adjective becoming a verb – which language cannot capture without contrivance. Therefore the next lines read

   QU
  (about eight or ten letter i can't pronounce

  s t r e t c h i n g

  g o n e - o n - t o -

Wondering over helpless departures from what one sees and feels sensually if forever partially – the hares' semi-articulate motion, signed ineffectively with a drawn line – to words one can't even *re*-sound, is tragi-comically qualified, mid-poem, through what might well be a reference to Beckett's *Krapp's Last Tape*. Krapp's one *present* moment of sensual enjoyment, in his eulogistic and repetitive process of replaying tapes of himself talking *about* a moment of sensual enjoyment, occurs as Freudian joke when he unexpectedly pronounces 'Spoooooool!' with prolonged relish. This recollection of the famous *fort-da* game Freud tells us his grandson invented in response to anxiety about his mother's presence and absence, which involved hurling a cotton string over the edge of his cot and spooling it back, punctuates the black comedy of loss in this play where even such physically pleasurable enactment has become symbolic, a word, whose very presence depends upon the absence of the thing it references. In O'Sullivan's poem the same word appears in a white space mid-page during the 'Address of the Ash' (17) – which as we recall is that symbol of forces that save speakers from drowning. Here, 's-P-O-O-L-I-N-G' between 'BLUE' and 'BELLOW' (a partial-pun on "below") becomes similar engagement in sensual enunciation, but this time without mourning, one that remakes both realms in her work instead of becoming hemmed in by the tragic parameters of Beckett's play. What happens directly after the collision with the geese – 'THE CROSSING OF RUSHES & MORE BLOOD | BLED UNTIL IT WAS HER | word | BARE like BASKET from BATTLE – | BEGINISH ————————————' (17) – depends upon the percussive sounding of *more* inadvertent collisions, whose result is a sign cut into experience, which in turn makes it malleable or misspellable, and "owned" by the speaker in a different sense: in complement to understanding the landscape as 'LIP RINSED PLAINS'. The lower-cased 'word' moves between the two realms, dropped as the speaker becomes deciduous, 'f[alls] to leafing'; it is the dying product of her translation, but nonetheless a necessary vessel which is *not* a "beginning" but something 'beginish', something with which one is constantly remaking relations through recognition of such making's natural and positive connection to "decomposition", too.

Indeed, the whole of the 'wintry' situation in this work is '*without mourning (or ceremony)*' (my emphasis), her speaker realises while watching the geese flying in 'the rain shuttered steep of their shrouds' – grieving', as the poem's epigraph originally anthropomorphised them. Instead, the speaker now describes them as 'burying on', which we suddenly recall was depicted far more positively in the initial lines of the poem:

    dandelion
      earths under we all rising humming over
        even the season we weep in

            | |
            | |
            | |

               (10)

Dandelions – a symbol of commonplace fertility that appears often in O'Sullivan work – are always just 'under . . . / even the season we weep in', or just below surface-level, "buried alive", even in winter, as the 'sun-word – sheer / *all seeing* –*sees* –'. The sun leaves noun-hood in neo-Steinian fashion to become movement, *directionality* – 'sun-word' or *sunward* – in her play with it and its effects here. The latter become, though not fully perceivable, a present physical continuum or flow from earth toward sky, a 'rising' as we saw her image it 'Christically', through earth's crust and its continuous cycle of change. Connected to the words that we saw the child will into 'RISE[ing]', 'we' rise in the above quote too, with "the word made flesh", inevitably to 'leaf' or fall in terms of the de-composition of pre-fabricated speaking in exchange for speaking *now*. Whereas the lovingly-depicted mother in this poem – who is connected to 'feathers' and birds through her 'feather dipping feet' – elects to make returning to the flow a death-wish, a repeated pull towards 'drowning' (14) in the quarry's deep pool or, alternatively, imaginative death in the cornfields *'behind [the father] / piling and binding to the ways of spelling'* (15), the child who tells her story ends it by developing another kind of interrealmic existence that depends on decompositional artisanship, on 'winter ceremony'. Invoking 'time now –', 'i' becomes intent on 'counting to the life asking after, asking after,' – a practice that recognises its own linguistic belatedness by (un)working narrative progression to reach back to what is always lost, 'the life'. Though her speaker cannot avoid what O'Sullivan calls the 'Seeing eye of the story [that] counts'(1997, '– that bread should be –', 34), and the reductiveness of the kind of *accounting for* that itemizes the unitemisable peacocks in *red shifts*, this child's strategy nonetheless reformulates the connection between linguistic and other realms to suggest the possibility of a perpendicular suspension, a "de-composition" that looks intriguingly like a crucifixion – a non-violent version of that meeting, that Coffey-esque crossroads – on the very last page, as the poem's many down-falling vertical lines are suddenly and tenuously connected to the horizontally escaping ones, and the child speaks:

i'd say animal

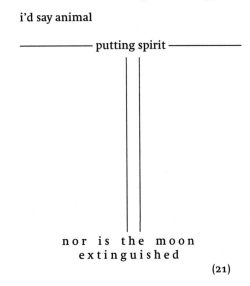

(21)

Such infusions of words *and* 'spirit', by her definition of that word, undo the Levinasian 'said' through the 'say[ing]'[19] – here the generic word 'animal' – by admitting other dimensions to what is too easily identified and therefore lost (like the 'HARES'' indescribable motion, and the human *otherness* in what Levinas by synecdoche refers to as 'the face'). The poem's last lines above recall the first ones, 'd o w n o f m o o n / d e e p l y / l' l o n g' (9) – the incoming of such otherness into the work. Neither reference effects capture of the unknowable orbiter that nonetheless "in-fluences" the flow of life in her sacred space of undiminishment; it therefore remains '[un]extinguished' at the poem's end. The child similarly interacts with otherness in ritual acknowledgement and celebration of those rings of fluid being, and makes inevitably 'counted life' be 'now' *because* representation is allowed to be incomplete and decompositional, be inspiriting *because* the approach is self-consciously both ceremonial and deconstructive: aware of its own artifice signed in symbolic excess that nonetheless allows the interrelations ongoing in the act of "worlding" to become apparent. That such practice has roots in ancient ones belies the story of "spiritual" progress, or at least complicates it in ways that dovetail with O'Sullivan's upturning of word-roots and making present past 'colliderings' that remain palpable in the linguistic landscape.

A moving example of O'Sullivan's location of primitive ceremonials underwriting both modern Christian practice and cultural/familial

relations can be found in '– that bread should be –', which returns to
the Great Irish Famine's devastation of Skibbereen, from which half of
O'Sullivan's family hail. Its title is a shortening of what O'Sullivan tells
us 'was the oft repeated phrase during the Great Irish Famine 1845–52':
'that bread should be so dear and human flesh so cheap' (1997, 23). The
shortening of that phrase for O'Sullivan's own title seems to suggest
that the Susan Howe-like project of the poem is, in important part, to
approach the silences in [her own] history:

whole families without a trace my —————————————

                                   dealt —————————

        it occurs: ————————————————————

      the unstory

        – that bread should be –

                                          (1997, 39)

While Howe's work often centres on historical absence itself as subject
in her work, O'Sullivan in hers regards 'the unstory' as still present. It
'occurs' and has substance in the making of 'bread' or sustenance out
of the 'hacked' and 'shatter[ed]' ancestral landscape; the 'low ground'
is a 'long black crêpe rolled in the mouth's threshing / gleam & misty
blood dripping so many red threads' (26). Shards of 'the found – the
disremembered', of tactile and sonic phenomena (like bits of the Irish
ballad 'Old Skibbereen') appear, among them the re-presencing of the
speaker's 'hand' and a 'his' hand (that of 'the father' (28), it would
seem) and, of course, the inevitable counting – but in this case,
'rounds, Rosary' (27). Though repetition usually amounts to
'Perish[ing]' in the poems ('Doubtless', 2003, 47), the sonic space made
here with this physical *activity* 'Shone Blue'. Such sensual reference to
the colour associated with the mother of Christ raises expectations
that the capital 'B' following the capitalised 'Rosary' will be 'Blessed
Virgin' – but the story moves *differently* into

                                               B

                                         u

                                            c

                                              k

                                            l

                                                 e

                                                   d

– very like '<u>the buckled raved sheens</u>' that in *red shifts* gave us Coffey-esque beauty as ephemeral flow. Here, the word gives us the letters as the "sacred" beads themselves, buckled by the hand's fumbling touch, by desire – as the physical things of language that may be essentially meaningless in themselves but are continually re-*made* to mean in their 'collision' between linguistic and non-linguistic realms. The page's penultimate and Howe-esque, upwards slanting diagonal paste of phrase, 'SAYING / DECADES', is O'Sullivan's picture of history; erring ('buckling') in words reinvents the past and all time in her redefinition of *presence*, as 'saying', continually erupting between "story" that (ac)counts and flesh or "life" that is desirous and *active* – *not* abjectly waiting for the end of deconstructive apophasis to be "born":

Seeing eye of the story counts   yet it is

   tilted, rigged, dragging at the haemorrhage of uns –

my body, (sever, sever who shall she see?

                       |

                 skulls

            keened out in the rain
     & back on the rain would come the tottering twist

   (stank, stank bone jointed   re-twining

its own circle

                   (34)

These are the 'uns' *used* – her 'use of the *UN* . . . the found . . . the disremembered' as I quoted it in the first paragraph of this essay – that, as in the water cycle alluded to in the last lines above, flow back into the work that is buckled enough, 'damaged' enough: the body/boat 'haemorrhaged' enough to tilt and drag at what has been elided rather than gliding smoothly over it. As her epigraph to 'Doubtless' (2003, 31), from Tom Lowenstein's meditation on the Inuit people, puts it:

The places themselves stayed as ancestors had known them. But where the ancestors had fought or died, seen visions or shamanised, they left knots, whorls, vortices of human implication in the landscape. To be in a place of death or vision was to relive the story and extend its relation-ship with the present.[20]

The 'circle' of the lines as they come round in the poem quoted above is like this – is like those flowing Celtic circles in *red shifts* which remain 'whorls, vortices of human implication in the landscape'. Such 'landscape' becomes textual in O'Sullivan's work, or palimpsestic with the terrain in which the body moves. 'A traveller's own moment of life stretched back and spread far', as the other epigraph from Lowenstein has it; in that continuum of meaning's "deferral" even the seemingly direct experience of travelling into a space is not one's own, but links one to ancestors through the linguistic overlay of the physical that makes immediate connection to them and to the world both impossi-ble and unavoidable. Thus the poet is the erring translator between text and texture, the jagged connector of the several riven planes of being in their perpetual mutual displacement, the music-maker of collision. In that sense, she *is* interested in "origins" and "births" – but ones that are *continually* happening:

> The works I make Celebrate Origins/Entrances – the
> Materiality of Language: its actual contractions &
> expansions, potentialities, prolongments, assemblages –
> the acoustic, visual, oral & sculptural qualities
> within the physical: intervals between; in & beside.
> Also the jubilant seep In So of Spirit – Entanglement
> with vegetations, thronged weathers, puppy-web we agreed
> animals. Articulations of the Earth of Language that is
> Minglement, Caesura, Illumination.
>
> Heart
> At once several times TUMULT & Beak-Sup Dusting/
> Believing/Convulsions break out in the next line. SILENCE
>
> introduction of
> sound:
> introduction of
> sight:
> introduction of
> texture:
> *

(2003, 64–65)

Such 'Illumination' is the result of identifying 'Believing' with tactile 'Beak-Sup Dusting', and with attending to 'Convulsions' that 'break out' into new introductions to sound, sight and "text"-ure in the next line – all of which *precludes* invoking either silence or the void in order to reinstate the old (w)holy transcendent. O'Sullivan's earlier use of the last six lines above occurred in *AN INCOMPLETE NATURAL HISTORY*, where they are spread in three groups across the top of an A4 page; the very next lines after their respective colons 'break out' in choc-au-bloc words and names of creatures piled down the page, each demanding singular attention – including prepositions – by appearing between full stops. While Beuys has suggested his interest in the degrees of mystical ascesis – the *cogito, meditatio, contemplatio* that her Irish forebear James Joyce parodied as modernism's neo-Thomist aesthetic "vision"[21] – O'Sullivan remoulds asceticism's rejections of the world into what she describes above as 'Minglement, Caesura, Illumination': i.e., *engagement* with it through embrasure of each differing thing. Which includes "the word" itself, whose arrival in the work as both historical (incarnate) and timeless (deferred) meaning-making material is, for her, *l'invention de l'autre*, the future and past happening now.

In other words, I might summarise by suggesting that rather than engaging in post-Romantic mimetics, as some of her finest readers such as Robert Sheppard and Keith Tuma have argued, in order to effect a Hopkins-esque *capturing* of the world's mysterious "inscape" through "instress", O'Sullivan's update of such revolutionary meta-physical projects more clearly lets it go, lets difference be, absorbing the damage that this does to linguistic control and thereby taking it in (like a latter-day shaman) to transform perceptions of self as well. Her work returns the history of metaphysics to the ongoing natural (including linguistic) processes that continue to inflect it and that are utilised by it as material: all of which becomes her '*INCOMPLETE NATURAL HISTO-RY*', and illuminates the 'Christic' image in her 'Order of Mammal' construction photographed for the cover of *In the House of the Shaman*. Her works' (holey, holy) incompleteness, their sacrificial affirmation of lack in confrontation with otherness that generates continual, collab-orative creation, pre-empts the paralysis that comes with waiting for the end-time that might give meaning to the present. Simply put, while Beckett's *Waiting* speakers are left with the stage direction, 'They do not move', O'Sullivan's bypass stopping or ending by suggesting some erring, or wandering: '& then maybe you go to another place'.[22]

Works Cited

Altieri, Charles. 'From Symbolist Thought to Immanence: The Ground of Postmodern American Poetics' in *Early Postmodernism: Foundational Essays*. Paul A. Bové, ed. Durham and London: Duke University Press, 1995 (originally published 1973), pp. 100–139.

Beckett, Samuel. *Disjecta: Miscellaneous Writings and a Dramatic Fragment*. Ruby Cohn, ed. New York: Grove, 1984.

——————. *Endgame* and *Act Without Words*. New York: Grove Press, 1958.

——————. *Waiting for Godot: A Tragicomedy in Two Acts*. New York: Grove Press, 1954.

Caputo, John D. *On Religion*. London and New York: Routledge, 2001.

——————. *The Prayers and Tears of Jacques Derrida: Religion Without Religion*. Bloomington: Indiana University Press, 1997.

—————— and Michael Scanlon, eds. *God, the Gift, and Postmodernism*. Bloomington: Indiana University Press, 1999.

Coffey, Brian. *Advent*. London: The Menard Press, 1986.

Davis, Alex. '"Poetry is Ontology"': Brian Coffey's Poetics' in *Modernism and Ireland: The Poetry of the 1930s*. Patricia Coughlan and Alex Davis, eds. Cork: Cork University Press, 1995, pp. 150–72.

Derrida, Jacques. 'Structure, Sign and Play' in *Writing and Difference*. Alan Bass, trans. New York: Routledge, 1978 (originally published 1967 by Èditions du seuil).

Dorward, Nate. 'Maggie O'Sullivan's Red Shifts'. ALIENATED.NET: POETECHNOLOGY (2002-01-06; 10:24:27; topic: literature reviews).

Dostoevsky, Fyodor. *Notes from the Underground*. New York: Dover Publications, 1992.

Duncan, Robert. *The Opening of the Field*. New York: New Directions, 1960.

Duncan, Andrew. *The Failure of Conservativism in Modern British Poetry*. Cambridge: Salt Publishing, 2003.

Eckhart, Meister. *Meister Eckhart, from Whom God Hid Nothing: Sermons, Writings and Sayings*. London: Shambala Press, 1996.

Eliade, Mircea. *Shamanism: Archaic Techniques of Ecstasy*. Willard R. Trask, trans. Princeton: Princeton University Press, 1964.

Fischer, Norman. 'Spiritual Practice and the Avant-Garde'. *Five Fingers Review* 10: *Vanishing Points: Spirituality and the Avant-Garde*. San Francisco: Five Fingers Press, 1991.

Fredman, Stephen. 'Mysticism: Neo-paganism, Buddhism and Christianity' in *A Concise Companion to Twentieth-Century American Poetry*. Stephen Fredman, ed. Oxford: Blackwell, 2005. 191–211.

Gibbs, Robert. 'Introduction: Levinas Texts: "God and Philosophy"' in *The Postmodern God: A Theological Reader*. Graham Ward, ed. Oxford: Blackwell, 1997. 45–51.

Grant, Michael. 'Afterword' in *John Riley: Selected Poems*. Michael Grant, ed. Manchester: Carcanet Press, 1995.

Howe, Susan. 'The End of Art'. *Archives of American Art* 14: 4 (1975): 2–7.

Jarvis, Simon. "Quality and the non-identical in J.H. Prynne's 'Aristeas, in seven years'". *Parataxis* 1 (spring 1991): 69–86.

Johnston, Devin. *Precipitations: Contemporary American Poetry as Occult Practice*. Middletown, Connecticut: Wesleyan University Press, 2002.

Kennedy, David and Keith Tuma, eds. *Additional Apparitions: Poetry, Performance & Site Specificity*. Sheffield: The Cherry on the Top Press, 2002.

Lacoue-Labarthe, Philippe. *Poetry as Experience*. Andrea Tarnowski, ed. Stanford: Stanford University Press, 1999.

Marriott, David. Review of *Shadow of Spirit*, eds. Phillipa Berry and Andrew Wernick. *Parataxis: Modernism and Modern Writing* 5 (Winter 1993–94): 63–5.

Matthias, John, ed. *23 Modern British Poets*. Chicago: The Swallow Press, 1971. (Roy Fisher's 'City' is reprinted here from his *Collected Poems* (Fulcrum Press, 1969)).

McCaffery, Steve. *Prior to Meaning: The Protosemantic and Poetics*. Evanston: Northwestern University Press, 2001.

Mellors, Anthony. 'Maximal Extent: Charles Olson and C.G. Jung'. *fragmente* 8 (1998): 67–90.

Montgomery, Will. 'Dark here in the driftings: the sacred in the poetry of Susan Howe'. *Parataxis: Modernism and Modern Writing* 10 (2001): 87–102.

Moriarty, Dónal. *The Art of Brian Coffey*. Dublin: University College Dublin Press, 2000.

O'Leary, Peter. *Gnostic Contagion: Robert Duncan and the Poetry of Illness*. Middletown, Connecticut: Wesleyan University Press, 2002.

O'Sullivan, Maggie. *AN INCOMPLETE NATURAL HISTORY*. London: Writers Forum, 1992.

—————. *FROM THE HANDBOOK OF THAT AND FURRIERY*. Writers Forum, 1986.

—————. *In the House of the Shaman*. London: Reality Street Editions, 1993.

—————. Maggie O'Sullivan / Dell Olsen: 'Writing/Conversation: an interview by mail'. *How2* work / book, November/December, 2003.

—————. *Palace of Reptiles*. Willowdale, Ontario: The Gig, 2003.

—————. *red shifts*. Buckfastleigh, South Devonshire: etruscan books, 2001.

—————. 'winter ceremony' and 'that bread should be' in *etruscan reader III: Maggie O'Sullivan, David Gascoyne, Barry MacSweeney*. Buckfastleigh, South Devonshire: etruscan books, 1997.

Pound, Ezra. *Literary Essays of Ezra Pound*. T.S. Eliot, ed. London: Faber and Faber, 1954.

Prynne, J. H. *Poems*. Edinburgh and London: Agneau 2, 1982.

Riley, John. *The Collected Works*. Tim Longville, ed. Wirksworth, Derbyshire and Leeds, Yorkshire: Grosseteste Press, 1980.

Rothenberg, Jerome, ed. *Technicians of the Sacred: A Range of Poetries from Africa, America, Asia, & Oceania*. New York: Anchor Books, 1969.

Sheppard, Robert. 'The Performing and the Performed: Performance Writing and Performative Reading', 'In-Conference' section, Romana Huk, ed. *HOW2* 1, no. 6, 2001.

Taylor, Mark C. *Erring: A Postmodern A/theology*. Chicago: University of Chicago Press, 1984.

Upton, Lawrence. 'Regarding Maggie O'Sullivan's Poetry'. See the website www.student.yorku.ca/~gbbetts/naipc3.htm

Waldrop, Rosmarie. Interview with Rosmarie Waldrop in *Postmodern Poetry: The Talisman Interviews*. Ed Foster, ed. Hoboken, New Jersey: Talisman House, 1994.

Williamson. Aaron. 'Sorceric Battery', Review of Maggie O'Sullivan, *In the House of the Shaman*. *Parataxis: Modernism and Modern Writing* 6 (Spring/Summer 1994): 86–9.

Wolosky, Shira. *Language Mysticism: The Negative Way of Language in Eliot, Beckett, and Celan*. Stanford: Stanford University Press, 1995.

Notes

[1] For one summary of the impact of modern mysticism on American poetry see Fredman. He suggests (as do others, like Anthony Mellors in *Late Modernist Poetics: From Pound to Prynne*, 2005) that *all* twentieth-century avant-garde poetries, including those in the L=A=N=G=U=A=G=E vein, have been affected by the mystical properties folded into their aesthetics from the start by such cornerstone figures as Ezra Pound and H.D. (and later, Robert Duncan) – even if only in terms of perpetuating 'the esoteric quality' of such poetics. More broadly, Steve McCaffery has amply documented the 'religious glossolalia' (165–69) and Judeo-Christian mystical roots at the heart of early twentieth-century sound poetries across Europe – a tradition out of which O'Sullivan's work quite self-consciously grows. It isn't difficult to argue that modernist art forms from *zaum* and *dada* and *merz* to the present have, in their anti-art, negative forms, continued to pursue what Hans Richter calls 'the restor[ation] to the work of art its primeval magic power, . . . the incantatory power that we seek, in this age of general unbelief, more than ever before' (see *Dada Art and Anti-Art*, trans. David Britt (New York, Oxford University Press, 1965), p. 59).

[2] I think of the reference to O'Sullivan in David Kennedy and Keith Tuma's co-written memories of readings in their introduction to *Additional Apparitions*: 'Somebody leaning over . . . as Maggie O'Sullivan was reading in New Hampshire [at the conference I organized in 1996, *Assembling Alternatives*] and asking almost seriously "Is she really a witch?"' (Kennedy 25).

[3] See, for example, Altieri, Johnston, or Peter O'Leary's *Gnostic Contagion: Robert Duncan and the Poetry of Illness* (2002).

[4] Maggie O'Sullivan/Dell Olsen: 'Writing/Conversation: an interview by mail, November/December 2003', *How2* work / book, p. 3.

[5] I refer to the title and terminology in Johnston.

[6] See earlier quote and note 4 above, and 2003, 68; 1983 (unpaginated).

[7] Taggart 22. He writes (with post-Poundian emphases) in 'The Spiritual Definition of Poetry': 'What engenders seeing is the imagination's power to connect one thing with some other thing, fusing them fast, to produce a new third thing. The process is metaphor; the new third thing is the image. . . . The history of poetry in our century is only superficially the history of the struggle to make it new. More enduring is the struggle to regain the definition of poetry as spiritual ascesis, a definition obscured equally by the decadence of nearly all postroman-tic poetry. . . . For it is ourselves in a present that is always forgetful who are unconscious and who must dig and discover in language for what eternally exists, really and unchangeably. (Cf. Robert Duncan: "The creative experience of Man is a Word in its Mutations barely overheard in generation after generation, lost into Itself in Its being found.") . . . The notion of free will, the choosing that Duchamp would make the artist's essential function, is trivial in such experi-ence. . . . Form (content) is not imposed upon language but received from it. It chooses you' (Taggart 22, 23, 24).

[8] Johnston 18. The quote from Olson is from *Collected Prose*, Donald Allen and Benjamin Friedlander, eds. (Berkeley: University of California Press, 1997), p. 183.

[9] These quotes are compiled in Wolosky (119) from a long tradition of Beckett criticism.

[10] I quote the title of a poem in Riley's *Collected Works* (38).

[11] This seems to reference the well-known anonymous work, *The Cloud of Unknowing* (circa 1370). Its exhortation to enter the cloud or intellectual darkness that undoes traditional representations of God in some ways resonates with Riley's indictments of systemic linguistic hierarchies. But its reliance on the spatial segregation of a 'God outside philosophy', as Levinas puts it, exemplifies the simplifying inversions of negative theology. As Robert Gibbs puts it in his expli-cation of Levinas's phrase, 'To consign God to outside consciousness or to a consciousness outside reason is to allow philosophy to persist as immanence . . . to leave reason and its field of thought intact' (48).

[12] See note 7 above.

[13] I quote a well-known phrase in Maritain's *Creative Intuition in Art and Poetry* (New York: Pantheon, 1953). Alex Davis very helpfully explicates the impact of Maritain's thought on Coffey's work, suggesting that such worldly making requires a conception of the poet as 'artifex' rather than visionary (152).

[14] J. H. Prynne, 'Letter to Andrew Duncan', *Grosseteste Review* (1984); quoted in Jarvis, 72; Jarvis then very satisfyingly brings up Hegel's quote (73).

[15] From 'The Meridian' and quoted in Lacoue-Labarthe, 79.

[16] This line with its Miltonic echoes also appears in the "blue" printed section of *FROM THE HANDBOOK OF THAT & FURRIERY*.

[17] See for contrast Norman Fischer's contemplation of spirit as 'the something that will be nothing, that contemplates itself' (206).

¹⁸ See the beginning of '– that bread should be –' (26; and below) for a related use of the word 'crêpe'.

¹⁹ As with Derrida, for Levinas a paradoxically impossible but possibly utopian sociality lies beyond replacement of the 'said' by the 'saying', an incomplete and responsive rather than identifying and assertive mode of interaction (see Sheppard for an extended contemplation of O'Sullivan's relationship to Levinas). But as McCaffery writes, 'Levinas identified a language without words as a pure communication' (165); in my reading of her project, O'Sullivan avoids such purist idealisms.

²⁰ The quotes from Lowenstein are from his book *Tikigaq: Whale in Ancient Land, Sacred Whale: The Inuit Hunt and Its Rituals*; see O'Sullivan 2003, p. 31.

²¹ See the famous passage in James Joyce's *A Portrait of the Artist as a Young Man*, during which Stephen Dedalus articulates his developing, schoolboy aesthetics to the irreverent schoolboy Lynch. He uses terms and concepts that demonstrate in an inadvertently damning way his supposedly secular ideas' dependence on St Thomas Aquinas's thought.

²² This phrase appears in both 'riverrunning (realisations' (2003, 70) and *FROM THE HANDBOOK OF THAT & FURRIERY* (unpaginated).

A Natural History in 3 Incomplete Parts

Peter Manson
(London: Magenta Press, 1985).

Maggie O'Sullivan's book *A Natural History in 3 Incomplete Parts* was published by her own press, Magenta, in 1985. The texts included in the book were written between June 1984 and April 1985, and the book was printed and bound by the author in collaboration with the poet, printer and publisher Bob Cobbing, who had published a version of part one of the book, *An Incomplete Natural History*, the previous year. In an interview with Redell Olsen, conducted in 2003, O'Sullivan has described the process of making the book:

> "Bob Cobbing and I made [it] together at his place – (we constructed the entire book going from xeroxing my original pages, collating, binding, glueing, trimming the A5 pages, etc. and it took us a 5-day working week – Monday – Friday – to do this – working intensively from 10 til 5 every day and getting to grips with the brand-new binding machine Bob had just bought!). We'd planned to launch it on the Saturday, so it simply had to be done that week!"

A Natural History is one of the many extraordinary multicoloured books which issued from Bob Cobbing's photocopier in the 1980s. The book itself is printed in alternating pages of reddish brown and dark blue ink. The wraparound cover is printed in two colours on orange paper, a process which could only be achieved on a monochrome copier by passing the paper twice through the machine, once with the blue toner installed, once with the red. As the interview suggests, it was a labour-intensive process, and in the end only around eighty copies of the book were printed. The book has recently been made available in black-and-white facsimile in O'Sullivan's volume *Body of Work* (Reality Street Editions 2006, henceforth *BOW*), alongside many other pamphlets and uncollected works from the 1970s and 80s. All page references in this paper will be to the text in *Body of Work*.

The book is, as the title says, divided into three parts. The contents page (*BOW* 70, Fig 1.) gives them the sub-titles "INCOMPLETE", "MORE INCOMPLETE" and "MOST INCOMPLETE", the space between the subtitles increasing as you go down the page, suggesting a project whose incompleteness can only increase, reality accelerating and expanding beyond the grasp of anything that could be called "a history".

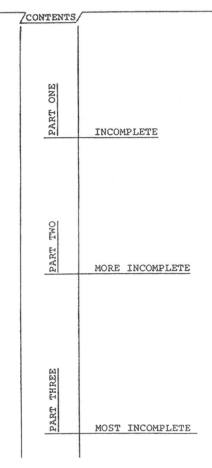

Fig. 1

The text is visually highly distinctive, composed on a manual type-writer and mostly in lower case, with occasional words picked out in upper case, or with initial capitals, or by underlining. Punctuation varies from passage to passage, but most commonly there is a full stop or period instead of a space between each word, so that the text seems almost nailed into position on the page. While this encourages the reader to read each word as an independent unit, not bound into a conventionally syntactic relationship with its neighbours, in fact the syntax often runs on quite independently of the punctuation. Sometimes individual words are omitted from the matrix, causing the dots to line up as points of suspension, so perhaps it's best to interpret the dots as rhythmic markers, discouraging the performing voice from modulating its stresses too naturalistically, rather than as strictly reliable signals of extreme parataxis.

The text signals very early on its kinship with the kind of open-field poetics that might be associated with Charles Olson or Susan Howe: "Skin of Open Fields, the" (*BOW* 72). For an open field to have a skin implies that this field has depth, like real earth, and the words picked out in capitals or by underlining do seem to stand out in an implied foreground against the ground plane of surrounding text. I'll come back to this, but for now it's worth noting the pleasurable contradiction between a text which is often, given the dots and the lack of declared line-breaks, denser than any page of prose, and the ease with which the skimming eye picks out the few emphasised words, quite out of sequence. An example would be in the text printed sideways in *BOW* 76, where capitalisation and underlining pick out the sequence RED . . . NARROW . . . . RED . . . LUNACY . . . But . . . JULY . . . BUT . . . TRESSES, the hidden buttresses only visible to a non-linear reader.

A possible source for part of the text (*BOW* 74)

scold-struck.melt.incline.dip.gate.goes.fruit-scent.air.opal.
desette.FLAUNT.each.blot.&.blur.torrential.almond.kiddler.
night.MOSTLY.BLOOD.CRISP.mostly.veil.couch.wick.in.
vert.&.coil..b/ween.shudder.burst.several . . .

is John Bunyan's poem "Upon A Sheet Of White Paper" (numbered XLVIII in the posthumously published book of emblems *A Book For Boys And Girls Or, Temporal Things Spiritualized*) where the phrase "blot and blur" occurs twice:

UPON A SHEET OF WHITE PAPER

This subject is unto the foulest pen,
Or fairest handled by the sons of men.
'Twill also show what is upon it writ,
Be it wisely, or nonsense for want of wit,
Each blot and blur it also will expose
To thy next readers, be they friends or foes.

Comparison.

Some souls are like unto this blank or sheet,
Though not in whiteness. The next man they meet,
If wise or fool, debauched or deluder,
Or what you will, the dangerous intruder
May write thereon, to cause that man to err
In doctrine or in life, with blot and blur.
Nor will that soul conceal from who observes,
But show how foul it is, wherein it swerves.
A reading man may know who was the writer,
And, by the hellish nonsense, the inditer.

The sheet of white paper, both subject and substrate of the poem, is implicated in an act of communication whose entire process takes place to the exclusion of women. The sons of men are the writers, the reader is a reading man, and even the paper itself is an erring, written-upon man. O'Sullivan's poetry could in the circumstance have no finer aim than instead to "FLAUNT.each.blot.&.blur". It is worth recalling that this book is called a History, and that her major project of the latter half of the 1990s is called *her/story: eye*.

One of the book's tours-de-force is *BOW* 78, an extraordinarily densely-woven text drawing on the science, mythology and phenomenology of insects:

Pollen.Primitive.Sting.Hatch.Firebrat.Tubular.Realm.Phose.Pest.
Ant.Anatomically.Furnace.Infernal.Warm.pigs.Pipes."Know.Feelers.
Noise.Green.Glanding.silk.or.Venom.Wasp.Antennae.Lock.Button.
Earth.The Next.Step.&.Seal.INSECT.INSECT.INSECT.INSECTS.Bumble.
Bees.Butterfly.Moths.Brine-fly.Wellheads.Weevil.Water.else.
Spring.Field.GrassHopper.Distant.they.as.Great.Air.to.find.Lo.
Locust.would.be.longer.Longer.Fly.Beetle.Mosquito.Suck.third.
Cylinder.Mine.zone.Certain.seeps.Air.peed.Pale.Green.Butter (. . .)

The page is topped by a set of three underlined headings, "introduction of sound:" "introduction of sight:" and "introduction of texture", and in fact this is one of the pages which is refunctioned in the middle section of the book by the introduction of literally collaged material which partly obscures the text.

This middle section is subtitled "More incomplete" and has an epigraph from *Canto CXVI* by Ezra Pound, "If love be not in the house there is nothing". I think it's significant that O'Sullivan doesn't quote the next line in the Pound poem, "The voice of famine unheard." The voice of famine, unheard and unquoted, resonates strongly in O'Sullivan's work: half of her family is from Skibbereen in West Cork, one of the areas most severely stricken by the Great Irish Famine of 1845–52, and she has dealt explicitly with the famine in such later texts such as — *that bread should be* –, published in 1996. This part of *A Natural History* pays moving tribute to both of O'Sullivan's parents, the gentleness and self-effacement of the mother,

> Peel tender mother
> Delving
>
> (like noBODY at all)
>
> (*BOW* 87)

contrasted with the volatile portrayal of her dad,

> STUB.SKITE.&.CATCH.THEM.CAUSAL/John.L./caraway.
> Cork/LOUD.F's.&.BLINDING/boot-nail/muttonvestment/
> WILD/gentle/WILD/meridian.January.slunk.slung.
> elliptical.daddle.
>
> (*BOW* 89)

Ireland intervenes more violently later in this section of the poem, but in the meantime there's the paradox of *BOW* 90, which consists of the line

> THIS.IS.RED.&.THIS.IS.PINK.THIS.IS.RED.&.THIS.IS.PINK.

repeated 25 times, with a final emphatic THIS. The text is in fact printed in blue, reminding the reader that what they are looking at is not the original typescript but a photocopy of it, possibly an unreliable copy. O'Sullivan, like her mentor Bob Cobbing, is a poet who fully acknowledges the fact that modern printing technologies like offset litho and photocopying are basically kinds of photography, and a photograph can be of anything you like, even a poem.

The collaged material in part 2 of *A Natural History* includes BOW 100 (Fig 2.), a map of the Greenham Common cruise missile base, site of a series of women's protest camps in the 1980s and 90s, overlaid by a press cutting naming 15 victims of the use of rubber and plastic bullets against civilians in Northern Ireland.

The facing page shows a photograph of a striking worker, murdered in Mexico in 1934 (Fig 3). The interruption of text by image and image by image is appropriate to the themes of invasion and violation which the collaged materials introduce, and the meaning of such text as

Fig. 2

```
Vassal. madrigal. django reign blistering navybricolage.
Decayed Beam, ski tar pulls thigh, runs thick lesion:
scratching, dancing, mixing, aX another
```

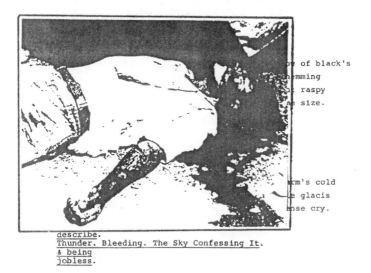

```
                                                  of black's
                                                   running
                                                   raspy
                                                   size.


                                                 rm's cold
                                                 e glacis
                                                 nse cry.
describe.
Thunder. Bleeding. The Sky Confessing It.
& being
jobless.
```

```
Billow churn, jazzy curve. Bee zen. of Glovewort.
Utter Glaze. fridge roseflocking mutagenic. fridge Acanthus,
lash prim thistle twist of pure nutmace, low flambé lead
split:• erosion. But child, Bead & reel, yellowed air soft
mightily, i bleed & soak & pool olive, prolonging
sund sund sundering


real rain.
```

Fig. 3

remains visible is altered by its new context. "Fire, as in / the Sun" becomes a comment on the use of plastic bullets, and the lines "describe./Thunder. Bleeding. The Sky Confessing It./ & being / jobless" now emerge from beneath the photograph of the murdered worker. The overlaying of elements implies a low 3-dimensional relief of which the book only gives us a 2-d snapshot. The idea that the poem might be a uniquely constructed physical object that we only glimpse in reproduction becomes stronger in O'Sullivan's later work (see for example the drawn and painted passages in *murmur*), but it's already strongly suggested by *A Natural History*.

The epigraph to Part 3 of *A Natural History in 3 Incomplete Parts* is the Zen koan, "Come in all that is outside", and appropriately, the section is sub-titled "MOST INCOMPLETE". At its heart is the text "SINGULAR VERBS & PLURAL SUBJECTS" (*BOW* 110), a ritual of incorporation set out almost like a recipe on the page, and foreshadowing more recent O'Sullivan texts like "NARCOTIC PROPERTIES" from *Palace of Reptiles*. The litany of things to be brought within the remit of the poem begins with the lapidary, herbal and bestiary,

> BRING
> asher wristing Pearl Smock, amethyst/
> Incandela.
>
> BEAT & SAY &
> Near Lift the Sun's
> myrtle tie satin maché hangdish.
> BRING
> Hobday. Scrub hawk, woodish clove hearse,
> Voice Thorn, seethe glazer, Welted May

and ends by admitting, as if in the hope of defeating by naming, some very human instances of violence:

> blade o/head.
> implacable brutality
> skirts the edge of gown,
> Vast Needle
> stoking twilight,
> baked mutter, satin bluesy isle of aloe antic
> w/loaves & Bowl
> &
> Sink in the Bone.
> Shrapnel.

The book draws to a close with echoes of the structure of a textbook: an alphabetized, index-like list of LEAD VOCALS (*BOW* 117), a list of sixteen COLOUR PLATES where one longs for the images that could live up to these captions: "JAM-SHOT MUFF SLIT SEEDLER", "RAT-LICKED BAIZE ORCHID" or "MALLOW-MITTENED TEASY INTER-SECTION" (*BOW* 120f.) Two sections headed "READING WRITING (a DOCUMENTARY)" (*BOW* 122f.) might set up expectations of a documentary on the making of the book, David Attenborough style, but their texts imply no such metatextual distancing, casting the same weather eye on human and non-human, even vegetable, life and death. One ends,

> wild plum ever silken, fucking shot
> <u>knife took</u>
> <u>u/neath</u>.

the other

FREEZEWORT
KeptCoal
<u>IN THE DAY'S EYE</u>.

If the book isn't in any conventional sense a natural history, it's because O'Sullivan recognises that even natural histories tend to be written by the winners, and she sees neither the possibility nor the point of victory. In the book's albeit perpetually outrun project of inclusion, empathy and malediction, extending far beyond the reach of cultural and biological determinacy, there is, however, much cause for optimism.

Bibliography

Bunyan, John, *A Book For Boys And Girls Or, Temporal Things Spiritualized*. London: R. Tookey 1701. Quoted from the online edition at http://www.mountzion.org/johnbunyan/text/bun-boys.htm (accessed 21st February 2007).

Olsen, Redell, online interview with Maggie O'Sullivan at http://www.asu.edu/pipercwcenter/how2journal/archive/online_archive/v2_2_2004/current/workbook/writing.htm (accessed 21st February 2007).

O'Sullivan, Maggie, *A Natural History in 3 Incomplete Parts*. London: Writers Forum 1985.

O'Sullivan, Maggie, *Body of Work*. Hastings: Reality Street Editions 2006.

O'Sullivan, Maggie, *murmur*. Online at http://www.maggieosullivan.co.uk/murmur.html (accessed 21st February 2007).

O'Sullivan, Maggie, *Palace of Reptiles*. Willowdale, ON: The Gig 2003.

O'Sullivan, Maggie, *— that bread should be —*. London: RWC 1996.

Agonal States: Maggie O'Sullivan and a feminist politics of visual poetics

Nicky Marsh

Out of Everywhere: Linguistically innovative poetry by women in North America & the UK, edited by Maggie O'Sullivan, has been a major contributor toward the establishment of a recognisable body of experimental poetry by contemporary women. The editing of the anthology was both expansive and self-aware, displacing the nationalist and formalist fealties routinely assumed by anthologies whilst also interrogating the connections between gender and the 'linguistically innovative'. The success of the collection was indicated by reviews such as that by Marjorie Perloff, potently entitled 'The Coming of Age of Language Poetry'. Perloff celebrates the anthology for moving away from what are cast as the implicit formalisms of 'Language poetry' – technique is, she contends, 'always and only technique: the new sentence, as many readers have noted, can be used as advertising copy as easily as in poetry' – and toward an examination of the 'larger cultural and social perspectives' surrounding the 'historical, the literary and mythological'.[1]

One of the most striking ways in which *Out of Everywhere* seemed to focus on these 'larger cultural and social' implications of 'technique' is in its inclusion of a wide range of performance, of inter- and multimedia work, and of visually innovative poetics. The anthology includes the work of that 'most painterly' of poets Barbara Guest, as well as poems by writers such as Denise Riley explicitly influenced by contemporaries in the fine arts.[2] The opening pages of the collection, featuring the work of Susan Howe, Joan Retallack, Tina Darragh and Paula Claire, are especially striking for the range of visual innovations that they incorporate. An attempt to even speculate a rationale for the

opening of the anthology seems more fruitfully served by an examination of these visual poetics than by a search for any specific genealogi-
cal, geographical, political or generational affiliation. I want to use the
attention to the visual and to the material shared by these writers – and
their disparate interpretations of what this can mean - to suggest two
cues from which to begin to read O'Sullivan's early work of the mid
eighties and its complex relationship to a politics of gender. Firstly, I
want to locate O'Sullivan within a tradition of visual poetics, to
explore her gathering of a range of poetic practices that foreground
the physical and abstract properties of language as much as its referential and communicative implications. Howe's fidelity to Charles
Olson's 'tumultuous page consciousness',[3] Retallack and Darragh's
exploration of the chance-intention dynamic and Claire's corporeal
rendering of semiotics, offer multiple strategies for an enlarged poetic
register. Such writing, as the emerging critical vocabulary for it
suggests, complicates the familiar presence-absence dynamic of critical
linguistics by bringing the social procedures of reading and the physical presence of poet, reader, and page into the semantic field. Secondly,
I want to indicate what O'Sullivan's drawing from these various traditions suggests for her own writing as it offers important ways of re-
conceiving the connections between an experimental poetic and political critique. I want to make apparent what O'Sullivan's interrogation
of poetic liminality – the spaces between reference and abstraction,
between the natural and the social, between the material and the
metaphysical, between public and private, between interiority and
exteriority – suggests for the interconnections between a material poetics and a feminist critique. O'Sullivan's early writing, I want to suggest,
offers us new models for understanding the sculptural qualities of the
poetic and the poetic qualities of the sculptural.

Out of Everywhere opens with an extract from Susan Howe's *The
Bibliography of the King's Book*. This extract represents Howe's meditation
on the nature and possibilities of the iconoclastic through a transgres-
sive use of both lineation and the page. Its first page contrasts the horizontal presentation of the 'Language of state secrets' with the vertically oblique exploration of the 'misapplying of law and history'.[4] This
idiosyncratic use of the space of the page becomes increasingly unre-
strained throughout the extract until its final, explanatory page. Its
concluding lines – 'must lie outside the house / Side of space I must
cross / / To write against the Ghost' – ascribe Howe's capacity to 'write

against' the authority of historical 'ghosts' to the illicit movements of her poetics.[5] The discovery of agency in the outsider's ability to move across the charged and dynamic space of language is a familiar trope in Howe's writing: apparent in her embrace of Melville's 'stammer', in Hope Atherton's feminised 'excursion' beyond community, and in the 'removes' of Mary Rowlandson.[6] For the latter two figures, especially, the ability to write from the outside of discourse is necessarily frustrated and partial: Rowlandson speaks with and against the biblical rhetoric handed to her and Atherton through the contradictions of his ordered neologisms. Howe has explicitly identified this interest in the dynamic materiality of language – her shift from visual to text-based work – with the ambiguously 'permission-giving' influence of Charles Olson.[7] The influence of Olson's 'Projective Verse' on the development of visual poetics such as Howe's has recently been theorised in increasingly gender-specific ways.[8] Alan Golding, for example, has described the ways in which Howe's attention to 'graphicity' makes explicit connections between 'normalizing print conventions and questions of patriarchal authority, tradition, custom, and propriety'[9] and Kathleen Fraser has placed these poetics in a broader overview of contemporary writing. Fraser attributes a feminist impetus toward visual experimentation to both Olson's understanding of the page as a 'site in which to manifest one's *physical* alignment with the arrival of language in the mind' and to the contemporaneous attention to 'screens, grids and underpaintings' emerging from abstract and expressionist women painters.[10]

The work of Joan Retallack and Tina Darragh included in *Out of Everywhere* point, conversely, to conceptual traditions of proceduralism in which writing becomes formalised inquiry. Retallack's 'Afterrimages' and Darragh's 'adv. Fans – the 1968 series' are both aleatory texts focusing on the materiality of signifying in order to reconsider the respective implications of the intentional and the arbitrary in the making of meaning. Each page of Retallack's poem contains its own mirror image and the 'reflected' version is determined by a chance procedure which allows only fragments of the original text to remain visible. The difficult work of making syntactic sense of Retallack's knowingly elliptical stanzas in 'Afterrimages' – 'sage of the ectopic eye / logical series of unsolicited occasions' – gives way to readings capable only of registering impressions of sight and sound – 'ec / s'.[11] In moving between these two simultaneous 'versions' of the poem we are asked to review the physical properties of perception alongside the cognitive processes of reading: to consider how much is produced by the eye and how much the eye is able to retain. Retallack's description of John Cage's work - 'chance and design startlingly reveal their utterly intermingled contingency, not as idea but as initiating experience to be undergone by composer and audience' - seems an unsurprisingly apt description of this writing.[12] Darragh's extract in the anthology, from 'Adv. Fans - the 1968 series', positions a palimpsest of fragmented cut and pasted dictionary pages (one superimposed upon another so that their original meaning is lost) against definitions attributed to having first been said in 1968. In doing so it displays and disrupts the steady formation of hegemonic discourse. The definitions to emerge in 1968 - shopper, teleplayer, hostess apron - reflect less the possibility of social revolution ubiquitously associated with the year than with a familiarly gendered postwar fascination with technology and consumption.[13] At the same time, the poem renders the dictionary - the privileged repository of such definitions - partial and literally obscure, mocking the reification suggested by its very ambition to subject language to taxonomy through its literalised objectification. This concern with denaturalising the rule-bound processes by which language accretes and stores meaning is wide-ranging and often dryly self-reflective in Darragh's writing. Her collection *Striking Resemblance* (which includes poems dedicated to both Howe and Retallack) extends the processes suggested by 'Adv. Fans' to the masculinism of colloquial speech, to genre, to translation, and to the framing of the physical page.[14] The writing functions through a combination of proceduralism and parody that makes continually evident the fertile gaps between intention and nonintention in language use.[15] For both Darragh and Retallack, such moves are motivated by an explicit commitment to the political. Retallack thinks of her own work in terms of a *poethics* 'of everyday life and work where forms of art and the art of life interpenetrate within a coherent framework of values' and Darragh's concern in 'Adv. Fans' is with understanding 'what went wrong with language in 1968'.[16] The chance procedures that motivate the fragmentary appearance of the work of both poets in *Out of Everywhere* strive to fully realise notions of cultural responsibility: to heighten the reader's awareness of the choices (and the limits to the choices) that their participation in the production of meaning involves.

These poems are followed in O'Sullivan's anthology by those of the British performance-poet Paula Claire. Each of Claire's six texts in

O'Sullivan's anthology corresponds to a description of a specific performance. The poems transcribe a range of what might appear to be random codes (the sound of a jetplane, the patterns created by an electron photomicrograph, the tracings of an open flower) into visual poetry through the use of multimedia strategies including 'recitative, chant, song and sound poetry' and 'music, walking and picnics'.[17] In each case, the authority suggested by the poem's very specific source material is rendered playful and ironic. Many of these poems, the appended notes tell us, were first performed at Bob Cobbing's Writer's Forum and can thus be read as a series of 'scores' with physical notations providing 'a signal to the body as well as to the voice'.[18] Eric Mottram's description of the Writers Forum highlights the speculative treatment of performance by these writers as they inferred 'design-performance, performance designs: parameters between words, sounds, noise, and non-verbal signs and visuals'. Mottram explicitly names the work of Claire when describing performances which 'create works and, indeed, create the acoustic occasion of the works by altering the room or hall's acoustics. Performance is a matter of movement from inside the body-mind system, outward for the performer's satisfaction, toward a possible other person, a participating audience.'[19] Claire's frequently wordless writing augments the possibilities of both performance and the text. She both literalises and estranges the act of translation, the constant process of coding and decoding that reading and semiotics requires, and makes the viscerality of the body of poet, reader and page integral to this.

This attention to the expansive pluralising of the poetic space that occurs in the opening pages of *Out of Everywhere*, clearly contributes to the development of an increasingly sophisticated prosody and vocabulary for innovative poetics.[20] These poetics require a reading practice capable of including a range of media, of performance, of semantic and non-semantic elements of signifying. In these pages these practices rely on a dynamic of regulation and release – the outlining and the subversion of rules – in which the traction suggested by the materiality of the physical text is central. For each poet, such potential is given a social, political and historical realisation more complex than that suggested by the neat presence / absence dyad of much critical thought. In Howe's work the physical word is given an almost messianic etymological alchemy, in Darragh's work it is made the unsteady sum of culture's authoritative social processes, in Claire's work it embodies the trace of a physical performance. The attention to the visual and the material in this poetry indicates a desire to exceed the parameters of the poetic: to force radically socialised and self-aware reading practices able to form new critiques of power and authority. Any feminist critique that we might wish to ascribe to this writing would seem to exist in this most de-essentialised and plural of forms. The complex, equivocal relationship with feminism suggested in the critical work of Howe and Retallack, for example, which accepts the primacy of gender critique to an analysis of power whilst distancing itself from second-wave feminism's risk of essentialism or identitarianism, are suggested in these poetics.[21]

This dynamic between regulation and release, and its footing in an attention to the social implications of a materially rendered language, is clearly apparent in much of O'Sullivan's poetry as it draws upon the ideograms and word-grids, chance procedures, and textual and physical performances suggested by her peers. Her poetics seem concerned with making manifest the energy of such a dynamic in order to destabilise received political and conceptual structures. Her writing of the mid eighties is – as titles such as *Concerning Spheres, States of Emergency, Divisions of Labour* and *Unofficial Word* suggest – frequently directed against the enervating lines of a culture of demarcation.[22] O'Sullivan's movement between these well-policed boundaries suggests a realisation of literary possibilities that finds contemporary parallels in descriptions such as Deleuze's of the 'fold'- incorporating the dual movements of 'implying-explaining, enfolding-unfolding, involving-evolving'.[23] The expansive poetic leverage later utilised by such a movement both draws upon the insights about the social properties of the physically-realised text suggested by the poets included in *Out of Everywhere* and, I also want to suggest, directs us toward more comprehensive ways of realising their implications. O'Sullivan's realisation of the 'agonal states' between modernity's dichotomies, can be read as unfolding sculptural models of the poetic which, in Elizabeth Grosz's influential description of a Deleuzian architecture, is capable of evacuating 'the inside' in order to 'confront its outside'.[24]

A Natural History in 3 Incomplete Parts, written in 1984 and published the following year by O'Sullivan's own Magenta Press, is a poem which embraces its own incremental incompletion.[25] It is comprised of small self-standing passages, the compressed units of power so characteristic of O'Sullivan's work, laid horizontally and vertically on each page. The passages of compacted lists and associative descriptions that comprise most of the collection are disrupted by, and interspersed with, words and phrases emphasising movement or half-understood commands directing the reader beyond the frame of the poem. One page, for example, is entirely filled with a dense, evenly-spaced, listing of single words and neologisms.

> Pollen. Primitive. Sting. Hatch. Firebrat. Tubular. Realm. Phose. Pest. Ant. Anatomically. Furnace. Infernal. Warm. pigs. Pipes. "Know. Feelers. Noise. Green. Glanding. Silk. Or Venom. Wasp. Antennae. Lock. Button.

Initially the page seems to evoke the tensions that Kathleen Fraser ascribes to the formal word grid she finds in successive generations of visual poets.[26] The page's compartmentalising use of the full stop encourages us to read each word or neologism individually, whilst the insistent frame of the grid forces the associations between words into view. At the same time, the page asks to be read as a form of textual performance. It is framed by three phrases directing the reader to the 'introduction of sound', 'introduction of sight' and 'introduction of texture'. Such an injunction stresses a different aspect of textual materiality, one that suggests the radically performance-orientated 'scores' of the Writer's Forum. O'Sullivan has, of course, been active in the development of these poetics. Her account of her own writing practices, for example, describes her 'embracing traversing CONTOURING the infinite heart of the page's spatial flow' in order to allow 'the musics & airs of the verbal word/sound patterns in the ear'.[27] The directions alluding to such processes in *A Natural History* physically charge the movement between the individual word and its place in the frame by directing us to a reading beyond that offered by the silent page. The detailed, incremental associations between words – with insects, with movement, with accumulation, with generation and degeneration – become increasingly resounding and active. By the end of the page it seems as if this compacted word grid embodies the furiously productive and regimented movement of insect life that appears, only from a distance, to be either anarchic and threatening or random and isolated. In place of such misconceptions we are given an impression of activity, of plurality, of fertility, of metamorphic repetition: 'jaw. into. Snap. dune. Many. times. Moth. larva.' The word grid's formal tension between an individual reading of each word and a collective associative process is given a clear thematic resolution.

Later in *A Natural History* this page, along with others from the poem, is repeated. These pages are now obscured by the crude imposition of images from the contemporary media. These images, including a partially-concealed map of Greenham common, a bald list of 'PEOPLE KILLED BY RUBBER AND PLASTIC BULLETS' and snatches from tabloid headlines – 'Man killed after RUC "go berserk"' and 'MAN DIES AS POLICE FIRE IN IRA RIOT' – make harsh reference to the political violence of eighties Britain. The poem's previously rather opaque references to Ireland (apparent in O'Sullivan's allusions to her parents and to the 'Emerald city') can be more confidently connected to the poem's evocations of violence: the explicitness of 'SASH CARNAGE' and the uncomfortable domestication of 'dishpan glass & bomb & gun & knife & fisty'. The poem's fluid negotiation of the tension between the individual and the collective is entirely concealed in this repeated page of the poem by these literal references to the violence of the state and its gratuitous depiction in the mainstream press. The page seems literally blocked: the literalism of the lists and photographs of the dead numb the processes of interpretation and movement that much of the rest of the poem seems intent on enacting. The radical politicisation that seemed to follow from O'Sullivan's realisation of the social processes of reading - shared by the poets who open *Out of Everywhere* – are thrown into relief. The issues of responsibility, knowledge and authority that these actions suggested are sharpened by a reminder of their literal political negation.

One model for further developing these implications of O'Sullivan's realisation of the social implications of the material text – although certainly not the only one – is provided by Joseph Beuys.[28] The similarities between Beuys and O'Sullivan's sculptural poetics are fairly clear: the shamanistic attentions of both to the possibilities of transformation are rooted in the elemental energies of the everyday and the seeking of alternatives to an overwhelmingly commodified and debased culture. Beuys' fascination with such possibilities was not only with the 'fat' and the 'felt' of his most famous works but also with Celtic myth-making and the transformative processes suggested by bees, wax and honey; by trees, diamonds and coal. In his tour of Ireland in the early seventies with *The Secret Block for a Secret Person in Ireland*, for example, he sought out 'the basic energies of fuel and butter, compressed peat briquettes, sandwiched with best Keryygold butter, or hexagonal coke'.[29] For Beuys, as for O'Sullivan, such aspirations are motivated less by a nostalgic desire for a premodern united Ireland or Germany than by a desire to re-engage the violent divisions that seethe through modernity itself.[30] According to Bernice Rose, for example, Beuys' movement between dichotomies aimed to establish a 'a flow of energy between them that made them mutually dependent, no longer in opposition but part of an ineluctable, life-giving circularity'.[31] The similarities between the aims of the sculptor and those of the poet are more than merely thematic. Rose reads Beuys' notations for performance as 'scores' that mediate between the 'concept and spatial effects of objects'[32]. This emphasis on the text as a series of traces constituting a broken relation to an impossible whole demands – like O'Sullivan's poetics – a reading that includes physical place, temporal occasion, status as an object. Howe's shards of history, Darragh's chance procedures, and Claire's performances are given an encompassing corollary in a Beuys-derived model of sculpture.

The explicit influence of Beuys upon O'Sullivan is not hard to discern. He is, along with figures such as Bob Cobbing, Barry MacSweeney and Basil Bunting, an important figure in O'Sullivan's literary pantheon. 'Plight', the last section in *States of Emergency* (published in 1987 by Paula Claire's International Concrete Poetry Archive Publication press) is dedicated to Beuys. Its exhilarating movement across a violent, natural terrain seems at least partly motivated by the implied presence of the 'abdicator, incendiarist, relinquisher, / tatterer, batterer, menacer, heretic, / hooligan'.[33] O'Sullivan was, in the period in which this text was written, working as a researcher and was the sole credited researcher for the BBC Arena documentary on Beuys directed by Caroline Tisdall and Christopher Swayne, first broadcast in June 1987.[34] One of the more idiosyncratic aspects of the documentary, which otherwise presents a thorough but fairly uncontroversial chronological and critical narrative of Beuy's work, is its filming of the then N.U.M President Arthur Scargill's response to the presence of Beuys' *Plight* in central London in 1985. *Plight* is an installation featuring a small room, lined with rolls of felt, containing a piano upon which is positioned a blackboard and a thermometer. Unsurprisingly, as Scargill is filmed walking slowly around the room, his commentary compares the sensation it evokes to mining, describing a profound sense of enforced seclusion and abandonment. His conjectures on the more abstract significance that can be attributed to the presence of the piano, blackboard and thermometer focus on the parallels they suggest with the political isolation that accompanied his own activist attempts at altering these working conditions. He suggests that the piano (silenced by the rolls of felt insulating the walls) and the blackboard (placed without chalk) indicate the possibility, and the immediate withdrawal, of communication outside of the room and that the thermometer is a 'gauge' for measuring this political climate. The immediate context for Scargill's interpretative soliloquy was, of course, the ignominious failure of the Miner's Strike in early March of 1985 (the detrimental impact of which continues to reverberate in British Trade Unionism) and his own subsequent vilification in the British press. Scargill's decrying, when announcing the end of the strike, of a 'Government aided and abetted by the judiciary, the police and the media' has been proven increasingly accurate in subsequent years.[35] That the BBC was able to associate the Scargill of this period with a European intellectual and political radicalism rather than with only the failed 'loony' extremes of the left is in itself noteworthy. O'Sullivan's documentary was successful in not only giving Beuys' work a striking political immediacy but, as importantly, with allowing a figure such as Scargill – routinely presented in most media of the period as menacing, irrational and potentially corrupt – to use this art to articulate an intellectual critique of his own marginalisation.

Such an extended development of the transformational possibilities of Beuy's installation of *Plight* can be read back into O'Sullivan's poem of the same name from *States of Emergency* (which was published in '87, but written in the second half of '85). The 'Conjure' of the poem's first words can be read as pertaining not only to the occultist aspirations of Beuys but to the dark, contested properties of the element which the 'sea gave up'. Just as the industrious activities of insects in *A Natural History in 3 Incomplete Parts* is both augmented and obscured by the presence of conflict in Northern Ireland then the possibilities suggested by the processes of coal and carbon are linked in O'Sullivan's 'Plight' to the social and political violence of mining. Again these connections are forged through O'Sullivan's attention to the physical energies stored in the processes and possibilities of a physically realised language. The poem's references to 'grunt/scab chant // wound /WAKED' as well as to 'rag Vile Stunt' or 'clashed / bloody cotton / clotty halo' can be read as attempts to articulate the complex web of associations – from primordial energies to state violence to the destruction of rural communities – that the Miner's Strike came to embody. The 'agonal state' of O'Sullivan's poetics can be read once more through its simultaneous rendering of a violent crisis in the political realm and a violent crisis in the possibilities of representation.

In my final reading I want to link O'Sullivan's attention to the concurrence of political and representational failure to the question of gender. Although rarely isolated as an individual concern, an interrogation of masculinity and femininity are clearly integral to O'Sullivan's undoing of hierarchical dichotomizations. Indeed, the complex associations of femininity – with the body, with the degraded, with artifice, with power and with powerlessness – provide lucid ways of understanding the connections between matter and violence in O'Sullivan's early poetics.

The subtitle to O'Sullivan's 1986 publication *From the Handbook of That & Furriery* describes it as a piece 'for Voice & Slides'. The cover notes to the poem give details of its first performance at Sub-Voicive in December 1983 and of a later performance in the following year in which the text was realised using 'auto slide projection, my voice, my voice on tape and collage performance.'[36] The suggestion of multiple presence and absences – of body, voice and sound – that these references to the performed versions of the poems indicate are also apparent in its published presentation. The front cover of the poem contains a handprint made in bright red poster paint. The handprint carries the irregularities of the individually made mark: the pooling of paint at the base of the thumb, the smudged, excess of paint at the tips of the fingers, a textured feathering where the arch of the palm fails to make contact with paper. Such indicators render the hand of the author – or of the book's maker – both present and absent. The same sense of the book as a trace of another happening is present in its title. *From The Handbook of that & Furriery* seems to be incomplete in at least two ways. Its opening word suggests an alternative whole – *The Handbook* – from which this text is derived. Yet *of that & Furriery* suggests a diversion away from itself, as if it were about to become one thing and, instead, became quite another. This becoming is left tantalisingly opaque by the title. 'Furriery' is a wonderfully odd word. It can sound like a childish verb, suggesting the process of gaining or of increasing fur. Yet the literalism of taxidermy that it also implies – the 'art of dressing and making up furs' – checks the infantilism of this sounding.[37] Furriery indicates an ambiguity about the properties of fur – not entirely unparalleled in Beuys' attention to fat and to felt – suggesting violence, possession and death as well as insulation, warmth and protection. This equivocation is held taut by its complex associations with femininity itself: with comfort, desire and artifice and with the abjection of the de-possessed animal. The poem's accompanying visual text makes apparent how these potent ambiguities are embedded in the material-ity of language itself.

The opening page of the poem is made from two intersecting images carefully shaped like shards of glass or pieces from an impossible jigsaw. One of them is filled with Arabic lettering and the other with a musical score. This format is reproduced throughout the poem, as a variety of languages (English, German, Spanish, French) and alphabets (Chinese, Cyrillic, Arabic, Roman) are fanned onto the page in irregular and shifting patterns. Typography's most 'potent aspect', according to art theorist Johanna Drucker, its 'refusal to resolve into either a visual or verbal mode' is usefully prised open in these images. For Drucker, typography makes apparent the fault lines within semiotic theory, requiring us to read not for phenomenology and post-structuralism's over-determined choice between the transcendent and the corporeal but for the simultaneity of the 'physical, substantial aspects of produc-tion as well as the abstract and system-defined elements.'[38] In such a reading neither aspect of signification, 'presence as substance or absence as difference can ever be left fully alone: each continues to irrupt into the domain of the other and interfere in the happy play of signifiers and in the dismal insistence on self-evident appearance.'[39]

In *From the Handbook of that & Furriery* O'Sullivan brings this produc-tive tension between an abstraction of signification and the self-evident appearance of the material word to a state of crisis. The frag-ments of typography that comprise each alternate page of the poem insist that the non-referential treatment of language as typography is clearly privileged over semantic meaning. On one page, for example, we are presented with four uneven strips of lettering, suggesting at least two kinds of formal and compositional contrasts. Firstly, most obviously, the physical presentation of these typographic excerpts encourages us to read them as opaque objects. Often the distinctions between extracts is stark: ranging from shifts in colour and font size to the differences between the multiple notations of the musical score, the fluid hand-written calligraphy of Chinese script and the squared dense blocks of the Cyrillic alphabet. Secondly, we are reminded of the different ways in which words, paragraphs, pages and texts are able to make relational sense. The Westernised reading practices of moving from left to right, top to bottom and front to back is denaturalised, not only by the contrasts between language forms but by their arrange-ment on the page. Often passages are not only shaped in ways that cut across words, sentences and lines but the whole segments are placed upside down, inverted, or at an impossibly obtuse angle. Yet this typographic sensitivity to the material word is shorn of the dynamic that its doubling as understandable language would imply: the tension that Drucker describes between the referential and the typographic is pared away. Even if these semantic units were complete, the chances of happening upon a reader able to read all of these languages is slight, and their referential meanings clearly negated. Drucker's naming of the necessary 'social conditions, context and claims for the political effects of signifying activity' are only ever shadowily present in these passages: their absence seems far more apparent than their presence. The complex systems of cultural difference and literacy that their contrasts necessarily evoke are denied content – we are left with only negative definitions which eventually empty themselves out, echoing Drucker's larger critique of the contradictions of post-Sausserian linguistics. The poem is clearly aware of the implications of this potentially reifying treatment of language. The sense of movement and dynamism of these typographic swathes seems fuelled by a latent violence. The cutting of the passages is overt, their shapes almost consistently sharp – suggesting knives and scythes – and their interconnections often only serve to intensify this sense of incision or shearing. If these languages are not quite caught in a struggle for domination, then they are presented as oppositional, being played out in a conflict that seems to be not of their own making.

The poem that accompanies these images provides an alternative way of understanding such acts of objectification and appropriation. The 'furriery' offers multiple ways of thinking through the violence of possession. The poem seems to revel in the physical violence that taxidermy affords: 'sometimes.raw.head.bloody.bone.in.street.too'. This violence is consistently linked to both the literal labours of furriery and to an associated taxonomic power to categorise and objectify: 'Mode, sorting, treatment of raw kin.and to a.' – the potential slippage between 'kin' and 'skin' in this instance revealing the high familial stakes invested in these processes. Two sections of the poem 'reasons.for.not.performing' and 'reasons.for.not.setting.up.hierarchies' further develop these connections. Both sections itemise, in lists which fail to quite correspond with one another, a number of loosely associated words. 'reasons.for.not.performing' is a list of horrifying physical mutilations suggesting the effects of hunting, of experimentation, of vivisection, of caging: '"crushing"', '"drug tests"', '"Freezing"'. 'reasons.for.not.setting.up.hierarchies' is, conversely, a list of substances suggesting transformation: the ability to negate ("'insecticide'", "'fire extinguisher'"); to clean ("'washing liquid'", "'washing powder'", "'bubble bath'", "'oven-cleaners'"); to alter ("'bleaches'", "'shoe polish'", "'eye make-up'", "'nail polish'", "'ink'", "'paint'") or to move ("'brake fluid'", "'zip lubricants'", "'anti-freeze'"). The more wryly enigmatic example of the "'church candle'" suggests the possible and perhaps metaphysical combination of these properties. Yet clearly such actions are not understood as benign. The title to the section, and the broader context of the poem, nudges us toward understanding such actions as dangerous, potentially reckless and contaminating.

Both lists move us toward an understanding of artifice, the attempt to control the lines between the natural and the cultural, as a site of potential violence. This association is clearly gendered throughout the poem, already replete in the notion of 'furriery' as a site of luxury, fetish and violence. The opening phrase's suggestion of a nursery rhyme or fairy tale – 'Maids. Of. Honour. / Queen. Of. Hearts' – genders a paradigmatic startling encounter, 'torture, versus. . . . . / "a.most.unlilkely.hero."', which begins a submerged dramatic narrative which runs throughout the poem as yet another way of staging 'what. men. talk. About / the.rips. &. Tears' and '"the.women. who.yearn.to.wear.them"'. The scythes of objectified typography that the published poem's representation of slides suggests are given their own gendered corollary in this text's obsession with the 'exquisite. / clockwork.dolls.that.swell.&.speak.why.dead./ the. Pelvises / the. fire.of.it . . . . . . their sex (ual). Organs, cavities.' The very last lines of the poem '"(U / how. does / your. garden / grow?")' bring together these responses as the whimsy of the question is rendered vaguely menacing by its explicit interpolation of the reader.

The poem's interrogation of femininity is complex. On the one hand, the association of femininity with furriery makes clear its subjugated status – its function in the poem as a trope for objectification. The visual slides that accompany the worded text, playing out this objectification through a typographic rendering of language, make evident both the violent implications of such an act and the role of language within them. Yet, as the very last lines of the poem suggest, neither femininity nor language can be entirely freed from such a struggle, as both are deeply complicit with the violent desires – for meaning, for pleasure, for possession – that the poem is concerned with both critiquing and embodying.

O'Sullivan's poetics successfully realise the 'agonal states' that resonate between the familiar boundaries of modernity – between reference and abstraction, between the natural and the social, between public and private. Yet her writing also makes apparent the more difficult knowledge that such a movement can never be innocent – that the violence which it draws upon and which it expends is necessarily equivocal, often risking failure or even reversion. This denial of a privileged 'innocent' space from which to write clearly extends to O'Sullivan's treatment of the relationship between femininity and language. Hers is a model of literary feminism which knows itself to be deeply implicated in the processes which it seeks to critique. Yet it is precisely this powerfully indeterminate energy, apparent in the work of other contemporary women poets who obscure distinctions between a visual and a language based poetics, which allows for the radical socialisation of this writing. It is the subsequent need to expand conventional assumptions about the relationship between representation and reading that follows from such an awareness that facilitates the power of these texts to exceed the apparent parameters of the poetic.

Notes

[1] Marjorie Perloff, 'The Coming of Age of Language Poetry', *Contemporary Literature* 38. 3: 558–587 (1997), p. 587

[2] Kathleen Fraser, 'Translating the Unspeakable: Visual poetics, as projected through Olson's "field" into current female writing practice' in *Translating the Unspeakable: Poetry and the Innovative Necessity*. (Tuscaloosa, London: University of Alabama Press, 2000), p. 178.

[3] Fraser, 'Translating the Unspeakable', p. 184.

[4] Susan Howe from: *A Bibliography of the King's Book or, Eikon Basilike* in *Out of Everywhere* ed. Maggie O'Sullivan (London: Reality Street Press, 1995), p. 11.

[5] Susan Howe from: *A Bibliography of the King's Book* in *Out of Everywhere*, p. 18.

[6] Susan Howe 'Encloser' in *The Politics of Poetic Form*, ed. Charles Bernstein. (New York: Roof Books, 1990); 'Articulation of Sound Forms in Time' from *The Singularities*. (Hanover: Wesleyan University Press, 1990); 'The Liberties' in *The Europe of Trusts* (New York: Sun and Moon, 1990).

[7] Susan Howe, 'Since a Dialogue We Are'. *In Relation* Acts 10: 167–169 (1989).

[8] Craig Douglas Dworkin, '"Waging Political Babble": Susan Howe's visual prosody and the politics of noise'. *Word and Image* 12.4: 389–405, (1996).

[9] Alan Golding, Susan Howe's Visual Poetics. In *We Who Love to be Astonished*, ed. Laura Hinton and Cynthia Hogue, (Tuscaloosa: Alabama University Press, 2001).

[10] Kathleen Fraser, 'Translating the Unspeakable', p. 186.

[11] Joan Retallack, *Afterrimages*. (Hanover: Wesleyan University Press, 1995), p. 7.

[12] Joan Retallack, *Musicage*. (Hanover and London: Wesleyan University Press, 1996), p. xxvii.

[13] Tina Darragh, 'adv. Fans – the 1968 series' in *Out of Everywhere* ed. Maggie O'Sullivan (London: Reality Street Press, 1995), p. 28.

[14] Tina Darragh,. *Striking Resemblance*. (Providence: Burning Deck Press, 1989).

[15] The procedures of 'adv fans' most obviously evokes Tristan Tzara's instructions for the Making of a Dadaist poem. See Jena Osman, 'The Poetry of Tina Darragh' in *Telling It Slant: Avant-Garde Poetics in the 1990s*, ed. by Mark Wallace. (Tuscaloosa and London: Alabama University Press, 2002).

[16] Joan Retallack, *Musicage*, p. xxv and Tina Darragh, 'adv. Fans – the 1968 series' in *Out of Everywhere*, p. 28.

[17] Paula Claire, 'BLACK(W)HOLEWHITE(W)HOLE 1986' in *Out of Everywhere*, p. 41.

[21] Joan Retallack, ':RE:THINKING:LITERARY: FEMINISM: (three essays onto shaky grounds)' in *Feminist Measures: Soundings in Poetry and Theory*, edited by Lynn Keller and Christanne Miller (Michigan: The University of Michigan Press, 1994) and Susan Howe, *My Emily Dickinson*. (New York: North Atlantic Books, 1985).

[22] Maggie O'Sullivan, *Concerning Spheres* (Bristol: Broken Ground Press, 1982); *States of Emergency*. (Oxford: International Concrete Poetry Archive Publication no 11, 1987); *unofficial word*. (Newcastle on Tyne: Galloping Dog Press, 1988).

[23] Gilles Deleuze, *Negotiations: Gilles Deleuze 1972–1990*. (New York: Columbia University Press, 1990), p. 201.

[24] Elizabeth Grosz, *Architecture from the Outside: Essays on Virtual and Real Space*. (Cambridge, Massachusetts: The MIT Press, 2000), p. 71.

[25] Maggie O'Sullivan, *A Natural History in 3 Incomplete Parts*. (London: Magneta, 1985), unpaginated.

[26] Kathleen Fraser, *Translating the Unspeakable: Poetry and the Innovative Necessity*. (Tuscaloosa, London: University of Alabama Press, 2000).

[27] Maggie O'Sullivan, 'when on the page i begin i search', in *Word Score Utterance Choreography*, ed. Bob Cobbing and Lawrence Upton. (London: Writer's Forum, 1998).

[28] There are other models of sculpture that could be usefully included in this analysis. The work of Eva Hesse, for example, provides a useful corrective to the more exuberant showman aspects of Beuys' shaman persona in ways that seem useful to consider in relation to O'Sullivan's poetics. In place of the ironically grand sweeps of Beuys' social sculpture, Hesse offers an attention to the elemental qualities of transformation and of their reliance on the dichotomies between the inner and outer, presence and absence and to the nuances of absurdity and repetition. Her reliance, moreover, on 'serial and modular repetition; notions of architectural scale and scaffolding, by means of lattices and grids' provides an

alternative way of literalising sixties aesthetic discourses of minimalism that influenced painters such as Agnes Martin. See Rosalind Krauss, 'Eva Hesse: Contingent' in *Eva Hesse*, ed. Mignon Nixon. (Cambridge, Mass: The MIT Press, 2002).

29 Caroline Tisdall, 'Beuys and the Celtic World', in *Joseph Beuys: Diverging Critiques*, ed. David Thistlewood. (Liverpool: University of Liverpool Press, 195), p. 117.

30 Bernice Rose has suggested the politicisation of these 'batteries' of stored energy which became 'a kind of aesthetic prosthesis for the split society, a means of empathetic healing.' Bernice Rose, 'Joseph Beuys and the Language of Drawing' in *Thinking is Form: The Drawings of Joseph Beuys*, edited by Ann Temkin and Bernice Rose. (New York: Thames and Hudson in association with Philadelphia Museum of Modern Art and The Museum of Modern Art, New York, 1993) p. 107.

31 Bernice Rose, 'Joseph Beuys and the Language of Drawing', p. 84.

32 Bernice Rose, 'Joseph Beuys and the Language of Drawing', p. 101.

33 Maggie O'Sullivan, *States of Emergency*. (Oxford: International Concrete Poetry Archive Publication no 11, 1987), unpaginated.

34 *Joseph Beuys*, directed by Caroline Tisdall and Christopher Swayne, (London: BBC, 1987).

35 This vilification, specifically the rumours of Scargill's financial corruption, reached their height five years later when *The Mirror* published a series of stories suggesting Scargill had embezzled money from the Miner's Fund and accepted money from Libya. Scargill was not finally exonerated of these accusations for another twelve years: Roy Greenslade, 'Sorry Arthur', *The Media Guardian*, (May 27, 2002).

36 Maggie O'Sullivan, *From the Handbook of that & Furriery*. (London: Writers Forum, 1986), unpaginated.

37 *Oxford English Dictionary*, online edition.

38 Johanna Drucker, *The Visible Word: Experimental Typography and Modern Art, 1909–1923* (Chicago: University of Chicago Press, 1994), p. 43.

39 Johanna Drucker, *The Visible Word*, p. 43.

'Ear Loads': Neologisms and Sound Poetry in Maggie O'Sullivan's Palace Of Reptiles

Peter Middleton

EAR LOADS

– I SING –

THEY CAME TO ME –

OCCIPUTAL DISTENTIONS

LINGERED, CHISMERIC, CHISMIC,
SCAR
CUMES,
CON-
CONDY-
CREO-
KAKA-
CATE-
CUA-
COOT-
E-
COB-
OD-
CL-
CR-
SWISH OF

(– WRENS CROSS MY PATH –)

TREMORING BUSTLE & MUTE
                    Maggie O'Sullivan, *from* 'Doubtless'[1]

To read 'Doubtless' and the book where it appears, *Palace of Reptiles*, is to
be filled with 'ear loads' of clongy, phonempathic language songs, creating whisdomensional rituals cut with the unknown. Maggie
O'Sullivan's spondeeeling non-lexical vocables have such wonderful
sonic associations that one wants to break out into one's own creashin-
ing, arkhaptic neologisms (and trying to do so I realise how subtle and
wide-ranging hers are compared to my efforts). Charles Bernstein's preface to a collection of her earlier books, *Body of Work*, applauds 'dialogic
extravagance in the articulated, dithrombotic, honeycomb pluriperversity.[2] He calls her style 'clinamacaronic' (playing on *clinamen, macaronic*,
and the German *kleine*), an especially apt neologism; the sequence
repeatedly swerves away from expected syntactic or syllogistic climaxes,
and employs so many strange words or recognisable words made foreign
by unexpected prefixes and suffixes, that it might well be borrowing its
macaronics from an unknown language just emerging into perception,
like the Borgesian language of Tlön. The passage above reflexively
describes its use of liminal phonemic inventions as the fruit of
'occipital distentions', which one can take to mean intentional distor-
tions of the rules of language by the back brain. What form of sound
poetry is this? It accommodates familiar lexical items, short bursts of
regular syntax, and intimates both lexical and syntactic placement for
many of the non-lexical sounds. It is both phonemic and non-phonemic,
both purely sensuous sound and semantically active lexis. How therefore might readers (and listeners—O'Sullivan is a consummate
performer of her work) respond to those 'ear loads' of 'chismeric'
sounds of Tlönic language?
    'What is the function of sound poetry today'? asks Stephen Voyce in an
interview with Christian Bök, and then qualifies the question by adding
that he is interested in how things have changed since 'the groundbreak-
ing work of the 1970s by poets such as the Four Horsemen, Henry Chopin,
or Bob Cobbing'.[3] This is a question that might equally be put to Maggie
O'Sullivan, who was mentored in Cobbing's poetry workshops,[4] and
whose poetry and performance, though very different to Bök's, similarly
dances along the borders of sound, sense and disorientation. Bök's
response to the leading question's inadvertent functionalism and its

invitation to dogmatic generalisation is to shift ground to the poetics of sound poetry. Earlier generations of sound poets, he says, 'justified their work by saying that such poetry allows the practitioner to revert to a more primitive, if not more infantile, variety of humanism.' Bök proposes instead that we think in terms of the achievements of civilisation and adopt a cyborg poetics: 'I think that most of the theories about sound poems are too "phono-philic" or too "quasi-mystic" for my own tastes as an intellectual, and I think that modern poetry may have to adopt other updated, musical theories to express the hectic tempos of our electrified environment.' Salience of the acoustic in Maggie O'Sullivan's poetry, especially her use of non-lexical word-like assemblages of recognisable phonemes, readily elicits characterisation as a primarily sound-based poetry that courts animist, bodily, zoomorphic spirits to express themselves in raw, passional sounds that can be reductively explained as primitivist (as can the work of an artist on whom O'Sullivan researched for the BBC, and who could also be mistakenly taken for no more than a primitivist, Joseph Beuys). As an alternative to grounding the phonic in a prerational culture, Bök follows what he calls a 'techno' standpoint towards the practice of sound poetry. Techno probably wouldn't help us understand O'Sullivan's practice, but I think Bök's emphasis on the value of a rationalist poetics for sound poetry is well worth pursuing when considering her poetry's use of sound. One way of doing this is to consider the history and concept of neologisms as a backdrop for her use of words that are on the margins of language or even entirely outwith semantic range.

As the passage above shows, the neologisms have a special context that requires acknowledgement even before considering the individual words themselves. These poems take time, time to happen, sound out, reveal thought, and they respond best to immersive reading and attentive listening. Nothing remains the same long enough to enable a truth claim to assert strong rights over the reader. Each line, each word, and sometimes each phoneme, mark shifts of being, changes of perspective, transformations of feeling, altered understanding, hits of new perception. She can be a good modernist and doesn't explain this process as a stream of mental event, or provide a capacious subject whose identity might be the locus for all these verbalising moments. More radically still, her poems don't unfold in evenly spaced verbal moments. Typographical and visual use of the space of the page, as well as painterly marks in some books, stretch and slow elapsed time, and the changing intensities of expression create wide differences in the scale of the poem's instants. The poetry can feel very small or terrifying large, imminently integrable or a rubble dump where horrors lurk (I can think of no other poetry that has learned as much from the contemporary genre of horror fiction and film). Even the words 'slip, slide and sometimes perish' in a manner alarmingly literal, so that words seem familiar, old, new and damaged, keeping the element of surprise on their side. It's within this altered sense of time and spacing that the neologisms occur, so many that the poetry might be called Adamic, although the power of naming often seems less a gift and more a desperate ruse in the face of unknowable and unsayable forces, entities and events.

News, new products, new celebrities, new words. Writing during the excitements about liberty after the French Revolution, Louis-Sébastien Mercier said: 'Neologers are everywhere, in the market halls just as in the Roman *Forum*, in the stock exchange, just as in the Senate. They are everywhere where liberty makes genius fruitful, where the imagination operates without constraint upon the models of nature, where thought can enlighten authority and defy tyranny.' Neologisms are still everywhere. In parapraxes: my mother on the telephone is telling me that she has heard from the sister of a New Zealand cousin who has just visited, and refers to the 'hister,' conflating 'heard from' and 'sister'. My son used to call yoga 'loga', hearing the words 'low' and 'lower' in the word. Misprints and mis-translations frequently create neologisms. On holiday in Italy I notice that a menu explains that a Calzone pizza is 'struffed' with ham. Scholars and scientists often invent words. The ecologist Charles Kendeigh coins the term 'biociation' as a condensed form of 'biological association' and 'consociality' to describe a climax community. An entire academic industry grew up around the neologism *différance*, which Jacques Derrida coined in order to demonstrate just how much philosophers and theorists ignored the rhetorical implications of ambiguity. *Différance* is an example of a neologism that somehow clings to its outsider status even while it becomes so widely recognised that it must be older than many ordinary but recent words. Politics takes up and drops words all the time. Back in 2003 we found out, or were led to believe that we were finding out, whether the government sexed-up, or should this be 'sexed-up,' (just how new is this phrase?) its dossier outlining the dangers of Iraq's weapons of mass destruction. A friend of mine is explaining how a seeming opportunity came to nothing: 'then it fuzzled out again.' I think I know (or seem to—this is not a moment in the conversation to ask for a definition) what she means: it was fucked up, it fizzled out.

'Sexed up' and 'fuzzled' are neither just everyday echoes of Finnegan's Wake speak, nor sharp displays of semantic compression, nor just a new productivity of speech capable of replacing two or more words with one. Much of their force lies in the mixture of creativity on show and the slight fuzziness of meaning. Linguistic creativity is also a sign of power or agency, of being able to exercise some control in situations (men, everyday life) which often render us somewhat helpless. Even the childish mispronunciation of 'yoga' provides evidence of emerging intellectual powers, at least for doting parents. Residual imprecision is important too, because it allows, as Derrida knew, room for imagination and new ideas to develop. Listeners are left to fill in their own interpretation as a contribution to the shared working out of what a discursive situation might mean to them, and this, like a mutual conversational game, is intersubjectively satisfying. Vagueness bonds people.[5] It is not that the ordinary clarity of words is a solidity like that of objects against which we can only kick. Words are usually old currency, smell of tired habits of mind and action, already carry too much historical clutter with them. And what is worse they often lie inert and almost useless there 'on the table top in front of you.'[6] As Pablo Neruda wrote, it can seem that we are faced with 'un golpe de objetos que llaman sin ser respondidos' ('a swarm of objects that call without being answered').[7] The doctors of language have applied almost every conceivable poetic medicine imaginable during the past hundred years to answer that call and get words back on their feet. Improved referentiality, elided referentiality; hyper-syntagmatics, sensory deprivation of single words; saturation with voice, deep impersonality; artificial languages, submission to the sliding signifier; and so on. This is not a list that is terminable.

Maggie O'Sullivan's poem 'Narcotic Properties,' from *Palace of Reptiles* (excellently produced by Nate Dorward's press The Gig) might be a new allegory of this history, as it instructs someone (a reader, a practitioner of magic) to 'PLACE A SMALL PALE-CREAM BOWL (TO SIGNIFY / abundance) / on the table-top in front of you'(16) and then to wash a series of 'LEAD ANIMALS' which presumably signify the ordinary idea of linguistic reference, each lead object being iconic of the class of animals in the world. What could be more appropriate than the idea of lead references? As one would expect, the procedure cannot hold firm the tidy relation of image to real object and soon the 'ABLE TREBLE FLIED / limbs' are caught in a language that is struggling for articulation and flying off in other directions, 'able' indeed, not just doubly but triply able, except that the word to name this power, 'treble,' falls short of being able, and suggests weakness, which the third word, the neologism 'flied,' confirms as it compresses together many equivocal terms (fled, flee, fly, flayed, lied, elide etc.). O'Sullivan's poetry has increasingly mapped this movement of modernist struggles to compel articulation from language that seems historically more resistant to recognising interconnectedness than ever before, and tracks this one particular move, that from ordinary language to neologism, with brilliant originality. Like a number of earlier modernist poets (W.B. Yeats, Robert Duncan, Ted Hughes all come to mind), she finds help for her poetics of the act of naming the world in occult and shamanistic writings, but unlike them resists the justifications and consolations of system. Her work also draws on utterly non-occult writers such as James Joyce, Gertrude Stein, more recent writers such as Clark Coolidge, Michael McClure, and Barry MacSweeney (the *Odes* especially), for whom the single word's expressiveness is a gift and mystery to explore, and above all on the women contemporaries she anthologised in *Out of Everywhere* (Susan Howe, Joan Retallack, Lyn Hejinian, Rae Armantrout, Wendy Mulford, Geraldine Monk, Karen MacCormack, Kathleen Fraser, Caroline Bergvall and many more), who have so extended our awareness of the interweaving of intellect, passion, body, gender, history, voice, text, the visual, and the acoustic, in our words. O'Sullivan brings something new to this genealogy too, a sense of the energy released as words break open, the word emerging only partially, neologistically, from utterance. Anguish, grief, joy, puzzlement, recognition, excitement, anger, pity—these and many other shifting emotions are integral to her work with those everyday avant-garde practices of neologism, the compression, display of creative power, and gifting of the friendship of making meanings together.

The OED offers these definitions of 'neologism' amongst others: 'the use of, or the practice of using, new words'; 'innovation in language'; 'a new word or expression'; or the 'tendency to, adoption of, novel (rationalistic) views in theology or matters of religion.' These definitions sound innocent enough (though those who adopt new rationalist perspectives from within religious communities have often been the target of attack—think of Spinoza or the current split amongst Anglicans) but the examples of usage tell a different story. W. Taylor says that neologisms are always quaint. Disraeli argues that neologisms help fertilise the 'barrenness of our Saxon', revealingly aligning neologisms with foreign cultural influences, since it is widely understood that the Normans and other immigrants have historically played this role. Thomas De Quincey sums up the doxa with typical epigrammatic flourish, making connections that persist up to the present: 'Neologism, in revolutionary times, is not an infirmity of caprice.' (1912). When speakers and writers use neologisms of whatever kind, they usually do so against a background of suspicion. Webster's dictionary is explicit about the dangers of neologising; a neologism is either 'a new word, usage, or expression' or 'a usu. compound word coined by a psychotic and meaningless to the hearer.' In this case the infirmity revealed by use of a nonce word is taken as a sign of madness (some forms of schizophrenia do manifest themselves as rhyming glossolalia).

H. W. Fowler, in his classic account of good usage, *The King's English*, whose title underlines the nationalist sentiments that support his views of language, sums up common-sense beliefs about neologisms at the start of his book *The King's English*. He is wary of a widespread impulse to make individual lexical innovations in the form of what he calls disparagingly, 'nonce-words,' relying on the submerged pun on nonsense to convey his disapproval and adding a catalogue of failings:

Most people of literary taste will say on this point 'It must needs be that offences come; but woe to that man by whom the offence cometh.' They are Liberal-Conservatives, their liberalism being general and theoretic, their conservatism particular and practical. And indeed, if no new words were to appear, it would be a sign that the language was moribund; but it is well that each new word that does appear should be severely scrutinized. [. . .] The progress of arts and sciences gives occasion for the large majority of new words; for a new thing we must have a new name; hence, for instance, *motor, argon, appendicitis.* [. . .] Among other arts and sciences, that of lexicography happens to have found convenient a neologism that may here be used to help in the very slight classification required for the new words we are more concerned with—that is, those whose object is literary or general, and not scientific. A 'nonce-word' (and the use might be extended to 'nonce-phrase' and 'nonce-sense'—the latter not necessarily, though it may be sometimes, equivalent to nonsense) is one that is constructed to serve a need of the moment. The writer is not seriously putting forward his word as one that is for the future to have an independent existence; he merely has a fancy to it for this once. The motive may be laziness, avoidance of the obvious, love of precision, or desire for a brevity or pregnancy that the language as at present constituted does not seem to him to admit of. The first two are bad motives, the third a good, and the last a mixed one. But in all cases it may be said that a writer should not indulge in these unless he is quite sure he is a good writer.[8]

A changing world will require new words, especially for the discoveries of science and the inventions of technology,[9] and a living language will require renewal by inspired additions to the lexicon, even if the inventor may be reviled at first. These inventors are likely to be writers (Fowler doesn't seem to consider the enormous contribution made by everyday discourse to the fund of new vocabulary, except in the case of low slang), who labour under a moral obligation not to invent words unnecessarily. The good (male) writer is allowed to invent occasionally, a permission which could almost be a sign of such status: we can recognise the really good writer by the appearance of such coinages, a claim legitimized in English by the enormous prestige of Shakespeare and his many apparent neologisms which subsequently entered the language as useful terms of everyday discourse. But if you are not Shakespeare, not certain that you are a 'good' writer, then watch out. Fowler was writing a century ago, but *The New Princeton Encyclopedia of Poetry and Poetics* (1993) is not much more encouraging: 'Neologisms (new coined words) tend now to be associated with novelty more than freshness, and sometimes with strained effects. The very word indicates they are not common currency.'[10] You know that a poet is onto something important when the reference books deplore the very linguistic practice they are improvising with.

Behind such negative attitudes lie fears of social upheaval that anarchic linguistic invention appears to be an omen for, as De Quincey implied. Daniel Rosenberg has recently argued that the preoccupation with neology during the French Revolution marks the 'consciousness of change so crucial to the period.' (367), and that its opponents thought that language was one of the most active zones of conflict.[11] One of the most unusual attempts to set the revolution on its proper course, to improve the expressiveness and articulacy of the language available to the new nation, was the dictionary of Louis-Sébastien Mercier, *La Néologie, ou vocabulaire de mots nouveaux, à renouveler, ou pris dans des acceptions nouvelles* (1801). The issue was where power over language lay, with the arbitrariness of institutions or with the people, and a prime target was the authority aggrandized by the *Dictionnaire de l'Académie française*. 'Mercier adamantly insisted with his contemporaries that new words must be accepted when they address reasonable needs. But his vision of neology extended much further—to words produced by imagination and even by happy accident,' (Rosenberg, 374), and he recognized the importance of the street as the source of vital new words. This awareness of the sociality of even acts of verbal invention is why he can say with such conviction that: 'Neologers are everywhere, in the market halls just as in the Roman *Forum*, in the stock exchange, just as in the Senate. They are everywhere where liberty makes genius fruitful, where the imagination operates without constraint upon the models of nature, where thought can enlighten authority and defy tyranny.' (Rosenberg, 376) Mercier's great work is set out as a dictionary because he believes that this force of change lies in the word rather than grammar and syntax, and he offers a list of words that he believes the world needs: *anecdotiser, ininventif, ininflammable, inabstinence, paroler, républicide, scribomanie*, are a few that give the flavour of his inventions (compare O'Sullivan's coinages such as *amuletic, engouled, outlered, unheavied*). To make neologisms was to celebrate creativity, freedom and a confidence in a revolutionary future—all ambitions that partially explain the anxious tut-tutting that most linguistic and literary authorities direct towards neologisms (a fascinating recent study of inventiveness of current American slang by Michael Adams celebrates many of these same virtues, claiming that slang engages in 'a veritable canasta of language play' and consequently displays many poetic characteristics).[12]

The extreme case of Mercier suggests that neologisms are signs of social instability, of aspirations to intervene in the historical process. He was particularly aware of the significance of onomatopoeia and its alleged role in the origins of language in pre-civilised peoples. Philippe Roger explains how Mercier justifies his neologisms with a discourse of Rousseauist primitivism that I believe also resonates with many features of Wallace Stevens'[13] interest in onomatopoeia and neologistic sound words:

> L'idiome du sauvage n'est pas un paradis perdu, ni un Éden qu'il faudrait retrouver. Il est en chacun de nous de «faire» un tel idiome. De telle sorte que l'inévitable apologie du Huron centrant la parole sur le verbe, l'incontournable référence à «*l'onomatopée* familière à tous les sauvages», ne sont guère pour Mercier que l'occasion d'insister, une fois de plus, sur la centralitè du mot, cette «charpente rèelle» qui suffit à l'èdifice de la parole et de la pensèe. Le mot: tourjours lui. Si Mercier, linguistiquement parlant, n'a que faire des sauvages, c'est qu'il a les mots: les mots «rudes et sauvages», justement, qui «dominent la grammaire». C'est qu'il suffit de cette croyance, elle-même sauvage, aux mots pour faire du nèologue un barbare bénéfique. En ce sens, la profession de foi «je serai un barbare» résume au plus juste le projet néologique de Mercier.[14] (Roger, 346)

O'Sullivan's poetry is also very interested in 'un barbare bénéfique', and in the roots of ononmatopeia, but like Roger's version of Mercier, she sticks with words, however neologistic. Primitivism elicits a technologically sophisticated, rational as well as affective response in her poetry.

Palace of Reptiles plunges the reader into a world of neologizing, and in doing so it refuses a certain type of Modernist contract with the reader (exemplified by Ezra Pound's *Cantos*): time spent looking up a word, a reference, a history or an academic source will be rewarded with new knowledge of our historical condition. It takes only two lines in the opening poem, 'Birth Palette,' to meet unknown words whose Modernist credentials will be decidedly ambiguous, and they are just heralds of what will follow:

> Lizard air lichens ivy driven urchin's pry to a pounce.
> Scribbled terrestrial traor, the paw actions tainy blee
> scoa, blue scog. In eat, gashed harmonica stresses to
> skull icon, jigged but shower, Crushtative bundles,
> Doe, Owl, the Hare mantled in a planetary pivot.
> Vulture-Jar, dragonfly & waterbeetle are we,
> each veil of the glide species. (11)

Start by looking in the dictionary for the first words suspected of neologistic tendencies. 'Traor,' 'tainy' and 'blee,' are all unfamiliar, but are they neologisms or simply very rare words tucked into a corner of the OED or Webster, or perhaps the lexicon of some other language? The first word I find in my OED, just visible in the field of the magnifying glass, is the word 'blee,' meaning 'colour of the face,' complexion, and by extension, appearance or form. The dictionary is unusually disparaging about the term: 'a purely poetical word in M.E., which gradually became obs.in the course of the 16th or early in the 17th c. (not in Shakspere); but being frequent in ballads and metrical romances it has been used by one or two modern poets.' Blee is clearly a word which the OED regards as unnecessary, 'purely poetical,' and one which could have conveniently been forgotten if not for these annoying poets—the 'one or two' says it all. It is not often that dictionaries insult the words in their care. This entry is a reminder that there is a politics and economics of the lexicon, and some words are entrepreneurial while others are virtually unemployable. Although recent literary theory and linguistics has insisted on a functional equivalence of signifying capability distributed amongst all signifiers equally, writers and even lexicographers often recognize that words vary in their power to do cultural work.

The dictionary has no listing for 'tainy' but it could be an adjectival form of 'tain' (tin) which is listed, although this adjectival or adverbial form would be even more unusual than this already obsolete noun. 'Traor doesn't figure at all, and might be all that is left after the word 'extraordinary' perished, appearing where we might have expected some such phrase as 'extraordinary *landscape*'—or *history* or *life*. 'Scog' is tricky. The dictionary lists a range of words, 'scoggin,' 'scoggery,' 'scogh' and a whole range of variant spellings, although not, as far as I can see, the simple root 'scog,' and provides a series of meanings including buffoonery, a wood or copse, a valve, and branchings of these core meanings. No wonder the dictionary occasionally has a go at poets. The boundaries of individual words are hard enough to demarcate, their spellings, pragmatics and semantics all promiscuously mingling with others over time, by usage and misusage, without the poets keeping alive obsolete words that were never needed in the first place, or what is worse, improvising their own. I hope no-one sends a copy of *Palace of Reptiles* to the office of the dictionary. If they see this and her other volumes they may have a panic attack at the thought of its implications for their project.

But just a minute. Webster *has* heard of 'scrog' and blames it, sorry attributes use of the word to regional British English: '*dial Brit*: a stunted shrub, bush, or branch : scrub.' A stunted word. Webster has not however heard of the word 'tain,' nor does it throw any light on 'traor.' A search of the Internet yields further support for the idea that this is a fusion of two phonemes from the word *extraordinary*, although from the website www.vancourier.com I learn that a Mali musician has the surname Traor: 'In the musical powerhouse of Mali, Rokia Traor, stands out in a number of significant ways. Traor, is a female singer/songwriter, a rarity in the West African nation. She also writes lyrics that emphasize independence for women, not exactly a common refrain in Mali's patriarchal society.'[15] In fact this is a relatively common surname in Mali, and another musician has the same name (a later issue of The Vancouver Courier spells the name Rokia *Traore*, a reminder of how spelling and names are also subject to 'occiputal distentions'). Although I am reasonably sure that the poet did not intend such an allusion, now that I have found the name it starts to set up a side-performance in the interpretative arena. The idea of a woman singer songwriter of great power whose work emerges from the desert terrain of sub-Saharan Africa, a scribbling terrestrial Traor, won't go away now. Even the less useful information that SCOA is a much-used acronym, variously employed by the Sprint Car Owners of America, the South Central Orienteering Association, and the Saluki Club of America, starts up a speculation that this or other words might be an acronymic, acrostic, or some other hermetic code for nouns that cannot be spoken without prolixity, and the risk of a danger hinted at everywhere in this poetry's traces of a buried violence.

The internet is especially interesting as a means of finding out whether a word is a pure neologism because the internet is the nearest thing we have to a complete documentation of all current usage; if a word has any circulation at all in any type of discourse it is likely to turn up somewhere on an internet page. Consider some of the oddities in the poem 'Theoretical Economies,' a poem in the form of instructions for a magic ritual or conceptual art-work. A search for 'hundridder' in 'Theoretical Economies' yields nothing, so it comes close to certainty that it is a complete invention though it does sound like a variant on 'houndrider' or 'houndridder,' the sort of gothic name that Tolkien and other fantasy writers devise. 'Gorple' turns out to be a place in Yorkshire. 'Walkenon' is also a neologism although there are people with the surname Walkenon. The phrase 'zanza-zinc' may not be a neologism, since 'zanza' is apparently a trade-name for a number of companies including a record company. These neologisms and neo-neologisms occur after the early passages of the poem offer a pastiche of what might be a black magic ritual or an allegory for the reading of a poem in hope of transformation, personal or social. We are told to hang up a banner, place small simulacra beneath it, and then 'drip / random li(n)es of order' onto this 'toy medium' (to borrow a phrase and its implications from Daniel Tiffany).[16] The results are what the poem 'Doubtless' describes as 'STILL STILLS OF BROKEN LETTERS' (36), a deliquescence of order, syntax, capitalized words, word fragments, and these simulacra of words, the neologisms. The ending of 'Theoretical Economies' hints at a purgatorial state of transformation, a late winter moment before new life:

RED

BEES
APART
owl-sha
conks   clays-under   splashing.   Abundance.   weeps. (21)

The missing half of the hyphenated addition to 'owl,' probably the word 'shaman,' is 'man' in this oozing, watery landscape where the industry of bees is more promise than actuality.

The neologisms in 'Birth Palette' are of course not singular words, they are firmly embedded in a complex poetic structure that exerts its own field of force over them. English language conventions governing word-order encourage a first reading of the opening line in which adjective, subject-noun, verb, and object-noun follow in a neatly jointed sequence. 'Lichens' would be the verb to represent the action of the air on ivy, and the second half of the line, 'driven urchin's pry to a pounce,' a subordinate clause that describes the particular ivy. This explanation represents a possible split-second interpretative stance that is likely to be abandoned just as quickly; the metaphorical usages and syntactic foreshortening required are too unlikely. The opposite alternative would be a non-syntactic reading that just takes each word as an ostensive gesture—there's a lizard, notice the air, see those lichens and the ivy—or what might be identified as a series of one-word sentences—it or they are driven, the child's curiosity will lead to something, perhaps to the attempt to seize hold of its object of attention. Neither account is quite satisfactory, not least because the most salient aesthetic display is the fugue of phonetic sound shapes that are both sonic and visual. *Lizard | lichens; lichens | driven | urchin; to a | traor | scoa; lizard air | scribbled terr*; or the many variations on the vowel combination of *i* and *e*. This patterning holds together the field of meanings generated by the commonality of words for animals and inanimate landscape from which tentative propositions do emerge—'dragonfly & waterbeetle are we'—only to dissolve again in a paratactic shift of syntax—'each veil of the glide species.'

Extended out over the two pages of the poem these effects cohere into an intense image of a wild, Darwinian landscape, in which all sorts of animals, even domesticated ones, express a predatory attention to other life which they will consume if they can. Moon, sky, sea, earth and water are the scene of this life. We humans find all kinds of animal metaphors and symbols of ourselves in 'the glide species' on an 'earth scalded,' and the challenge is to understand the extent and responsibility of our empathies and recognitions, our 'heart size,' as our 'options falter.' You could say that the poem belongs alongside a British pastoral tradition running from the Romantics to Ted Hughes, and be reassured that those men did not write in vain, but you would miss the degree to which it conveys the resistance of this wild plenum to appropriation for spiritual insights or implicit allegories of the instinctual drives, as much as genetic modification by any commodifying form of inquiry. Her poetry also sidesteps a negative theology of poetic language, and doesn't claim pure otherness for the wilderness beyond all cognition, nor an absolute unknowability that could only be presented in the non-emotive, anti-rhetorical manner of *soi-disant* science. This poem will not let itself be confined to one register and introduces phrases from both financial reports (phrases that could be read as inversions of the poetry's entire metaphorics, so that all these animals become signs in a zodiac we might read for its horoscopical politics of the Stock Exchange) and neuroscience (the line from the later part of the poem, '"twas all moon down in the brainstem",' could elicit a reading in which spider, 'lemony pig', and 'deers' could all be archetypes or 'asterisms,' working like starry psychic aneurisms in the skull's cosmos-containing brain).

At this point some comparisons with other contemporary poets who use neologisms occasionally will be helpful for underlining just how richly semantic neologisms can be. Philip Whalen's poem 'Sauced' is a well-known poem thanks to its inclusion in *The Beat Scene*, where it represents a Beat aesthetic, joyful drunken synesthesia.[17] It is also an example of a poet playing with the idea that neologisms are psychotic. The line, 'A Trio for Jaybird, Telephone & Trombone,' inverts and transposes the syllables as if this *were* a musical composition, creating words such as 'trambone,' and 'telebone.' Even in this early, and relatively simple poem, the neologism knowingly plays with ironic self-reflection on the social stigma of the self-invented word, especially the tendency to treat them as signs of mental aberration. A more subtle use of neologism occurs in Fanny Howe's poem, '16:18,' from the sequence of poems *O'Clock*:

> Sometimes a goodbye
>
> seems a bee's
> done buzzing
>
> earily: purrs
> in hair, furred
>
> for the sting.
> Fear's then
>
> a hurt-leap.
> Time comes in
>
> like the words
> *Sit down.*
>
> Your nerves
> reverses.[18]

The poem uses 'earily' for the pun eerily/like or in the area of an ear, and 'hurt-leap' for the pun on hurtle/hurt leaps, interrupting abruptly the smooth flow of cognitive intake through semantically recognised words. These neologisms also contrast with the opaque ordinariness of the phrases used for everyday exchanges, and which in the current painful situation carry enormous unarticulated force. Emotional turbulence associated with a moment when simple phrases of welcome are failing creates the condition in which the signifying excess, and slight eerieness of the neologisms, becomes possible.

In his text 'Albany', Ron Silliman writes that 'Rubin feared McClure would read *Ghost Tantras* at the teach-in,' and one can see why even someone as used to street theatre as Jerry Rubin might feel that yippie agit-prop might not be ready for a poetry of such unregenerate sound poetry and its visceral neologisms.[19] This is the first tantrum, I mean tantra:

GOOOOOOR! GOOOOOOOOOO!
GOOOOOOOOOR!
GRAHHH! GRAHH! GRAHH!
Grah gooooor! Ghahh! Graaarr! Greeeeer! Grayowhr!
Greeeeee
GRAHHRR! RAHHR! GRAGHHRR! RAHR!
RAHR! RAHHR! GRAHHHR! HRAHR!
BE NOT SUGAR BUT BE LOVE
looking for sugar!
GAHHHHHHHH!
ROWRR!
GROOOOOOOOOOH![20]

Rubin's fear is the poetry's force. This is a practice that Maggie O'Sullivan might seem to endorse at times. She prefaces *In the House of the Shaman* with one of those deceptively legitimate uses of ordinary language with which Gertrude Stein challenges us: 'And each of us in our own way are bound to express what the world in which we are living is doing.'[21] McClure assumes that expressing the world means that 'a dahlia or fern might become pure speech in meditation' if we are able to 'listen to inner energies a-roar.' Silliman's opening (incomplete) sentence in his prose poem 'Albany' implicitly dissents: 'If the function of writing is to "express the world".' The statement is left unfinished inviting the reader to receive this as both the answer to a missing prior question about texts, and the first half of a conditional statement whose consequence will have to be inferred by a reader, unless the second sentence ('My father withheld child support, forcing my mother to live with her parents, my brother and I to be raised together in a small room') is taken to say implicitly: 'then here is what I must say.' Although the second sentence of 'Albany' does exemplify expressive, autobiographical utterance, the 'world' has become the poet's situation, where he is 'coming from.'

When Silliman was interviewed by Manuel Brito, he pondered neologisms in two short poems, 'Blod' by Aram Saroyan and 'Thumpa' by Robert Grenier:

Thus, as is virtually always the case, nonsense is a particularly complex instance of sense itself, not its erasure or Other. Here, *thumpa* is a 'non-word' that points to a surprisingly large body of other 'non-words,' all of which exploit the social category of the non-word as an aspect of their own agency. The onomatopoetic loses its force if we don't acknowledge its special condition and thus becomes 'only' a word.[22]

Aren't O'Sullivan's nonce-words almost illegal immigrants to the linguistic community, seeking asylum from scenes of horror that the poetry cannot directly name? What else could the adjective 'terrestrial' qualify after all? 'Traor' marks the impossibility that any of these well-used abstractions would answer to what is needed here. The phrase 'scribbled terrestrial traor' suggests that the text is attempting to reflect on its own process, its hastily written vision of the earthbound, mundane world, so that the third word becomes a sign of some kind of failed articulation. Is 'traor' then a guesstimate that doesn't make it as a word, an attempt to utter a sound that will become the necessary word? Can one discern the faint outlines of words such as 'trawl', 'traitor,' 'treasure' or 'extraordinary?' It certainly seems significant that the first of these occurs in a reference to the act of writing. One can imagine an unlikely reading of the phrase as meaning something like: I scribbled so fast the word 'terrestrial' came out as 'traor.'

My discussion of neologisms has so far concentrated on modern poetic tradition, but neologising has a much wider range than this, in scat and comic books, for instance. Frank Miller's Batman knows all about the necessary extremities of scat. Some moments of intense engagement can only be greeted with a cry like 'SKRRAKK,' although the good bourgeois of Gotham probably share the views of the television news presenter who explains that the dark knight is known for his 'wild animal growls, snarls, werewolf surely.'[23] Is O'Sullivan's practice a form of poetic scat, a Bob Cobbing-inspired update of Ella Fitzgerald, a counterpart to Bobbie McFerrin in *Beyond Words*? Scat? There would seem something a little like cheating in making poems of invented words if the words were only scatting. Lost for a word whose phonemes will fit exactly into the tune? Make one up. Scat is actually very difficult to do, because the precise articulation of the words, and the degree of semantic coloring that remains in the nonce word are extremely hard to control with the voice attuned to familiar grammar and lexical coloring. Fantasy writers know that sparing use of strange-sounding neologisms can evoke their otherworldy scenes very effectively. Ursula K. LeGuin places a glossary of 'Kesh', the language of the people documented in her novel *Always Coming Home*, a culture living far in the future whose economy is ecologically far advanced though reticent in its use of technology. 'Goutun' means the 'twilight of morning' and 'kach' a city, and 'aïbayaï' is ''handmind', physical work done with intelligence, or the results of such work'.[24] In the last example, the invented word requires a more familiar invented portmanteau creation to explain it, and this points to one striking feature of these words: they are most evocative when they refer to something that is slightly beyond our understanding or perception. The neologisms in *Palace of Reptiles* and the other books do work with these auratic effects, yet this, like the scat, is only a part of what is happening.

One way to follow the phenomenology and event of these words further is to ask about the neologism itself. What is a new word, how can it be? Isn't a word no longer new the moment it is uttered or written into the record of our interactions? Isn't the neo logic that of the almost new, the almost fresh, already slightly eroded by exchange in the wet mouths of users and the fading neurones of memory? Neologisms proliferate. There are Joycean punning neologisms, prelinguistic cries, words patched together into temporary association, in-group words, private twin languages, evanescent jargon, the comic book language of Batman, the quasi-neologisms of trade names—this is only a small selection of the possibilities. They are troublesome too, they may not after all be new, but simply misapprehended or unfamiliar. Misprints are easier, they can be ignored once the disturbance to smooth reception has been set aside. The inventions of scholars and writers are trickier, because of the extended claims that will accompany the word itself, and the challenge to the reader to accept the word into specialist use and comprehend the existing verbal deficit that makes its coinage necessary. Often it is only another specialist who could decide on the viability of a new term, or even know just by reading the account in which it occurs, whether it did gain any sort of temporary currency.

But to write like this is misleading. Neologisms are not only ubiquitous, their diversity resists such rationalising taxonomies. Such putative words form an infinite set whose cardinal number is higher than that of actual words, because for every proper word (but what one is beginning to ask is such a word) there will be a nearly unlimited range of variants that shade off into entirely non-semantic vocal or alphabetic effects. No firm set of categories? Does this mean that generalisations about the scope and character of neologisms are impossible, or unreliable, or at best highly provisional? It would do if a mapping of neologisms relied on taxonomy, but the problem is different, and not unlike the difficulties that once afflicted the field of research from which this metaphor is drawn, biology. Once observant scientists began to check the members of a species in great detail they tended to find that they were all different, and also noticed all sorts of half-way hybrids. A marine biologist friend of mine once complained that the biggest problem in making a census of river fish in the Wye was the abundance of intermediate forms of the fish that then resisted classification. The answer to such dilemmas that researchers have developed over the years is to recognise that all living organisms are variants, that none of them are pure forms of the species, because that is how the complex chemistry of genetics actually operates.

Maybe neologisms are not all as easy to spot as the ones whose alphabetic form is dissonant. When we read the word 'traor' in O'Sullivan's poem we reach for the dictionaries, perhaps run other searches, and conclude that it is her own coinage, because the arrangement of the letters and sounds does not correspond with any existing verbal paradigm. Our word recognition faculties make their demarcations on formal grounds, and this seems entirely obvious. But some neologisms will not be identified by this method. All words in actual use have traces of neologism in them, usually concealed by the familiarity of forms. The poets were right. Words are hairy, fleshy, wild; they usually dress to hide it. Some modern linguists have recognised that linguistic value must work like this, that words must always be twisted a little, revalued slightly, misunderstood, even, in the eyes of the philosopher John McCumber, be poetically interactive, where poetry is a synonym for the beauties of distortion (beauty is mostly achieved by simplification of elements).[25] When the politicians talk of 'weapons of mass destruction' we don't know what they mean, not least because what they mean will only become clearer, if it does, in the future, and its use in the present is interdependent on its many other uses, most of which cannot practically be known by one individual. Robert Pippin describes the dilemma of modern moral life in terms which illuminate my point. He says that 'what I am in fact thinking consciously about my own attitudes, or what I think about others, might but need not have much relevance to what opinions and beliefs may rightly be (eventually) attributed to me about such matters. I may never have 'actually thought' the opinions I do have, and what I consciously tell myself I believe may not at all be what I believe.'[26] This is also the epistemic problem with meaning in language for modernity. What is said, in ordinary conversation, in the newspapers, on television, in our popular novels and other textual arts, lives with an awareness that what is meant consciously may not have much connection with what will be seen to have been meant when the event has had more time to realise itself in our historical awareness.

Linguists and philosophers who have pursued these arguments are primarily concerned to refute models of perfect communicability, the supposedly noiseless transmission of thought from one mind to another with no loss, and no creative development, that they allege inheres in the standard models of language. For those who try to work creatively with language to discover more about the world, even this recognition remains constrictive. There are also an ethics and an aesthetics of this neologistic condition that are potentially of great interest to poets. If meaning is not appended to the word like charms on a bracelet, from where it can be readily identified with the help of a dictionary, but instead meaning is always unfinished, hairy, not quite glimpsed, and still growly with the body's formation of sound, then how do we achieve the subtle understandings that meaning can bring? Create a waxed logical language of pure mentality? Or work with the words for better understanding? Logical languages have enabled thinkers to achieve remarkable insights, but they only operate within tiny subsets of the continuum. Working with the imperfections of language, which we ordinarily call style, rhetoric, and expressiveness, has a much better record. Words in use normally achieve the articulation of new insights only incrementally through intense usage by which gradually they unfold though to itself; even ordinary supposedly well-defined words (well-defined in the dictionary at least) can have a semantic deficit as far as understanding is concerned, if they are not hurrying about in verbal exchange.

Modern poetry has now run through a wide, inventive and extending repertoire of verbal techniques which seem at first hearing to bleach meaning from words, phrases, sentences and texts. Repetition, parataxis, catachresis, phrases without verbs, unconnected sentences, words from different registers crushed together, partial phonemes, absent contexts, absent referents, and sublimed abstractions—these and many others associated with writers since Stein, Pound, Williams, and other early modernists, have lifted poetic language away from the attested literalisms of science and the would-be familiarity of media speech. Almost all attempts to justify or explain these practices begin with the idea that ordinary language has become contaminated with ideology, worn out with over use, and lost all precision or accuracy as a form of thought. Always defamiliarize and dereferentialize: this is the cry. During the past twenty years it has become possible to interpret the entire works of pre and post World War II modernist writers, especially poets, as language projects. Signature styles and habitual preoccupations are now read as prolonged commitment to inquiry into features of language stained with invention for the poetic microscope: speech acts, nominalism, metaphor, assertion, the sentence, parapraxis, catachresis, logic, and phonematics. Noticing explicitly that William Carlos Williams often replaces the use of neutral direct statement to an anonymous audience with modes of address that presuppose a specific relation to a particular kind of recipient pulls interpretation away from the obvious tendency towards a biographical reading, however nuanced, of his poems as a record of the life of a doctor, artist, father, husband and lover. Now we notice continuities with the significant emphasis of lyric poetry of the past on its direct address to a lover or friend, often to named people, admire its ethnographic attentiveness to the different forms of social relation embedded in discrete communicative acts, and notice that it anticipates speech act theory. Charles Olson was once read as a new kind of historian. Now attentive readers are most likely to notice that he extends across three volumes an investigation of a voice, constructed largely through expressive use of commas and line-breaks, that is capable of introjecting all the histories that he can find of his own life-site or 'situatedness.'[27]

These earlier Modernist poetries appeared to resolve only slowly into language experiments. Contemporary avant-garde poets, however, often present their work first and foremost as a linguistic enterprise. The sentence, the phrase, the word, have all had their proponents, both formalistically and sociolinguistically. Or, as Maggie O'Sullivan expresses it: 'In words, other rooming for what is at RISK inside out in language. Oppositional dialogues, realities, cartwheels, sway substances, Language Undeniably, Ably drowsed, dowsed even.' (PR 68) But this tendency to see these bodies of poetry as linguistic projects makes linguistic concentration on one feature of language the only form of inquiry, making the mysterious *wh* that prefixes most interrogatives 'the onlie begetter' of late Modernist poems.

O'Sullivan is not quite of this company although she has almost always been read in this context. A brief parenthetical list of words that might initiate different forms of intellectual inquiry points to why. She plays with the sound of the interrogative in 'Theoretical Economies,' where the homonymic row and column reminds us that not all questioning sounds are the prefix to questions:

```
(whatll          wattle          wambs
wha
white
whe
who)
(21)
```

From the standpoint of the linguistically-turned reader, a neologism such as 'wambs' exemplifies O'Sullivan's own signature mode of linguistic inquiry into the edges of verbal intelligibility where the dictionary gives up on words that may or may not have some currency in speech or specialized discourse. Her poetry is of a scale to be considered alongside those other poets in the language laboratory.[28]

The poem 'Now to the Ears' suggests that the relation to Modernism is more self-conscious, more critical, and even its neologising less reducible to linguistic effect than our current assumptions about the aftermath of Modernist poetry might suggest. Up in the 'leaf dens' of a wild landscape, common animals, hare, crow, raven, thrushes, and other creatures call and dance, 'all summer long', as Yeats wrote. Near the end of the poem we have the single isolated line, 'the waste of it,' a trope which for almost all readers of contemporary poetry is now saturated with its uses in T.S.Eliot's poems *The Waste Land* and *Four Quartets*, poems that are actually linked by a similar line in *Burnt Norton*: 'the waste sad time / Stretching before and after.'[29] Allusions to Yeats and Eliot are unsurprising in contemporary poetry; these were the modern poets most widely read by young people at school and in Higher Education. The allusiveness is muted here, and it is not evident that immediate content recognition is the point, but this does not mean that we should ignore it either. As so often in contemporary avant-garde poetry, we sense that an argument is being conducted with the poetics now represented by these mentors of earlier generations. Eliot, as I alluded earlier, talks of words that 'slip, slide and sometimes perish.' Maggie O'Sullivan's words do actually slip, slide and break apart, but the result is not the breakdown of social hierarchy and loss of relation to divinity that Eliot fears. The scope of this contestation of the right to represent the modern condition comes into sharp relief in the final lines of 'Now to the Ears,' where punctuation becomes more prominent than the restrained vocabulary it hedges round:

sob –

tick (ticca) –

told. te. me.

Don't Only Dance

shimmish? (30)

A hyphen, a pair of brackets, three full-stops (periods), capitalized words, and a question mark, are a strong presence in a sequence of only five short lines and ten words. Their excess diacritical presence marks an emotion that has already been signalled by the content of certain words (grief, wastes, wailed, choke, sacrificial, skull, boned, bandages, tombs, torched, scream) which either express intense loss, mortality, or danger, and belong to a register of language for extremes of human suffering.

Consider this punctuation in more detail. The poem is centre-justified, and this as always takes away the line-break as an add-on reservoir of punctuation whose role as a pause for incorporation as metre, syntax and breath intake, is so integral to the history of printed poetry. On the spinal median the words spread out equidistantly towards equated line-endings and the consequent equivocation of stop. Ordinary left to right reading of the words is shadowed by a counter-current that is as much rhythmic as semantic. Simply put, the centering of a text as asyntactic and non-narrativized as this, turns every line into a phrase unit whose initiating moment of stress and intonation, the usual ways of voicing a metric, is delayed until the entire line is known and the reader has to negotiate this uncertain launch into the middle of its affairs. The line has always already begun when the first word in the line is read.

Now consider the dash. No poet can now use the dash without invoking Emily Dickinson, whose use of this flexible marker as a point of transformation that would otherwise require cumbersome phrasings and punctuations, remains a landmark as striking as Walt Whitman's use of ellipses for similar, if more limited, purposes, in the first edition of *Leaves of Grass*. The dash has something of the force of a gesture pointing out a salience—as if to say, 'so you see, this is what these words lead to.' Like Whitman's ellipses, it also allows time to pass; the unfolding expression can start in a new momentary configuration, fresh in the suddenness of new time. Most striking of O'Sullivan's innovations is however the semanticisation of the dash. In these final lines, it also becomes a code word, a neologism without letters. The fifth line from the end reads: 'sob –' and the dash could be a shorthand equivalent for the word, and for the sound which is almost certainly likely to be non-phonematic anyway. We can think of this as saying that the dash is a sign for the sob. Its recurrence in the next line could be a recurrence of the physical emission of grief after the two words that suggest time and a mysterious, because neologistic, 'ticca'. This word characteristically seems to be an amalgam of at least the words 'ticker' (clock, heart) and 'wicca' (pagan magic), and the mind tries to make this work before alert attention calls a halt and admits that although its sound is homonymic with that of the clock theme, the look of the word denies this. The dash adds its own noisy linguistic silence. Is the sequence of dashes a line of silent neologisms for the words that they accompany, a series of trans-formations that can only end in silence, the dash that promises more, but cannot tell us how that more will be connected to what preceded it? Rational interpretation wants to reject this possibility. Its appearance in one's response to the poem is part of how the poem's neologising creates doubt and glimpses of semantic possibility that cannot be reached.

The full-stops, and the capital letters in succeeding lines, have similar though opposite effects of lending weight, either at the beginning or end of the words, so that the line 'told. te. me.' takes forever to utter the three words as if this telling were uncertain, forgotten, or a burden, and the following line is continually abandoning what it was trying to say and starting again, except that in both cases the line seems (apart from the disjunctive punctuation) perfectly grammatical and therefore a unit itself, moving fluently on. The dance of syntax is resisted as the injunc-tion not to be like the birds and beasts of the air and earth and 'dance.' Here the poem might have finished, except that then it would simply leave us with warnings and fears. Instead it pulls off a startling new move, and ends with another mysterious neologism that once again shimmers on the edge of intelligibility, this time melding words for dance, quickness of movement, and light (shimmy, shim, shimmer, skit-tish). Iconicity of language makes this possible as much as the glimpse of the remaining outlines of words partially melted together. Because we don't and cannot know what this word's interrogative means or even what kind of action it invites—an answer, an action, an agreement—the poem leaves us with only our ears sure. We read back to the opening of the poem and there is the invitation again:

Now to the Ears

Having journeyed to the Place of the
GIVERS

there is here

flicker. fleur. de. feather. fly. VOICINGS

on the shape
of storm novembers— (27)

The poem seems occult when first read, because its literalness is not in the form of narrative or statement, but in a form of enacted ritual. Stormy Novembers are what is given shape here, the landscape of a wintry closing down, a dying back of plants and animals, the cries and loudness of land-scape unmuffled by foliage, and the symbolics of a season that tests our belief in renewal and continuity. Each successive line of the poem takes us further into the shaping of these Novembers, where there can be no arrival at a conclusive statement of what this experience is.

A poetry that works with the nonce word as a key instrument in the sound risks reductionism and consequent dismissal. It is no accident that Maggie O'Sullivan's work has sometimes met the kind of angry incomprehension that the Dada artists courted. Her poetry however, as I have argued here, is very far from any programmatic desire to shock readers and overturn convention. It is deeply traditional in its atten-tions to continuing crises of language and its deeply interwoven poetic critique of other contemporary and earlier Modernist poetics. Its use of neologism calls attention to the scandal of neologisms for our beliefs about language, and even some of our most advanced theories of the textual condition, but its mode of inquiry is pre-programmatic. The idea of a systematic inquiry of the kind practised by many of the poets of the past fifty years is set aside, and to some extent challenged, although never through such organised methodologies. Emotional intensity, its demands for recognition and transformation, its pointers towards intel-lectual possibilities and mistakes, is her preferred mode of poetic work-ing. Its 'stem-suns' to be 'worded later' from the 'wreakage' of language from the borders of nature and culture is a new Ecology in poetics that recognises the indeterminacy of speciation or exactness of words.[30] Language overspill, unfinished words. What did you say?

Notes

[1] Maggie O'Sullivan, 'Doubtless', *Palace of Reptiles* (Willowdale, Ontario: The Gig, 2003), 42–43. Hereafter PR.

2 Charles Bernstein, 'Foreword: Maggie O'Sullivan's Medleyed Verse'. *In*: Maggie O'Sullivan. *Body of Work*. Hastings, E. Sussex: Reality Street Editions, 2006, 7, 9.

3 Stephen Voyce, 'The Xenotext Experiment: An Interview with Christian Bök', *Postmodern Culture* 17:2 (2007), 38. Online at: http://pmc.iath.virginia.edu/text-only/issue.107/17.2contents.html.

4 See extracts from an interview with Maggie O'Sullivan in: Nicky Marsh, Peter Middleton, Victoria Sheppard, 'Blasts of Language': Changes in Oral Poetics in Britain Since 1965, *Oral Tradition* 21:1 (2006), 51, 57 etc. Available at http://journal.oraltradition.org/issues/21i/marsh_middleton_sheppard .

5 A referee for this article points out that there are different types of vagueness, notably the restricted code described by Basil Bernstein, which enables people with a shared *habitus* to converse in words that they hear as precise because the words are understood as referring to a shared contextual world, and the sort of vagueness, that I have attributed to *différance* and to O'Sullivan's coinages, which invites speculative filling in that can open up new areas of thought. An example of the first kind is found in the way Henry James derives comedy in *The Awkward Age* from the dissonance between high emotional tensions and the banality of verbal expression in the dialogue amongst the inner circle around Mrs Brookenham (as for example in the discussion of the 'boat' in which Aggie is supposedly afloat, a metaphor that completely baffles the outsider Mr Longdon (Book IV Chapter XV) Henry James, *The Awkward Age* ed. Vivien Jones (Oxford: Oxford University Press, 1984), 130). An example of the second kind of possibility is explored extensively in Gillian Beer's *Open Fields* (Oxford: Oxford University Press, 1996) where she argues that 'new scientific and technical knowledge allows the poet to contemplate with fresh intensity intransigent questions which grip language in all generations'(168). Her chapter 'Translation or Transformation? The Relations of Literature and Science' explores the issues.

6 Maggie O'Sullivan, 'Narcotic Properties,' 16.

7 Pablo Neruda, 'Ars Poetica', *Residencia en la tierra*, trans. Donald D. Walsh (London: Souvenir Press, 2003), 46–47.

8 H. W. Fowler. *The King's English* 3rd ed., (Oxford: Clarendon Press, 1931), 29.

9 For further discussion of science and language in poetry see the following articles of mine which are part of a larger project on science and poetry: 'Strips: Scientific language in poetry,' *Textual Practice* 23:6 (Dec. 2009), 947–958; and 'Can Poetry Be Scientific?', Philip Coleman ed., *Science and Poetry* (Dublin: Four-Courts Press, 2007), 190–210.

10 Alex Preminger and T. V. F. Brogan eds., *The New Princeton Encyclopedia of Poetry and Poetics* (Princeton, N. J.: Princeton University Press, 1993), 690.

11 Daniel Rosenberg, 'Louis-Sébastien Mercier's New Words,' *Eighteenth-Century Studies* 36:3 (2003), 367–386, 367.

12 Michael Adams, *Slang: The People's Poetry*, (Oxford: Oxford University Press), 177.

13 I also discuss this same material on the political history of neologisms in my essay on Wallace Stevens' fascination with non-semantic sound words: Peter Middleton, 'The "Final Finding of the Ear": Wallace Stevens' Modernist Soundscapes', *The Wallace Stevens Journal* 33.1 (Spring 2009), 61–82.

[14] Philippe Roger, 'Libre et Despote: Mercier Néologue'. *In*: Jean-Claude Bonnet ed. *Louis Sébastien Mercier (1780–1814): Un hérétique en literature* (Paris: Mercure de France, 1995), 327–347, 346.

[15] http://archive.vancourier.com/issues02/073202/entertainment/073202en1.html

[16] Tiffany argues that both lyric poetry and science work hard to make the intangible somehow perceptible, and that science has a long history of using models and 'toys' to do this, whereas poetry uses lyric images. The gulf between the enormous authority of contemporary science and the apparent epistemological bankruptcy of lyric poetry can be bridged in part by tracing the parallels in their use of toy media: 'Science has become the final arbiter of what constitutes a real body, whereas lyric poetry appears in the public eye to be little more than a toy medium, apparently immune to the obligations of realism.' His ideas could be extended to O'Sullivan's interest in models such as her 'lead animals'. Daniel Tiffany, *Toy Medium: Materialism and Modern Lyric* (Berkeley: University of California Press, 2000), 246.

[17] Philip Whalen, 'Sauced'. *In*: Elias Wilentz ed. *The Beat Scene* (New York: Corinth Books, 1960), 145. Collected in: *On Bear's Head* (New York: Harcourt Brace & World and Coyote, 1969), 262.

[18] Fanny Howe, '16:18', *O'Clock*, (London: Reality Street Editions, 1995), 55.

[19] Ron Silliman, 'Albany', *ABC* (Tuumba 46, 1983), no page nos.

[20] Michael McClure, *Ghost Tantras* (San Francisco: Four Seasons Foundation, 1969), 7.

[21] Maggie O'Sullivan, *In the House of the Shaman*, (London: Reality Street Editions, 1993).

[22] Manuel Brito, *A Suite of Poetic Voices: Interviews with Contemporary American Poets* (Santa Brigida: Kadle Books, 1992), 156.

[23] Frank Miller, *The Dark Knight Returns* (London: Titan Books, 1986), 21, 26.

[24] Ursula K. LeGuin, 'Glossary', *Always Coming Home* (London: Collins, 1988), 509–523.

[25] John McCumber, *Poetic Interaction: Language, Freedom, Reason* (Chicago: University of Chicago Press, 1989).

[26] Robert Pippin, *Henry James and Modern Moral Life* (Cambridge: Cambridge University Press, 2000), 54.

[27] These issues are further explored in my essay 'Charles Olson: A Short History,' *Parataxis* 10 (2001), 54–66.

[28] See my *Distant Reading: Performance, Readership, and Consumption in Contemporary Poetry* (Tuscaloosa: Alabama University Press, 2005). Issues of performance are also discussed in 'How to Read a Reading of a Written Poem. *Oral Tradition* 20:1 (March 2005), 7–34. Online version at http://journal.oraltradition.org/issues/20i.

[29] T. S. Eliot 'Burnt Norton', *Four Quartets* (London: Faber and Faber, 1959 [1944]), 18.

[30] Phrases are from 'Narrative of the Shields', *In the House of the Shaman*, 64–65.

This article previously appeared in the *Journal of Innovative British and Irish Poetry 2010*: Peter Middleton, 'Ear Loads': Neologisms and Sound Poetry in Maggie O'Sullivan's Palace Of Reptiles', Journal of Innovative British and Irish Poetry (2010), 1:2)

"The Saturated Language of Red": Maggie O'Sullivan and the Artist's Book

Marjorie Perloff

Page design, typography, *lettrisme*, phonetic spelling, the use of nonce words, glyphs, paragrams—these have always been central to Maggie O'Sullivan's poetry. Such volumes as *Unofficial Word* (1988) and *In the House of the Shaman* (1993) have been linked to American language poetry, but O'Sullivan, who makes her home in Yorkshire, England, draws on Celtic myth and ritual and on medieval folk motifs rather than on contemporary pop and media imagery, as do her American counterparts. In recent years, moreover, her books have increasingly been conceived as artists' books rather than as collections of individual poems. *Red Shifts* (1999) is a case in point, and two other recent books, not yet in print—*Waterfalls* and *Murmur: Tasks of Mourning*—display intricate interplay between the verbal and the visual, making use of elaborate collage material, (pen and ink drawing and watercolour on cartridge paper), impinging everywhere on the text itself.

Yet, because her derivation is from the poetry rather than the art world, one doesn't find O'Sullivan's name in studies like Johanna Drucker's *The Century of Artist's Books* or *Figuring the Word*, or in Renée and Judd Hubert's *The Cutting Edge of Reading: Artists' Books*—all three of these excellent volumes published by Steve Clay's Granary Books.[1] Despite the current lip service paid to the "interdisciplinary," poetry communities, it seems, even the experimental community of which O'Sullivan is a part, don't interact with "art world" book artists such as Buzz Spector or Ed Ruscha, Annette Messager or Susan King. Even Ian Hamilton Finlay, revered for his language art, is rarely included in discussions of contemporary poetry. It is a curious situation, given that artists' books generally give equal time to word and image. In Johanna

[123]

Drucker's words, the "artist's book" is one that, unlike the illustrated book which treats visual images as additives, figures that are potentially removable, the artist's book "gives equal status to images, binding, typography, page-setting, folds, collages, and text" (*Century* 14).

By this definition, *Red Shifts*, written between 1997–99 and published in the new series of Etruscan "exhibition" publications in 2001, is surely an artist's book rather than, as would be usual, a long poetic sequence. Consider, for starters, what happens when a shorter poetic fragment—in this case a three-page text sent to Charles Bernstein, in response to his invitation to participate in an International Poetics Symposium for *boundary 2* is incorporated into *Red Shifts*.[2] According to O'Sullivan, "Three months after I had sent this text to Charles I had a phone call from Nicholas Johnson of Etruscan books offering me a commission to do a book work, to which I agreed. I decided to continue working on the three page *Red Shifts* text, deepening, developing my explorations of the spatial and textual terrains."[3]
Thus the line

breathing-in-breathing-out

is replaced in the book by two inverted V-shapes—"b—r—e—a—t—h—i—n—g / in" on the left, "b—r—e—a—t—h—i—n—g / out" on the right—printed out on what was evidently a dot-matrix printer that produced rough-edge letters, giving the book a more "primitive" look than the "normal" *boundary 2* version. This visual representation of, so to speak, taking a deep breath, is repeated two pages later, typography and layout underscoring the difficulty of breathing which is one of the central motifs of *Red Shifts*.

Or take the transformation of the concluding passage on page 210 of *boundary 2*. In *Red Shifts* (p. 10), the catalogue:

suf—
thistle . . .
what . . .
twen—
dreamdery. . .

is centered and followed by four blank spaces and then the centered lines:

sure i sung all along the river for practise[4]
moon for all the   blanket just

The six-character space between **"the"** and **"blanket,"** gives the moon a mysterious role: we are not sure what it is "for," but it is not merely "blanketed" by clouds or a "blanket" in the sky. In the poet's **"dreamdery"**—the coinage linking dream to medieval ballad refrain with its variants on "hey derry derry down"—the inscrutable moon is perhaps "for the misbegotten," more broadly for all the nameless beings—animal, vegetable, mineral—the poet can imagine. **"Just,"** in this context is ambiguous—is the blanket of the night "just" or "just a blanket" or does the passage continue on to the next page? We cannot tell but visually the single centered column above the white space and trapezoid shape below create a superb scene of **"dreamdery"** activity—an activity not as prominent in the original poetic fragment, where the space between the columnar passage and the couplet (originally a triplet, with the line "pennant flut," later excised, preceding it) is reduced as is the space between **"the"** and **"blanket."** And although there is no period after **"blanket just,"** the anthologized poem clearly "ends" at the bottom of this page. Indeed, on the facing page, we find a short prose narrative by Alexei Parshchikov that begins with the sentence, "If I'm to peddle stories, I'll strive to pick from my mind a tape that concerns one tender airhead freak, my classmate, whose name was Arichkin" (211).

The anthology arrangement, reasonably enough, has taken us alphabetically from O'Sullivan to Parshchikov. The juxaposition of these two bardic poets—Anglo-Irish woman and Russian man—produces interesting semantic conjunctions, as do all the relationships in Bernstein's carefully chosen international anthology of experimental writing. But the fact remains that the sort of closure inevitable on the *boundary 2* page does not quite represent the ethos of what was to become *Red Shifts*. Indeed, in the case of the artist's book, the reader turns the page and is confronted by a startling image, of which more in a moment. For this poet, one surmises, bookwork made possible a textual heightening, not available in the traditional production of individual "contained" poems, whether in one's own collection or in anthologies.

How does O'Sullivan's bookmaking work? *Red Shifts* [see figures 1 and 2] is a square (6 × 6") booklet of fifty-two unnumbered pages, whose words and images are printed in red and black against a white ground. On its cover, a zigzag red path, etched against a white ground, and outlined in red, extends across from back to front. In the back, the zigzag path crosses the abstracted child-like image of what looks like a fish, whose round oversize eye stares at the viewer even as its skeleton is sketched in below. The spiky zigzag movement of the path, colored as if by a child who doesn't quite fill in all the outlines and makes smudges, continues on the inside cover, facing the title page, which bears a large red inkblot shape that calls to mind an octopus or perhaps a cartoon monster.

The title *Red Shifts* can be read in a variety of ways. Is "red" a noun, in which case it is the color that shifts, or a verb? If the latter, do the "red shifts" refer merely to "red" changes—changes in blood, for example, or to "shifty" designs, or does "shift" have the more specific dictionary meaning (see OED) of "displacement of rocks on a fault line," or—again in the OED—"a change in the position of a spectral line representing a change of frequency, for example that caused by the Doppler Effect"? *Shift* is such a "shifty" word hat it also denotes the computer key shift, here used to create the book e are looking at. Or the "change in hand position in order to play a different set of notes in a different register on a keyboard or string instrument." And finally, *shift* can mean "the change in the pronunciation of a sound in the course of the development of the language," as in the Great Vowel Shift.

This last meaning of *shift* may well be the most relevant in this visual-verbal narrative, whose consonants and vowels are always shifting and often coming back to their medieval, now obsolete values. But in any case the title, printed in lower-case italics, and on the title page, in childish handwriting, sets the stage for what appears to be an ominous event: we will watch the red make a shift

or note the geology or frequency of those red shifts, their varying notes on the poet's vocal instrument and their vocalic transformations. And further: the image of the Etruscan press logo—a red circle framed in black with a white cross in the middle—here suggests that the "red shifts" are somehow *Verboten*, off limits! One thinks of the Red Deeps, the secret meeting place of Maggie and Philip in George Eliot's *The Mill on the Floss*, the Red Deeps forbidden to the lovers once Maggie's brother Tom found them there. But the circle of the Etruscan logo is "squared" by the booklet itself, thus setting the stage for the tension between square and circle that goes on throughout the book.

The sense of anticipation is reinforced by the first two pages of *Red Shifts* where a wavy outline at the left is juxtaposed to another version of the zig-zag path, this time in darker red—almost brown—with three peaks, bearing the words "thrine / roam / awkward & slow / unable to stand / & bread / put out among the branches." "Thrine" is archaic for three, especially three children at birth or triplets. Is this a reference to the ballad of the "Three Ravens" (whose versions include one called "The Twa Corbies")? In the ballad, the ravens have picked clean the bones of the mysteriously slain knight; they are predators not, say, sparrows for whom "bread" has been "put out among the branches." Indeed, O'Sullivan's roaming "thrine," who are "unable to stand" may well refer, not to the three ravens, but to their human prey. And, as in fairytale, the "path," cut off at the end of the page, where the line, now wavy, ends, gives a visual analogue to the mysterious "story" itself.

The human voice emerging from the "thrine" now comes forward:

broke
breaking —raised arms –
cant hold my breath/ my breath
sobbing

savage
tonguesbled

sh --- sh --- sh--- sh --- sh -----
hurrish ---
—upped - up—up –up –
any bare syllable STARE –

incendings –
thresh – tilt /

"Broke" may refer back to the branches of the preceding page or to being "unable to stand," but here the voice is more definitively that of a person, "broke / breaking—raised arms"—the poet herself, it seems, who can't "hold my breath / my breath / sobbing." We never find out what is wrong, but the coinages that follow, like "tonguesbled"—a bleeding tongue on the analogy of "nosebleed" or at least a tongue that has bled—leads to no more than the "sh" of the next line, the inability to find one's voice. O'Sullivan's sobbing, voiceless speaker reminds one of Mouth in Beckett's *Not I* or perhaps Lil in Eliot's *Waste Land*, for we now read "hurrish — /upped –up - up – up –" ("Hurry up please, it's time!) even as "any bare syllable STARE" recalls the woman in Eliot's "Game of Chess." The rhyme of "bare" and "STARE" moreover, relates voicelessness to the fear of being seen and hence found out—this time a reference to his *Film*, where, in a play on Berkeley's *esse est percipi*, the terrified narrator makes frantic attempts to escape the camera eye. The note of fear is under-scored by the "incendings"—another coinage—foretelling some form of holocaust, an incendiary firestorm where one can only "thresh" and "tilt."

As possible analogues for the "sobbing" voice, Nate Dorward has suggested Wordsworth's Solitary Reaper or Tennyson's Lady of Shalott.[5] But, for the moment, the sequential structure of the book holds such analogues in abeyance: on the recto facing the sobbing presence, we meet a new set of "characters" in the form of "**sheeny**" (glossy, shiny) "**curlews**" and "**lapwings**," whose fates are bound up with the poet's, the "**tear of the wind**" (both "tear" as cut" and the "tear" of weeping) reducing them to "**black / feathers / blue**." But feather soon gives way to "**hoove lost**": horses, too, evidently, are the victims of "**ruptures crossing**," of "**rent—parture—t'tide**," of all that is "**sutured**" and "**deto-nates**," causing those alive, whether human beings, animals, or birds, to have "**FLED**."

What is happening in this scene? O'Sullivan's narrative is never straightforward, but there are constants throughout, in this case, epito-mized in the three-word line "**rent-parture—t'tide**." Curlews and plovers are water birds; in the poet's tale, the shore, with its "**waterflows**," described here as "**buckled raved sheens**," is the scene of that which has been "**rent**," subjected to cutting ("**parture**"), perhaps by the "**tide**" itself. Rupture, tear of the wind, suture: we are witnessing the cata-clysm associated with the mystery of the "red shifts." Indeed, the death note ("**heavying & freezy sank—**", p. 8, "**red / squawk / slaw / teared**"—p.9) becomes steadily more oppressive—"**amber sag lornly**"—where "lornly" recalls the plaintive "forlorn" of Keats's "Ode to a Nightingale." The phrase leads up to the blank space, already discussed, on page 10 and the distancing of the woman's song, **"sure I sung all along the river for practise."**

On the verso of this page, we find a mysterious red, white, and black faceless figure, whose appearance recalls that of magician or Druid priestess, although the figure's ribcage is exposed. This mysterious oversized figure is silhouetted against the familiar zigzags of the Red Shifts, but in the upper right there is a diagram of a maze and at bottom right, drawn in miniature scale, a house in black shadow next to a bare tree. Is the dark house the locus of **"dreamdery"**, the Druid emerging from the maze of the poet's mind? Does she cast a spell over it? If we look at the recto across from the fairytale image, a clue is supplied, not only to the identity of the figure but also to O'Sullivan's larger poetic narrative:

> **i have found this red**
> **is breathed**
> **or reply,**
> water's edge, ~~DECOMPOSITIONS~~
> **draw ing breath's**
> **broken fanging—**
> **Nion, the Ash, this 3rd**
> **letter of salvages**
> **bridge & gut**
> **aquacity staltic**

Here it will help to unpack some meanings. In Celtic legend, the Nion Ash tree, which grows beside water, symbolizes the power of the sea, as personified in the sea god Lir, one of the ruling divinities. Lir represented a mystical fusion of man and God through the medium or element of water. The Ash was also sacred to the trickster Gwydion as a tree of enchantment, from whose twigs he made his wands. In related legends, the staff of a witch's besom was made of ash as proof against drowning. To protect oneself from drowning in the sea, one would carve a piece of Ash wood into a solar cross and carry it on one's person. Ash leaves were placed in pillows for prophetic dreams and hung over doorposts to keep away evil influences and sorcery. Ash attracts lightning so one could harness the energy. Carrying the leaves was said to gain the love of the opposite sex. Representing the Third

Moon, Ash was the emblem of water magic, being the Moon of Floods. And the runic alphabet formed itself of ash twigs.[6]

O'Sullivan has always drawn heavily on the myths and shamanic legends of the Irish tradition in which she was raised, and here the voiceless, breathless speaker draws sustenance from the Ash's **"aquacity staltic"**—its water magic, whose rhythms are those of the peristalsis of the digestive tract (hence, perhaps, the exposed rib cage in the verso image). The Ash's ability to attract lightning ("this red"), producing powerful **"DECOMPOSITIONS"** at the **"water's edge,"** makes it the runic **"letter of salvages."** And we have already seen the poet singing **"all along the river for practise"** of a moon that may well be the Ash as Third Moon, the Moon of Floods that acts as "blanket" for the naked self.

From this point on, the narrative of O'Sullivan's poem *shifts* "redly" between magic chant, stemming from the extraordinary powers of the Ash tree, and the chaos and indifference of a "Nature, red in tooth and claw" as Tennyson characterized it in *In Memoriam*. On page 14, there is reference to the death of a loved one— **"cant eat it cant eat it ———|** **can't hold my breath/my breath** / sobbing ——— | ——— **sea's** **water."** A page later, this death reappears in the image of **"this tiniest skull"** and there are references to **"punctured crow," "eyes-uv bone"** and choking. The abstracted images of red human figures and black spidery shapes become more frequent: on page 22, for example, there are what look like red rubber stamp traces in orderly rows, between which we find the four words **"axe wind – thouznd feather".** One thinks of Gerontion's "gull against the wind," for the page contains no representational or even allusive forms. And when the text resumes, after another page of red and black tracery, this time over a field of grainy black diamond shapes, the text itself comes in for the first time as itself red!

The red text on p. 24 begins with the line "paddy.took.after.my grandmother's / people"—the first instance we have had of "ordinary" narrative, perhaps a story told by the poet's father about the family. References to "& feather the day" and "break cattle" follow. But realism never seems to be a serious option for O'Sullivan and page 2 is blank, containing only one line across the center:

        roarrr ——————————————rua————

where the morpheme "rua" may be the suffix of a mountain or volcano as in New Zealand's "Rotorua." After this line, in any case the text goes black again, the narrative continuing to deal with Irish farm life, its **"driven dirt & ——— | & beast-glance | bellowing the roads used drive them the 10 or 12 miles."** At the same time, earlier motifs come back to haunt the poet—"breathe breathe breathe breathe"—with many references to cutting, blemishes, and "hem-(mir) mohr (h)age," culminating in the psychic low point:

wept t'
at an angle

gob—drew- loop
—homeless—
'bandaged eyes the lightnin'
lip to ash

incised——

out of all ———

The amorphous black amoeba shape on the next page now sits on top of the red ones and the next two pages contain only the single word **"winzdroppt ———"** on the verso, the facing page displaying black veil inkblots over pink ground, with black diamond shapes and zigzag glyphs on the white ground below. The magic powers of the Ash tree seem to have given way to the **ash** of the dying fire, the **"bandaged "eyes"** of the **"homeless"** finding themselves **"out of all."**

From here on out, language becomes sparer. The white pages contain only a few words of broken text, and there is little typographical play. "The saturated language of red" (p. 36) is actually in sober black and the narrow veil shapes on p. 38 are, for the first time, brown, red, and violet, rather like rock formations seen from a distance. Beneath the visual image, we read the centered words "**trembling | shiver of land**," and the first line on page 39 announces "**sACRIFICE or bURIAL**," with a focus on "this. **crep. Ant,**" with its play on "discrepant" as well as on the "ant," seemingly made of "crepe," juxtaposed to the "big faced | ,power of **beasts**" beneath it.

Page 40 bears the list:

**1 pea) 1 ash) 1 ring) 1 tree)
sundered splash**

where the prominent rhyme ("pea" "tree"; "ash"/ "splash') is heard as a kind of mantra, a black-over-red straight line down the middle of the page intersecting the four subsequent words:

easel wink marine ecstasy

The "marine ecstasy" may be the fruit of the ash tree, as reproduced on the poet-artist's "easel" in a "wink." The straight vertical line continues onto the next page, which bears only the words "whence the whispers" aligned at right angle to the page, along the vertical line. That line finally plays itself out on the third page of its existence, extending from the bottom of the page two-thirds of the way up. It is a bleak moment.

But not for long, for now on pages 45-46, the mode shifts to elaborate incantation, the words in black, spread across the page, surrounding the red outlines of rock or pebble shapes. "**3 pieces of a bell**," "**3 drops of any drink**," "**3 inches of earth**," and "**3 shovelfuls**" on the verso are juxtaposed to "**7 eyes**," "**7 iridescent tail feathers**," "**7 moon sticks**," and "**7 flight that is**" on the facing page. This witch's brew of sacred numbers introduces, for the first time in the poem, the bird of "**irides- cent tail feathers**"—the peacock, who reappears on p. 47 in the lines "**reach of the peacock's / blistering blistering thresholds**," isolated on an otherwise blank page. But the recipe on pp. 45–46, far from produc- ing a magic elixir, once again leads to a further blank, to silence. The page that follows the busy red rocks ("Come in under the shadow of the red rock?") is again blank, with only the small units of "**foot-marked**" and "**owish—teries—aisles—**" and "**dimpled**," all three phrases printed as diagonals in the bottom right. And another blank page follows, at whose bottom we read "**hare in the field / hare's build of it, flaught ist˙,**" with its play on "flutist." The poem concludes with a recurrence of "**b-r-e-a-t- h-i-n-g**," this time printed as seven diagonals dispersed across the page, the letters becoming increasingly smaller, and the hyphens between letters disappearing after the third instance, ending with the 8-point font of "**breathing**". The facing page gives us the mirror image, but not quite matching, and the word "breathing" used seven times rather than eight, eliminating the first inverted V-shape "**b-r-e-a-t-h-I-n-g / in**" on the left. The concluding double-page watercolor contains a Miro-like red shape—animal? bird? or vehicle?— there being wheel and maze glyphs interspersed throughout and what looks like Cuneiform glyphs across the bottom of the page on a grayish-purplish background.

As a codex book, *Red Shifts* is inevitably read sequentially, and although the "narrative" never coheres into total intelligibility, the book's tale seems to be one of calamity and suffering, moving toward the diminishing of "breath," even as the Ash tree and peacock's threshold suggest the possibility of resurrection, immortality. The final visual image is ambiguous in this regard. The movement of the animal or bird or fish is from right to left, the glyphs beneath the shape telling its story. Happy ending? We only know that the red has shifted, that the red shifts and red/black/grey glyphs cannot be tracked in "normal" speech. And so the book finally emerges as intentionally "illegible," a book that can only be experienced, not fully translated into more coherent speech.

In a 1999 interview, O'Sullivan provides some pertinent background for the mode of *Red Shifts*:

> My background undoubtedly has shaped who I am / how I am in the world / my work. My father and mother had little schooling and my father worked as a labourer in and out of work all his life. We were brought up on the edge, locked out, without any voice. As well as the materiality, the primacy of language, that most preoccupies me, in what can be done underneath, behind, with-in the multidimensionality that is language, my work is driven by the spoken, sounded or breathing voice. Particularly I have always been haunted by issues of VOICELESSNESS — inarticulacy—silence— soundlessness—breathlessness—how are soundings or voices that are other-than or invisible or dimmed or marginalised or excluded or without privilege, or locked out, made Unofficial, reduced by ascendant systems of centrality and closure, configured or Sounded or given form & potency: how can I body forth or configure sounds sounds, such tongues, such languages, such muteness, such multivocality, such error—& tis is perhaps why the non-vocal in mark & the non-word in sound or language—make up much of the fabrics & structures of my own compositions.[7]

O'Sullivan's words here recall Susan Howe, and indeed these two poets have much in common. But O'Sullivan's language is more private than Howe's or than Steve McCaffery's—another poet whom she resembles so far as language play and deconstruction is concerned. To convey "The non-vocal in mark & the non-word in sound or language," O'Sullivan increasingly turns to the wordless image, as she does in the visuals of *Red Shifts*. Together with her "mis-spelt, mis-heard, mis-read, compound" words, her contractions, parts of words, word-clusters, and individual letters, O'Sullivan creates a dense field of force that literally mesmerizes the reader. Her aim, as she puts it in the same interview, citing Tom Leonard, is to oppose "the politics of dominant narrative language as would-be encloser of the world, language as colonizer," language that is "presumed 'invisible' to its referent" (91). This is no easy task and I must confess that even with the dictionary close at hand, and books on Irish mythology nearby, there are still many words and phrases in *Red Shifts* that remain obscure, as do the black-red-white images throughout.

And yet the "breath" and its cognate "breathe," along with "breathe in," "breathe out" organize the **red-wind-whisper-bird-shore** references so that each rereading yields new configurations of great beauty. The complex modulation of "red" is especially striking: we move from phrases like "i have found this red / is breathed" to the "red pulse & **cupptwig**" of the "house," where "**a strong hue does heavy deepen.**" Then, too, missing words play a central role in O'Sullivan's drama. Take the near-blank pages of "**'sometimes she cries**" and "**& sometimes she is / again**" on pp. 31–32. The first phrase is placed in the center of an otherwise blank page. The second, in contrast, appears at the bottom right of the facing page:

& sometimes she is
again"

Is **what** again? Obviously there is something missing in the second quotation, most likely the word "**silent,**" whose six letters followed by a space would fill precisely the seven spaces from the left margin that precede "again." Sometimes she cries & sometimes she is silent again." Here the white space of the page embodies the "silence" that is not put in words in the text. It is a very bold and brilliant artistic move, demonstrating that the verbal can actually morph into the visual. But it takes many readings of *Red Shifts* and comparable O'Sullivan texts to discover these magic moments. The poet's manifold *shifts* must be *read* and reread if their "red" is to be understood.

Notes

[1] Johanna Drucker, *The Century of Artists' Books* (New York: Granary Books, 1995); Drucker, *Figuring the word: Essays on Books, Writing, and Visual Poetics* (New York: Granary, 1998); Renée Riese Hubert & Judd D. Hubert, *The Cutting Edge of Reading: Artists' Books* (Granary, 1999).

[2] Maggie O'Sullivan, "red shifts," *boundary 2:* "99 Poets/1999: An International Poetics Symposium," a special issue edited by Charles Bernstein, 26, no. 1 (Spring 1999): 208–210.

This passage, beginning with the lines "black / feathers / blue" and concluding with "blanket just," reappears, in altered form, as (unnumbered pages 4–10 in the book.

3 O'Sullivan, email to the author, 7 September 2003.

4 O'Sullivan purposely misspells certain words like "practice" (here "practise") so as to call attention to them and heighten their morphemes: in this case, the spelling relates a word like 'practise" to "expertise."

5 Nate Dorward, review of Maggie O'Sullivan, *Red Shifts*, *The Gig*, 10, December 2001, p.

6 Thisis a précis of various handbooks on tree symbolism and online dictionaries and source books of Irish mythology.

7 O'Sullivan, "Binary Myths 2: Correspondences with Poet-Editors," *Stride*, ed. Andy Brown (Exeter, 1999), p. 90.

Preface to In the House of the Shaman

Will Rowe

What I have to offer is a preface, no more than one way of coming to the book, a book which every time you or he or she comes to it starts to move in different ways and at different speeds. That happens with other books, but especially with this one. It is difficult to be objective.

One point of departure is as valid as any other; it's a question of how the book brings them together. Eric Havelock, in his *Preface to Plato*, is concerned with how Plato instituted philosophy against poetry. What's under discussion is the writing of *The Republic* as something that was done against the grain of the language. The discussion in *The Republic* comes back several times to what the philosopher is concerned with, though of course *philia* means love. In order to take us back in to that moment, Havelock calls it a 'syntactical situation'. Before you can get to *ousia* or being there has to be a break with the language modelled in Homer, Hesiod, and other poets. Havelock summarises the situation:

> Is there any overarching discipline (*mathema*) which can train the subject to think about this kind of timeless object? [. . .] Plato replies in general terms that it will be a '*mathema* of that beingness (*ousia*) which always is and is not put into wandering by becoming and perishing.' The phraseology may [. . .] tempt the reader to think he is being asked to look at a metaphysical super-reality rather than at a syntactical situation. But it is the latter that Plato intends. The term *ousia* or 'beingness' is used to suggest that the several abstracted objects [. . .] compose an area of final knowledge outside ourselves. The contrasting syntax of narrative is here properly rendered as the realm of becoming (more strictly of 'birth'); the realm of the endless event-series. It is the realm of those multitudinous situations which happen.[1]

And with respect to the poetic form that Plato rejects, 'the original syntax of the poem has been destroyed'.²

The wording of *The Republic* is 'ekeines tes ousias tes aei ouses kai me planomenes upo geneseos kai pthoras' (485 b1). One English translation reads 'the knowledge that reveals eternal reality, the realm unaffected by change and decay;'³ which gives no sense of the phase-shift that Plato is bringing about in the language. The metaphysical freight runs along well-worn, silent tracks, as if they had always been there.

A twentieth-century phase shift runs through a piece of writing by Henri Michaux 'A crowd come out of the dark' ('Une foule sortie de l'ombre'). The scene is a sort of dream or vision, in which there is a coming into appearance. The crowds that 'all the while were emerging out of the dark and seemed, as they left it, to flow into reality', when looked at 'very closely', seem 'each to have only one leg, the one they stepped out with' and only half of a body. They are also 'conspirators of the purest kind [. . .] for as they left the void and entered reality they were so cautious, so mistrustful and so masterly in their mistrust, they partly concealed themselves even as they marched.' For the subject, 'it was as if I were present at the turning point of an era, as if the times were set in motion and, thanks to a new discovery kept secret till then, were showing forth their novelty before my very eyes.'⁴

This is the work of an 'astonishing film-maker' who 'was the inventor of another trick too: by some new mechanical technique he caused a sort of pure vibration to occur, something purely psychic conveyed through a means that was physical. Whatever it was, it gave the impression of life itself, of life in danger.' And then there is a further comment: 'the film and my own trembling were dramatically combined, the screen was invaded by my physiology.'⁵

In another text, 'Le jardin exalté' ('The Heavenly garden'), he writes 'A ruffling of mood, and nobody there, but all the parts, branches and leaves and twigs, were human and more than human, more deeply agitated, more shaken and shaking.'⁶ There is no word for 'mood' in the French, only the phrase 'exaspération sans personne', literally 'exasperation without person'. With the word 'mood', the translation puts a subject back in – a person who's having the experience. Then there's the phrase: 'The beauty of things palpitating in the garden of transformations.' Here the translation has put an object in, where there isn't one in the French: 'Beauté des palpitations au jardin des transformations;' literally, 'beauty of palpitations in the garden of transformations'. The English translation has put in an article (*the* beauty) and an object ('of *things* palpitating').

How the translation displays habits of reading and patterns of the language, is what I want to draw attention to. Here is another example from the second Michaux piece: 'L'infini chiffonnage-déchiffonnage trouvait sa rencontre.'[7] The word *chiffonage* is hard to translate: a literal version would run something like 'the infinite chiffonning-unchiffonning came together' (or, 'was assembled').[8] The English translation by David and Helen Constantine reads 'eternal ruffling and eternal smoothing here conjoined', which gives an idea of agency; the idea of a person doing it seems to hang around the phrase 'eternal ruffling and eternal smoothing'. Something else is happening in the English too. The French 'chiffonnage-déchiffonnage' means becoming chiffonned/ becoming unchiffonned, which belongs to the same domain as Plato's 'wandering by becoming and perishing'; Plato's word for wandering has the same root as planet, a wandering and – as we now know – trembling body, in the sense that these bodies do not move along smooth, Newtonian paths, but continually jerk and tremble. By a sort of short-circuit, the English expressions *ruffling* and *smoothing* give a premature concreteness. The fact that ordinary English gives a simplistic concreteness to abstracted qualities, making them seem like things, is something that Basil Bunting complains about in an essay written in 1930:

> The languages of western Europe are all strongly analytical. They break up the event into a series of abstract conceptions. They emphasise its qualitative liens with other events and in so doing tend to lose the conception of the event as a single complex occurrence and to substitute a series of semidetached simple abstractions. This entirely falsifies reality and causes us to live in a world of self-constructed phantoms.[9]

The examples he gives are words like 'blackness' or 'hardness'. Part of Bunting's point is that this concreteness comes in to simplify the real complexity of any event, where the notion of event includes – especially – any emotional event: 'simultaneity, interdependence, continuous cross-reference and absence of simplification are characteristic of all fact, whether physical or mental or emotional.'[10]

These split-off analytical bits correspond to the Lockean version of the individual, who is in a position to survey and shift around these (secondary) qualities, in an anticipation of New Labour Information Management procedures. Their concreteness has the lure of a fetish, using that word in a Marxian sense.[11]

Bunting's solution – or at least the one he puts forward in the essay, since his practice as a poet is more various – is to go for complexity of syntax; to regain, for example, some of the syntactical complexity of Elizabethan poetry. One of the characteristics of the writing of *In the House of the Shaman* is the use of expressions such as 'talonedings', which confuse a state (having talons) with a process. Here's the passage:

> Soundings   Talonedings   A Full Mist
> unbroths   Larger in the Heart
>   coiled, eaten   other wounds –
>   wisdoms, distressed & distressed –
>
>   a multiplicity – (H, 16)[12]

What I want to draw attention to is how the object – talons, for example – ceases to be a transferable mental impression, within a controlling catalogue of such. Equally, there is no recognisable subject as such, but instead, disparate becomings.

Then there is the use of a spatial term, 'yonder', as adverb 'YONDERLY', twice. The first time:

BECKONED MAGPIE YONDERLY EWE TO LAMB (H, 36)[13]

Treating a spatial relation as a mode, gives an event-torsion to space, and stops it being – as in the ordinary language – flat and fixed.
    Another characteristic of this language is making an object into a mode of action, as with:

SNOUTILY
    PAW seizes – (H, 37)

The language seems to be turning the short-circuiting round; instead of abstractions acquiring a simplified, manipulable concreteness, there are sensuously dense materials occurring as events. Perhaps neither abstract nor concrete. What type of events then? I will come back to this; each book of MOS's can be approached as a field defined by the particular type of event occurring in it. For the present, I want to suggest that this is where the intellect comes in, in the production of objects as events and not in the animation of abstracted qualities as is the case with capitalist individuation, as for example in the fetish word 'delivering' a service, where the receiver is (bourgeois) individual and not political subject. Knowledge and individuation are figured in the following lines from 'TO OUR OWN DAY':

> ill.me.
> dot.me.
> glue.me.cloven.
> cloaka Bones,
> a branding math-smudge (H, 34)

Here the self pronoun is subject to punctuation and marking which is called 'math-smudge'; if math(ema) is taken as intellectual discipline,[14] then it is here placed on the same plane as the biological construction of the body, without the clean lines of ordinary maths.

Some of the book's terrain has a Hopkins feel, as in the clusters of words which start to jam linear syntax: 'Squandering ooze to squeezed | dough, crust, dust; stanches, starches / Squadroned masks and manmarks'. This is from the poem 'That Nature is a Heraclitean Fire and of the comfort of the Resurrection', which includes the thought that 'nature's bonfire' wipes out man's 'mark on mind'. There is a phrase in this poem which metamorphoses into a line of Bunting's. Hopkins writes, again of 'Man', here as 'Manshape': 'nor mark / Is any of him at all so stark / But vastness blurs and time | beats level.' No 15 of Bunting's *First Book of Odes* replies: 'Nothing | substance utters or time / stills and restrains / joins design and // supple measure deftly / as thought's intricate polyphonic / score dovetails with the tread / sensuous things / keep in our consciousness.' Running through both, though rendered differently, is a question about the relation between writing, time, and the loss (or Blakean Los) of meaning. For Bunting, it is not the thought of resurrection that overcomes the recurrent residue of deadness but the lasting aliveness of 'thought's intricate polyphonic / score.' But thought, as Bunting's poems bear witness, is never safe from failure; it is the product of 'man's craft' and capability for multi-plicity; where it fails there is a failure of desire.[15]

The objects so far mentioned – in fact the vast majority of objects that appear in *House* – belong to nature and not manufacture. Of course human production is there in the making of the language. But so far as objects are concerned, they are biological or biomorphic. The shamanic enters the book as a relation between 'kinship with animals' – title of a section of *House* – and making a language. Let me briefly say that I haven't used the word shaman<u>ism</u> because it has become more and more a New Age term. Also, briefly, it is worth saying that 'kinship with animals' has nothing to do with Disney's Brother Bear, which of course asks to subject to identify with it. The relation with animals in *House* has a de-individuating effect, which is not the same as repressive dis-individua-tion. MOS's interest in the shamanic, on the other hand, is strongly related to the work of Joseph Beuys, whose action, 'I like America and America likes me,' of 1974, involved spending time with a coyote.[16]

In 'Coyote Concert II', given in Tokyo in 1984, the coyote's animal noises have become signs which Beuys performs as grunts and simul-taneously as dots and dashes which he writes on a board. On the coyote, in a commentary on a Northwestern native American coyote narrative, Jerome Rothenberg quotes Jung: he is 'absolutely undiffer-entiated human consciousness . . . a psyche that has hardly left the animal level . . . god, man & animal at once'.[17] The coyote language, in the graphic embodiment Beuys gives it, comes out as a sort of punctu-ation. MOS several times uses dots as a punctuation that doesn't punc-tuate in the syntactic sense but has dropped to another level, as in the passage quoted just now:

   ill.me.
     dot.me.
   glue.me.cloven. (H, 10)

The dots are not full stops in that they are actually – in the way MOS reads – closing the usual sound gaps between words.[18] They are doing something sub-syntactic.

In another place in the book, 'Bog Asphodel Song', there's the line 'bless the animals w/out punctuation'. Here is part of the context:

LIVE!

DANSING!

LOUD!

YELLOW!

Terrestrial
Motive.

YELLOW
learns leap.
Pollen Utterances,
BIG SOUND
little sound.

Neighbour of Louse & Spear,
Bless the animals w/out punctuation

What is this de-punctuation?

One of the things it might be doing is indicated in Gregory Bateson's use of 'punctuation' as a term equivalent to segmentation. For Bateson, what segmentation does to the flow of experience is to cut it 'into subsequences or "contexts" which may be equated or differentiated by the organism.'[19] This punctuation of what he also calls the 'stream of events', is what makes learning possible, at the lowest and most basic level of learning, without which the higher levels cannot occur. It is he says the first step towards 'abstract habits of thought'. The higher levels depend on learning to learn, that is on changing 'the set of alternatives from which choice is made' or on 'how the sequence of experience is punctuated.'[20] Learning = change = metamorphosis. In Ovid's *Metamorphoses*, it's the naming action that's up for grabs: what do you call it when the object is crossing the boundaries between god, human, plant, animal in all sorts of strange couplings – in fact ceasing to be object?

What happens when the action moves to the level of syntax? If, instead of taking syntax as producing lines above already-existing segmentation of the flow of experience, you bring it flush with that? One possibility would be Williams's 'So much depends / upon // a red wheel / barrow', where the segmentation of speech is brought flush with those of syntax and typography, and the poem works against syntax as a higher level. Perhaps relevant are the various moments of sinking down that are interspersed through MOS's book and are related to speech organs ('mouth / fell / out / here') or to the head ('Head nor / falls down/' (H 35)). 'Riverruning (realisations', a piece presented to the Poetics Programme at Buffalo (1993), includes loss of ability to speak: 'I scant, dwindled stammering before speech'.[21] Speech breaking down or being stymied also figures several times in *House*: 'gone i see the speechway broken' (H, 20); as does the physical impairment of the letter: 'the feet / hobbling / [to] the letter' (H, 21).[22] This impairment is related to body fluids as scoring ('BLOOD-LINES / on soil') and with writing becoming animal ('Horse it with a Bird'). Robert Sheppard in an essay on MOS's work speaks of 'alien writing systems'.[23]

MOS's work adds possibilities to the early 20c revolution of the word associated with Williams and others. 'Want as a Province of sheer Retinal Directory –' (H, 59): one of many phrases which exposes a recurrent movement, which brings together 'the raw and the cooked', unconsidered desire and the division of space as the gap in which place can be conceived;[24] where 'the eye has a haptic, non-optical function':[25] a field without depth. Rothenberg, in *Shaking the Pumpkin*, exemplifies the Cherokees' 'use of colours beyond their (mere) symbolic values [. . .] to achieve striking effects':

As the Red Cardinal is beautiful, I am beautiful
As the Red Dhla:nuwa is beautiful, I am beautiful
As the Red Redbird is beautiful, I am beautiful
As the blue Cardinal is beautiful, I am beautiful

The switch of colour will affect the spirit of the subject(s). It is sufficient, in some incantations, to bring about death.[26] There is nothing in the middle distance: not just no perspective but no space as such. Graduated scales are lost.

This type of effect in MOS's writing includes letters and the whole range of graphic signs, and in that sense is a development out of

Excla, a book written in collaboration with Bruce Andrews and published in 1993.[27] In the section of *House* called 'GIANT YELLOW', there's this:

> A pen ticks,
> Body of the Animal Altered
> HELD
>
> DREW
>
> [. . .]
> BORN.
>
> Meso-cysted
> BELLOW geometries (H, 60)

'Ticks' takes reading into minute movements – or creatures – 'altered' into change or making sacred; and 'drew', 'born', 'bellow', and 'geometries' move between rational apprehension and sheer becoming. As a need to go back through first punctuation, i.e. the segmenting which is shared by human beings and animals, and which is neither purely analogue nor purely digital,[28] this is an action which MOS's writing shares with some aspects of shamanic ritual languages.[29]

House several times goes into a syncopated cutting between suffixes and prefixes to other suffixes and prefixes. For example:

> elved X, chema-
>   tensions
>   chema-
>   nexions: poisons
>
>   pins, xins,
>   flicted (H, 56)

This is a type of jump-cutting between frame-markers with the frames emptied of content. Or if you take the suffixes and prefixes to be modifiers, then in all the modifiers there's a becoming material. The effect latches on to other words:

Auric   fin   spun   key   skins
Boundary between

[. . .]
—acro   pleural   petal   fugal

—thick   fat   spat   fast (H, 61)

Here perhaps there's a double exchange: from objects to modifiers and modifiers to objects. No scope for the short-circuiting Bunting felt to get in the way of careful attention. Language itself becomes a Heraclitean fire, which is already an implication of Hopkins's poem, where 'squadron', which originally meant a square of soldiers, becomes 'squandered'. Instead of the continuity of an extractable semantic content, words are consumed, as duration runs through them, where duration is the Open, the whole which is not giveable, as in Bergson.

Rather than word-fragments, these move towards being word-particles, particles which break away from words at a different speed or speeds and allow readers to abandon the desire of whole words. This happens alongside blurring of boundaries between organ and flesh, and exterior and interior of body:

Bury the edges,
pulped, each eye
plunged ajar,

          twisted
          every feather
          bled inside
          mesh
          w/body (H, 9–10)

Sometimes the language material is like Cobbing's, or Klhebnikov's soundings (e.g.: 'Hag Ma Lung Ma Lung Ma' (H 52)),[30] but it is more interesting when it undoes the distinction between organ and flesh, and inside and outside of the body. 'Dead Horse Bellies / Dead Syllabary Dead' (H, 10): if a syllabary is 'a system of characters representing syllables and (in some languages or stages of writing) serving the purpose of an alphabet' (OED), then another boundary is being crossed, between dead and living flesh/voice/writing.[31]

That transformation relates to the interweaving or interpenetration of damage and repair, which is a strong characteristic of *Murmur*, which was performed at Birkbeck College on 6th November 2003 and is as yet unpublished in book form.[32] The sense of damage and repair as coming from the same place is also to be found in *House*:

> tusk & wound
> succour
> on
> Key
>
>> Black & Sting
>> 3 Beams. 2 Fish,
>> Consistory ticking, Water between
>
> breaths
> to the mouth
> of each
> corpse
> All day & never – A slash, A
> scream, A smash, A burn pushed
> in
> side (each within the
>   gag
>
> BIRD OR FISH
>
> foot
> prints
> tenderer
> imaging (H, 23)

Damage to flesh and abilities to make signs ('gag') occur immediately alongside physical revival and making traces on the land ('foot / prints'); 'Consistory ticking' gives an image of time inside the sign, where 'consistory' (= court or council chamber) is a place of sumptuous language and 'ticking' is, as well as minute movement, a fabric for covering feather pillows, and what (onomatopoeically) a small blood-sucking parasite does.

Damage and repair occur, therefore, inside a relationship between signs and physiology, a relationship which is crucial to shamanic healing, where it may take the form of incantation, dance, and the laying out of sign-materials on the shaman's *mesa* or altar.[33] The *mesa* can be thought of as the shaman's book. Crucially, a shaman's healing action needs to be understood as part of a larger role, which is to be the one who questions the totality of the symbolic and in so doing reconstitutes it. As Rothenberg puts it, the flow of sounds and visual images in the shamanic ritual is 'world-making and self-making'.[34] Emptying the symbolic does run the risk, to use Olson's phrase, of God rushing back in, which is one reason why shamanism has become a New Age province. The context is those situations or practices which make symbols into 'wisdom', detached from the materials, times, and places of their making.

Dancing the word, the letter, the thing, the body is making languages out of disparate materials: 'a LESS-LESS identifiableness'.[35] This is not a subject making objects through language: an event has already happened to undo an abstract noun, the parachute of nouns hasn't opened.[36] Traveling each word, phrase, syllable, particle – each modifi-cation – is a new desire ('there are as many kinds of desire as there are kinds of objects whereby we are affected'),[37] traversing the times of words and wounds. But there are risks involved. Desire can be narco-tised into damage.

Shamanic techniques are highly various, and may include the use of hallucinogenic substances. In all cases though, there is an alteration of the relationship between body and signs,[38] by a return to or entry into the level at which pattern of any kind is made. The first part of *House*, which has the title 'ANOTHER WEATHER SYSTEM', begins with

> Contorted
> lure
> of
> Circles (H, 9)

The circle can be taken as the first turning upon itself or first folding of the segmented. Michaux writes:

> The circle is the first unthinking abstraction [. . .] A circle is that which
> runs between outside and in, between the thinkable and the imagin-
> able. [. . .] And it intoxicates [. . .] through repetition, our first drug.[39]

The lovely thing about this is how Michaux turns the lure of narcotics
inside out: we are the narcotic, we make it inside us.

MOS is not concerned with the mythic narrative of origins, but with
repeated dissolutions and beginnings: 'gone-thru || broke ||| falteringly,
|| tangled || sunken' (H, 9). In accounts of shamanic experience, this is
the territory of death and recovery: 'then the bear of the lake or the
inland glacier will come out, he will devour all your flesh and make
you a skeleton, and you will die. But you will recover your flesh, you
will awaken, & your clothes will come rushing to you.' Which is related
to the image of the muddled body: 'My body is muddled today; I
dreamt many men were killing me.'[40] Questioning the whole of the
symbolic involves a production of the body, not the interpretation of
an already-given body: 'ill.me. / dot. / me / glue.me.cloven. / cloaka
Bones, / a branding math-smudge' – to quote that passage again. This
production may fail; the process is risky.

'Another Weather System', which is the long first section of the book,
repeatedly offers damaged bodies and capabilities destroyed: 'Dead Horse
Bellies'; 'murder bullies'; 'TOAD SCREAM'; 'Mouth / fell / out / here'; 'Brains
Out'. The writing does not make a subject available to reading which
would make the materials into an experience. Eating and killing, living
and dying, do not accrue to a person who can carry them off as attributes.
Person, organ, perception, these super-ordinates are not allowed to function; the person-indicating pronoun is beside itself not above itself:

> i
> and
> and i
> there
> and
> i
> i
> while
> i
> i
> hear (H, 18–19)

So that this is not an analysis – where would it be carried out from? – still less an allegory (the final subject of all of Ovid's metamorphoses is the Imperial power). It is difficult to imagine being so destitute of resources to inform reading, that the economy of eating and killing, of damage and making, are the same, and not available to some other place called knowledge; '*HUNGER* / hooking the bill tearing the flesh lining the text.' (H, 14) The psyche has to be equal to it.

In Hopkins's poem, the human is 'squandered' by 'nature's bonfire', 'mortal trash / [. . .] to the residuary worm'; only 'the Resurrection' holds against such tremendous wastage, making it possible to write 'I am all at once what Christ is'. Read without the comfort of theology, the poem elicits Jeff Nuttall's designation of art, as the ecstatic encounter between ethics and nature – ethics becoming the grain of decision in the writing.

Shamanic practices, as Eliade suggests, are paratheological: they do not administer doctrine. Or, as Iain Sinclair has argued, the shamanic, in our time, occurs with a minimum of indebtedness to other systems.[41] Animals may be called upon as aids;[42] these are taken up in theogonic and cosmogonic narratives such as the *Popol Vuh*, the Quetzalcoatl cycle, or the *Huarochiri Manuscript*, to mention three American examples. The middle-American snake-bird god was helped, in his journey through the land of the dead, by worms and bees. Ustvolskaya found aid from ants when composing. It is the degree of boundarilessness which makes such aid necessary:

how winds, how rains, how snow, how ice, how floods,

how born or well or ill or artery or dead or healing

how Fog, Rear, Bloar Abrupted. (H, 19)

Any net cast over the onrush becomes part of it, and that would include all semiotic systems. Such suspensions, even if temporary, are all-embracing. Why, then, 'descend', to such a level? No answer can be given outside what the work makes possible. But the need to find other languages is part of it, as is song, shared with birds and other animals, and making earth inhabitable:[43]

you
too

stiffen swoop on ridge
you
too
topple turn hills many more turns
you
too
the Beasts do the rain not the Birds do another
you
too
call the pulsing home. (H, 17)

'Call', as both naming and voicing, each including the other, has a beautiful ambiguity, which spreads into 'pulsing', making voice both semantic (phone semantike) and animalic – in fact making any boundary between language and nature uncertain.[44]

What I am calling the shamanic is not confined to ethnopoetics in the restricted sense – i.e. as translation of non-Western materials. Rothenberg's idea of 'total translation' is concerned with bringing across all the elements of the performance event: from the scenario to the body movements to the sounds and visual elements, whether meaningful or not, if meaning is taken as what is framed socially as sense. MOS's long association with Bob Cobbing meant that she inherited a parallel idea of bringing into writing that totality of event and of using writing as a score for multiple performance. Cobbing is well-known for having been able to perform any visual material.

In a shamanic trance-state, the subject is given songs:
Anything, in fact, can deliver a song because anything – 'night, mist, the blue sky, east, west, women, adolescent girls, men's hands & feet, the sexual organs of men & women, the bat, the land of souls, ghosts, graves, the bones, hair & teeth of the dead,' etc. – is alive.[45]

Song is very important in MOS's concern to get the whole event into the writing. In fact there's an almost constant exchange between song and all the surfaces, emplacements and implements of writing. It is not irrelevant to note that her father, an Irish migrant to England, was a singer. There is in her work an underlying and recurrent songfulness, in constant interchange with seeing: 'When the stir of all Breath would to a Seeing turn' ('NARRATIVE CHARM FOR IBBOTROYD', H. 44), linking temporality with real-time movement. In her performance of *Murmur*, she includes a field recording of an Irish keening sung by Kitty Gallagher in Co. Donegal in 1952. The phrases, and the visual elements of the text also, become – to extend a metaphor from MOS's talk/text 'Riverrunning (realisations' – islands in a stream of song. Song is the birthing element, making pain bearable, pleasure knowable.

Notes

[1] Eric Havelock, *Preface to Plato* (1982 [1962]), 228.

[2] Havelock, 218.

[3] 1955, translated by H.D.P. Lee, 245.

[4] Henri Michaux, *Spaced, Displaced*, 1992 [*Déplacementes Dégagements*, 1985], 49–51.

[5] Michaux, 53.

[6] Michaux, 169.

[7] Michaux, 168.

[8] See J. p. Luminet, *L'univers chiffoné*, 2001, for the notion that 'chiffonning' describes the primary characteristic of matter, at both quantum and cosmological levels.

[9] Basil Bunting, 'Some Limitations of English', in Ric Caddell, ed., *Basil Bunting: Three Essays*, 1994 [1930], p. 23.

[10] Bunting, 24.

[11] Here I am thinking of Steve McCaffery's 'The Politics of the Referent' (1977). Blake's critique of Locke is also relevant here, as 'precursor' to Bunting's.

[12] The abbreviation H refers to *In the House of the Shaman*, 1993,

[13] See also p. 41.

[14] Recalling Alan Davies (and Nic Piombino's) essay, 'Blur'.

[15] There are many examples in Bunting's poetry. The earliest is at the end of 'Villon': 'How can I sing with my love in my bosom? / Unclean, immature and unseasonable salmon.'

[16] The action occurred inside a cage-like room in May 1974 in New York. Beuys's relation with the Coyote, which urinated on the New York Times, included an element of domination, something that is absent from the types of 'kinship with animals' presented in MOS's work.

[17] *Shaking The Pumpkin*, 1986, 366–7.

[18] see p. 10, for another example

[19] Gregory Bateson, *Steps to an Ecology of Mind*, 1972, 262.

[20] Bateson, 140, 262.

²¹ *Palace of Reptiles*, 2003, 60. 'Scant' = diminish or neglect, but also suggests song (loss of?).

²² see also H 61: '*Squabble-Speak / sub — / statuary – [. . .]* Sylla/ // bled Garjey' where the syllable *garg* connects with throat, gullet. Note the exchange between blood (body fluid) and writing. A continuation of strange nuptials?

²³ Bob Cobbing and Lawrence Upton, eds., *Word Score Utterance Choreography*, 14

²⁴ Edward Casey, in *The Fate of Place* (1998, 9), summarises Hesiod as proposing that 'as a gap, chaos is a primordial place in which things can happen.'

²⁵ Gillles Deleuze and Félix Guattari, *A Thousand Plateaus*, 494.

²⁶ *Shaking the Pumpkin*, 358.

²⁷ *Excla* offers a large expanse of writing-markings, scorings-scrivings: non-alligned graphisms (i.e. not aligned to the idea of voice as making meaningful sounds which writing then transcribes).

²⁸ Bateson, 262

²⁹ See Rothenberg's translations of the Navaho horse songs, which include meaningless syllables. Jumping backwards and forwards between the analogue and the digital may in fact be one of the characteristics of shamanic language.

³⁰ This aspect of the writing offers more to a reader when it consists of broken-off fragments of words, e.g. 'Indu Aka bead loshes quoises' (H 22), as opposed to stand-alone syllables. The two modes of course overlap.

³¹ So death is not a script written upon the flesh of the living as in Bunting's 'Villon': 'Remember, imbeciles and wits, / sots and ascetics, fair and foul, / young girls with little tender tits, / that DEATH is written over all.' (Section I)

³² *Murmur* is included on a CD of MOS's work published by Stem Recordings (www.stemredordings.com).

³³ See Jerome Rothenberg and David Guss, *The Book, Spiritual Instrument*, 1996, 31, 48. They discuss how the Peruvian shaman Eduardo Calderón works with intersections of various fields, the relations between worlds constantly varying.

³⁴ Rothenberg and Guss, 44.

³⁵ *eXcla*, section A 1.

³⁶ See Brian Catling's poem 'Small Light': 'the skull / [. . .] bobbing to rest / [. . .] with names.' (*Future Exiles: 3 London Poets*, 1992).

³⁷ Spinoza, *Ethics*, III, LVI.

³⁸ See Eric Mottram, *Towards Design in Poetry*, 1977, 5: 'a language might be made of anything: the body makes and uses systems out of anything.'

³⁹ Michaux, 103.

⁴⁰ Jerome Rothenberg, *Technicians of the Sacred*, 1984, 486–487.

⁴¹ Iain Sinclair, 'The Shamanism of Intent', in *Lights Out for the Territory*, 1997.

[42] It is worth noting that the relationship between writing and nature in MOS's books is not sealed off either from domesticity or from modern technology. See 'Narcotic Properties', in *Palace of Reptiles*. I am grateful to Harry Gilonis for drawing my attention to this.

[43] See the notion that song inscribes place into terrain, in Gilles Deleuze and Félix Guattari, *A Thousand Plateaus* ('1837: Of the Refrain').

[44] Steve McCaffery's statement, 'Performed Paragrammatism', offers a possible poetics of such writing: 'the restrictive sense of "presence" in Derrida's theory of logocentrism and the metaphysics of parousia . . . speech is prosthetic to voice and if one of the historical mandates of philosophy has been to erase or domesticate that wider domain of vociferation (grunts, screams, growls) i.e. the entire foundational, animalic strata of voice and presence that connect to flight, loss, becoming, heterogeneity and heterology.' (Bob Cobbing and Lawrence Upton, Eds., *Word Score Utterance Choreography in Verbal and Visual Poetry*, Writers Forum, 1998).

[45] Rothenberg, *Technicians*, 487. He adds: 'Here is the central image of shamanism & of all "primitive" thought, the intuition [. . .] of a connected & fluid universe, as alive as man is.'

Talk: The Poetics of Maggie O'Sullivan

Robert Sheppard

What kind of text *is* 'riverrunning (realisations' by Maggie O'Sullivan?
One answer to this question may be derived from inspecting the prove-
nance of the text and its various 'realisations', but before we can discuss
the text we have before us on the page, we have to pay some attention to
the various oral contexts through which it was produced. The text we
have is carefully described in an author's note as 'based on a talk I gave
for the Poetics Program at the State University of New York at Buffalo on
Tuesday 26 October 1993 and also at the Kootenay School of Writing,
Vancouver, on Wednesday 3 November, 1993'. (O'Sullivan, 2003, p. 57.)
   That little word 'talk' loses some of its informality and ephemeral
qualities in the context of North American poetry. While O'Sullivan
has 'talked' to my students at Edge Hill University after a reading,
answering questions, haltingly dwelling on some point she has not
finally thought through, and suggesting strategies for the students'
own writing, this 'talk' is not what is signified by the word in the
specialised context of language poetry. When Bob Perelman remi-
nisces on 'The Bay Area talks,' which he curated and edited into written form, he describes something altogether more programmatic,
even combative. He emphasises that the poets' talks

> were oriented toward the present and the future: the participants were
> attempting to construct a plural poetics in public. Talking out these
> writing values was at times clarifying, at times diffuse. The written talk
> that remains casts a dramatic, novelistic light on these thrashings-out
> . . . Their specific forms differ: some were protoacademic essays; some
> were performance pieces; some were group discussions of poetics
> centred around an initial speaker with the audience chiming in, inter-
> rupting, suggesting detours, wrestling over control of terms and of the
> verbal arena. (Perelman, 1998, p. 210)

[154]

O'Sullivan's first talk (which I envisage as falling into Perelman's cate-gory of 'performance piece') was dedicated to Charles Bernstein, who, as director at the time, presumably invited her to 'talk' to the staff and students on the poetics programme at Buffalo. If this is not visiting language poetry at its source, it is at least mooring one's barque in one of its more enduring tributaries. While not a creative writing programme, as that is commonly conceived, the poetics programme headed by Charles Bernstein attracted as its students practising writers (usually poets) who wished to further their study into questions of the philosophy of writing. 'The Poetics Program's emphasis on creative reading,' writes Susan Schultz, introducing a provocative concept into the lexicon, 'rather than writing also distinguishes it from the English department proper at SUNY-Buffalo and from English departments around the country whose emphasis is on literary criticism, not poet-ics.' (Schultz, 1997, p. 137) By the early nineties, the programme involved the contributions of writers such as Susan Howe and Robert Creeley, who were living reminders of Buffalo's role in the earlier projectivist avant-garde under the academic tutelage of Charles Olson.

Although O'Sullivan had already established links with language poetry, most notably in the collaboration with Bernstein's co-editor of the influential *L=A=N=G=U=A=G=E* magazine, Bruce Andrews, that was published in 1993 as *Excla*, delivering such a talk as described so colour-fully by Perelman was not second nature to O'Sullivan. When I have seen her trying to explain her work to sceptical students she becomes defensively strident or effervescently vague (but then, poetics, as I hope to show 'don't explain', as Charles Bernstein himself, echoing Billie Holiday, puts it! (Bernstein 1992: 160)). The 'talk', the 'colloquium', even the academic conference, are not very developed sites of public discus-sion of avant-garde practice in Britain.[1] This kind of event has histori-cally ended in embarrassment or silence. It was only in the 1990s that that changed somewhat and O'Sullivan's presentations (although delivered overseas) were part of this. That O'Sullivan herself may have been unsettled by the experience is revealed by a strange dream passage in the text:

> (Include a Nightmare – i am in the house i grew in my family abound me Charles Bernstein & 2 aides alarm the fading door they have bicycled in the rain i know this because when i move my air in greeting his hand drips all & of none clanging back the waters so nervous & so tore my tongue frets & webbing Bided the 3 settee & ask me every piling upofme my talk (O'Sullivan, 2003, p. 60)

Amid the slippery transformations of language ('abound' for 'around', for example) and with the elisions of the cut-up method, and even with the Flann O'Brien-ish arrival on bicycles, it is clear that an early childhood memory is invaded by the dedicatee of the final text, an only begetter, along with his henchmen. The three of them sit on the settee and presumably interrogate the dreaming O'Sullivan about her 'talk', which she clearly represents as an intimate 'every piling upofme'. '<u>Still</u> i cannot speak', the text announces (twice). (O'Sullivan, 2003, p. 60)

One can only imagine the guffaws with which this passage was received at Buffalo (a British audience might have allowed itself a wry smile), but O'Sullivan has never, to my knowledge, played anything for laughs, and the anxiety of the 'revelations' that might accompany the 'realisations' are real enough. Visiting the Headquarters of Poetics she envisages its leader possessing 'aides'. (But perhaps Bernstein is also the carnivalistic 'pantomimic wild brother' O'Sullivan also addresses. (O'Sullivan, 2003, p. 60).) British Linguistically Innovative Poetry and the British Poetry Revival poetry before it have not (until recently) infiltrated the academy as commentators – usually its detractors – claim of language poetry, and it is easy for those inside the academy to forget the intimidation its authority represents for writers outside of it. These 'aides' could be taking notes to hand to the Director of Poetic Prosecutions! Even Perelman, reflecting on the West Coast talks, notes: 'While I think this space remains useful it was not utopic: men talked more easily than women; different degrees of educational capital made for an uneven floor. A number of writers who attended the talks spoke (afterward, off the record) of being "terrified" to speak.' (Perelman, 1998, p. 215) In the face of her nervous aphasia it is not surprising that O'Sullivan defends her 'piling upofme' with piles of quotations from her own, and others', work that she clings to like comforters, and then distributes through the (written version) of the text. Barricades of anti-authority. It is fortunate for us as readers that this provocation to 'talk', this impossible speech, produced this 'writing' which we can subsequently 'read'. Perelman notes the ironies of 'talks' that appear more written than spoken; and of oral presentations, like Lyn Hejinian's 'The Rejection of Closure' (an important document of the language movement) whose original oral version 'ends with a more comically graphic depiction of openness' than the more 'conclusive' written essay. (Perelman 1998, p. 211)

The written version of Maggie O'Sullivan's talk opens with a consideration of the resonances of the word 'talk' itself, which are so different from those of 'song' or 'speech' (to which she will ultimately turn). It is almost as though she had first inscribed the name of the flexible 'genre' she was expected to deliver and then attempts to transform it, through interrogation. She opens:

TALK.
Tell-Tale.
Heard-Tell.
Tell-Tales.
Heard-Tell-Of.
Uttering – Tell-Tale. (O'Sullivan, 2003, p. 59)

The effects of talking – or 'talk' as we might say, without a definite or indefinite article – lead onto the act of telling, and that which is told is a narrative we call a 'tale'. Already the text is suggesting the negative implications of the act. 'Tell-tale' signs are those unconscious trails we leave to others' detection; a 'tell-tale' is a person who tells a lie against another or who breaks a confidence. The archaic note in 'Heard-Tell' is brought to the surface when a phrase such as 'I heard tell of' is considered. It not only reminds us that a tale must have a subject (an 'of') but that it suggests the spoken formulae used in archaic oral literatures, by those storytellers and shamans who professionally, as it were, 'tell tales', whose 'uttering' makes them a model for the contemporary poet, in O'Sullivan's view. At its boldest, 'utterance' is the theme of this 'talk'.

Before we reach the text's first textual manifestation, it received its second 'talk' outing, just over a week after its first, at the Kootenay School of Writing, which is a non-profit making organisation, and the nucleus of the many poets who emerged in Vancouver during the eighties, many of them women. (Perhaps the absence of a Kootenay nightmare is explained by this gender distribution.) A large number of them are associated with the magazine *Raddle Moon*, which operated out of the school's headquarters. Two of these Canadian writers, Lisa Robertson and Catriona Strang, were later featured in O'Sullivan's Reality Street anthology, *Out of Everywhere: linguistically innovative poetry by women in North America and the UK* (1996).

The text's first publication in 1995 preserves the Vancouver connection. It was published as part of a hundred page anthology of British poetry, edited by Peter Quartermain, which formed part of the magazine *West Coast Line* (Number Seventeen (29/2) which hails from that city. O'Sullivan's text stands out from its fellows in one important way. Whereas some other contributors – myself included – provided a generous sample of poems, and a 'statement of poetics' that I remember the editor requested, the O'Sullivan contribution cannot be divided in this way. Her 'poem' is a 'poetics', although it is not a 'statement of' but an embodiment of, the workings of her poetry and its underlining philosophy. It asserts its textual hybridity, not just in its transformation from 'talk' to text, but in its textual production and publishing context as well.

Its second textual presentation appears at first to be at odds with its hybridity, as a chapter of the academic book *Contemporary Women's Poetry* edited by Alison Mark and Deryn Rees-Jones. Subtitled 'Reading/Writing/Practice', in this volume, as Isobel Armstrong points out in her 'Preface', 'The voices of women poets, speaking about the way they write, are juxtaposed with those of critics writing about women's poetry'. (Mark and Rees-Jones, 2000, p. xv) Armstrong finds the resultant 'sound collage apposite because contemporary poetry persuades us to listen with the eye, see with the ear'. (Mark and Rees-Jones, 2000, p. xv) It is not surprising, since this seems to describe O'Sullivan's poetic practice, that Armstrong comments on O'Sullivan's work, 'whose haunting experiments with verbal installations make words into particles of sound as well as blocks of material we have to see from all angles'. (Mark and Rees-Jones, 2000, p. xv). This materiality is indeed a theme in 'rivverrunning (realisations For Charles Bernstein' as this version of the text is entitled. Armstrong's additional remark that O'Sullivan's 'refusal of self', which sits somewhat ill at ease in a book with a loose feminist perspective, produces 'lapidary poems, where the potentials in sound and language are sought in the tonguescape not simply of human but of animal and other sounds. Hers is an ecopoetics, an open field of sound, aware that the human self is not the world's centre'. (Mark and Rees-Jones, 2000, p. xvii) While this articulates many of O'Sullivan's concerns, it also mimes her style, quotes one of her neologisms. And while there is one favourable remark about O'Sullivan's work by the editor, Alison Mark, and several other references to her anthology *Out of Everywhere*, there is little to contextualise O'Sullivan's contribution for the (new) audience of her work, to help readers to see the materiality from various angles, to illuminate the non-human perspectives. Her piece is arranged contiguously, 'collaged', to use Armstrong's word, with Jo Shapcott's personal account of the influence of Elizabeth Bishop on her work, and Deryn

Rees-Jones' discursive poetics which takes on board issues of imperfect readerly understanding of defamiliarised text. O'Sullivan's piece itself might give the reader one such example, of course, although this point is not made. I do not mean to be negative about this lack of contextualising. In one sense, it helps to foreground the very materiality that is such an essential part of her work, as the reader is forced to engage with it, but it is a frustrating read for a reader unfamiliar with embodied poetics, if I may put it thus. The text is not so much collaged as spotlit in its difference and isolation.

It is worth pausing for a moment to consider where familiarity with such a discourse might be found. One obvious source, which links with the text's original occasion, and which points out an influence upon O'Sullivan, is the poetics essays and hybrid critical writings of the language poets. Bernstein's most famous poetics work is probably 'Artifice of Absorption', which is (in the form of) a poem; Bruce Andrews' essay on Susan Howe, 'Suture – & Absence of the Social', for example, is a collage of quotations from Howe herself. [2] Readers of *Contemporary Women's Poetry* would get some glimpse of this hybrid writing from Alison Mark's essay on 'Writing about Writing about Writing', and from Harriet Tarlo's borrowings and quotations from Rachel Blau DuPlessis in the final essay of the book, '"A She Even Smaller Than a Me": Gender Dramas of the Contemporary Avant-Garde'. (Mark and Rees-Jones, 2000, pp. 64–75; and pp. 247–70 respectively). These issues of the poetics of poetics – metapoetics – will be returned to later.

This essay was proposed before the publication of O'Sullivan's long-awaited volume *Palace of Reptiles* (2003), and it was with some surprise but much delight that I discovered 'riverrunning (realisations' (with its dedication returned to its rightful subsidiary position and with a number of textual changes) included as part three of that book. This decision emphasises the text's hybridity genre-wise; 'the eight poems of this book touch on multiple genres (elegy, celebration, performance art, poetics talk) in order to transform them' the book's blurb asserts. It also definitively declared it to be a primary, and not a secondary, text. (O'Sullivan, 2003, back cover). It must not be read as a supplement to O'Sullivan's *oeuvre*, but as its then-latest published manifestation. It meant that my prior decision to offer a reading of this work of poetics *as* a work of poetics became simultaneously a reading of a poem.

I have written on O'Sullivan's work elsewhere, and also on the nature of poetics, but I have only here related one to the other.[3] Poetics has had a number of definitions and of uses. Drawing from my own experience as a poet who produces poetics, and as a tutor of creative writing, for which I regard poetics a necessary complementary discourse, I have attempted to define the practice and products of poetics more closely. When creative writers 'read as a writer' (to drop once again into the jargon of creative writing pedagogy) they often produce writing that is distinct from literary criticism, as Schultz notes of the Buffalo programme. Its focus keeps shifting onto some text of the author's own, or, more usefully, onto some text that is not yet in existence. T.S. Eliot's essays, for example, sometimes read like a prospectus for his own work, as critics have long realised. It is precisely a *discourse* with a scope and rules, and even a history, of its own. As Jerome Rothenberg puts it: 'But the world we share, & our interplay with it, calls again & again for *discourse*: in the case of Poets, the setting forth of a poetics'. (Rothenberg, 1981, p. 3) On the one hand there are the hybrid works of the language poets, on the other, the more descriptive and autobiographical accounts in Marks' and Rees-Jones' book. For such a mercurial and discontinuous discourse, that can be found equally in writers' letters and creative works themselves as well as in statements and manifestoes; there needs to be a phenomenology of forms. Such an undertaking is beyond the remit of this essay. It requires, at the very least, the multiple definitions I have offered elsewhere, and from which I will select those most useful to the present object of study. Their contact with an existing act of poetics may well suggest directions for, and augmentations of, the larger project, to which I will return at the end of this essay. (See Sheppard 2002 for the original statement of these definitions.)

Poetics are the products of the process of reflection upon writings, and upon the act of writing, gathering from the past and from others, speculatively casting into the future (as Perelman is careful to stress about the 'talks' series). Poetics is a way of letting writers question what they think they know, letting writing dialogue with itself, to produce, to quote Rachel Blau DuPlessis, 'a permission to continue'. (DuPlessis, 1990, pp. 156) Poetics could be a test of practice; but practice will test poetics. The making can change the poetics; the poetics can change the making. Poetics steals from anywhere. As Bernstein says: 'One of the pleasures of poetics is to try on a paradigm and see where it leads you.' (Bernstein, 1992, pp. 161) The positions to which a poetics gets a writer are usually temporary and strategic. To look for truth value or even logic in its articulations may be beside the point for the writer, though it might not be for a reader or critic. (I shall return to this point in my conclusions). It speaks to a working practice as much as it speaks to its reader. Poetics may even involve strategic self-deception, and may therefore mismatch the writing that results. Poetics might even be silent about a major part of the poet's work. What appears at first to be critical blindness may be a strategy to get texts moving, to get the writer creatively into spaces that otherwise might not be accessed, or to divert attention away from the creative act. Again there are issues of the truth value of the statements to be faced, since some, like Rothenberg, see poets in epochal terms: 'I've attempted, like other poets so engaged, to create a new & coherent poetics for our time.' (Rothenberg 1981, p. 3)

Another danger of poetics is that it might look like self-justification, but if it does it has ceased dialogue with the activity of making, which is implied by the very root of its name. This can be avoided by embodying poetics in the creative work itself, as content, as theme or aside. This is also why it often appears as, results in, hybrid texts such as 'riverrunning (realisations' itself).

To explicate the enactments of poetics in 'riverrunning (realisations' is ultimately to risk violence to the text, in that its refusal to hierarchicalize its elements – it is laid out like a collage on a flat surface – must be resisted. There is at least some evidence that the text itself may have had more structure at one point, or that an attempt at a more discursive essay was abandoned and thrown into the intuitive action of collage. There exist a number of explicatory or autobiographical passages that suddenly intrude into the poetic flow: 'The works I make. . . . In 1984, I began my assemblages. . . . In 1988 . . . I stepped out. . . .'(O'Sullivan, 2003, pp. 64–8) There is a danger that such passages assume an authority over the possibility of interpretations offered by more poetic epiphanies ('A Blackbird, it gouged throb unscripted', for example) which point the reader away from, in this case, inscription itself, towards the animal world. (O'Sullivan, 2003, p. 62). These are traces of the act of making itself, appropriate to a *poetics*, of course. I have already shown the results of the intention to 'Include a Nightmare'; but the text also commands itself to 'Include Scene-Shifts' and 'Include guiDance', which both gesture towards the performing arts. The 'SOURCES' at the text's end alert us to a range of resources and unattributed quotations that add another dimension to it and to the poetics towards which it is moving. Sources range from academic texts (the word 'university' repeatedly jumps out of the bibliography as you scan it) though some of them are distinctly unusual and obsolete, to the more obvious Joyce and Bunting, a number of popular sources on Irish history and culture, through to Russian Futurist texts. While the presence of these conflicting elements points once again to the collage structure, it also points to the entangled thematics of the piece. The 'sources' are not made present merely in acknowledgement of borrowings, nor are they intended as an authoritive bibliography for budding scholars and poets, like Olson's famous 'bibliography' for Edward Dorn. Beyond the use they may have had as a barrier against exposure to the interrogative lights of the Buffalo Poetics Police, they point us to what O'Sullivan calls 'tributory' elements (con-tributory elements) of her work, the riverine metaphor of 'source' being appropriate to a list of 'SOURCES for riverrunning (realisations', as she calls them. (O'Sullivan, 2003, p. 71) It is necessary to read the non-discursive along with the discursive, the opaque along with the clear, the non-attributed along with the cited source, the poetic along with the auto-biographical, but it is also necessary to separate them, in order to determine how a philosophy of composition can be articulated apart from the activity of writing's dialogue with itself, from its various 'realisations', to use O'Sullivan's term. Poetics' conjectures might incite or provoke O'Sullivan or ourselves to further activity. What I am undertaking here is not poetics, but the poetics of poetics, a *metapoetics* if you like, which I conceive of as a critical activity.

Much of 'riverruning (realisations' pays tribute to 'tributory' artists, and acts of homage begin with the very title, of course, which incorporates the opening word of Joyce's *Finnegans Wake*, a word which connects its end with its beginning, and is a pun on an adjective most appropriate to the novel: 'riverine'. But the flowing of the river also provides Joyce with the setting, not only for the slumbering of his characters HCE and ALP, but of the famous 'Anna Livia Plurabelle' section at the end of Chapter One, which O'Sullivan quotes in the text, in which two washerwomen discuss the sexual indiscretions of HCE and discuss the life of 'Anna Livia' (O'Sullivan, 2003, p. 63; Joyce, 1975, p. 198) with her 'awful old reppe' of a husband as they clean clothes on the bank of the Liffey. (Joyce, 1975, p. 196) The 'telling' that O'Sullivan identifies as a chief constituent of 'talk', is one of the foci of this tale of gossip. 'O tell me all about Anna Livia! . . . Tell me all. Tell me now,' one of the women pleads. (Joyce 1975, p. 196) (They will metamorphose into tree and stone by the end of the chapter, while Anna herself keeps merging with the river.) After her opening meditation upon the word 'talk', O'Sullivan quotes (in capitals) one of Joyce's most famous sentences: 'Well, you know or don't you kennet or haven't I told you every telling has a taling and that's the he and she of it.' (Joyce 1975, p. 213; O'Sullivan 2003, p. 59). The circular structure of Joyce's dream epic and the open parenthesis of O'Sullivan's title both suggest that telling does not have a taling (or end) necessarily, but O'Sullivan does not pursue the sexual innuendo, 'the he and she', of the women's gossip. The sentence has a more talismanic presence for O'Sullivan: it is the first spoken by Joyce himself on the recording made by C.K. Ogden in 1928 of the *Anna Livia Plurabelle* (then still 'in progress'). Before one of her readings in the 1980s I witnessed O'Sullivan playing a tape of this to the audience: the surprisingly high-pitched 'half-sung/half-said' of Joyce's thin but mellifluous voice. (O'Sullivan, 2003, p. 59) Joyce is one of O'Sullivan's performative precursors in the use of neologism and pun, but a moment's comparison reveals the essential difference. While they are both concerned with articulating what feels like language being born, as I have argued elsewhere,[4] Joyce's vision is largely comic and essentially narrative (however 'plurabelle' that narrative proves), whereas O'Sullivan's language is transformative in a supposedly promissory way:

> turning & returning & stirring the phrases in the plate of promise, what promise of I can't
>> for you?
>> for me?
>> for whom?
> Poetry finds my life – Poetry as she has Arisen (O'Sullivan 2003, p. 63)

The poetry (and poetics) are striving for a function here. It is not the male Finnegan that will arise at the end of time, but a feminised poetry that is encountered as the already arisen, 'AS SHE ARRIVES OUT OF THE FUTURE, WORDS LIVING', as O'Sullivan writes, probably quoting the 'Futurian' Russian poet, Velimir Klebnikov, who, as Marjorie Perloff points out, with his 'neologism, paranomasia and glossolalia' is a modernist precursor to a number of contemporary writers, including O'Sullivan. (Perloff, 2002, p. 126) But neither Joyce, with his attempt to construct the collective unconscious through polyvalent language, nor Klebnikov's attempt to use 'beyonsense' to codify particular phonemic structures as universal meanings, ('"v" in all languages means the turning of one point around another') could completely satisfy an artist who believes in the materiality of language. (Klebiniov 1985, p. 147) Her materiality, her focus upon the component parts of poetry, could not be clearer:

> introduction of
> sound:
> introduction of
> sight:
> introduction of
> texture: (O'Sullivan, 2003, p. 65)

While this ultimately derives from Pound's triadic division of poetry into a poetry of sound (melopoeia) and image (phanopoeia), his third category ('LOGOPOEIA, "the dance of the intellect among words"') is replaced by an insistence not upon intellect but upon the material thickness and artifice of the medium. (Pound, 1954, p. 25) There can be none of the communicative transparency which still haunts Pound's poetics. But neither is intellect banished; it must appear sensually, in O'Sullivan's work, quite literally through the three qualities she lists. Although it appears from this checklist as though sound is primary, notice how, even in her most passionate assertion of the oral and aural (which involves a self-quotation from the poem 'Doubtless'), sight, along with smell, is present in an impressive synaesthetic compound, while the lineation, capitals and underlinings leave the reader unable to escape the 'texture' of O'Sullivan's poetic artifice;

> Marigold's plush & Boiling sheer
> geranium Tang.
> A Chirp. Braided, attended misbehaves
> animated by extension, lip drove, I eared/Listen out for
> the light –
> Ear-Loads I Sing! (O'Sullivan, 2003, p. 62. See also p. 42)

The great modernist master of materiality for O'Sullivan is Kurt Schwitters. By materiality she does not just mean grainy artifice (she quotes Basil Bunting for that), but materiality as an attitude towards materials, that is drawn from the visual arts. Indeed, it was as a visual artist in the early eighties that O'Sullivan discovered Schwitters' importance for her writerly poetics, while making 'assemblages or visual constructions' (which can be found adorning the covers of her recent books): 'ASSEMBLAGES, after Kurt Schwitters who made superb use of the UN – the NON and the LESS – THE UNREGARDED, the found, the cast-offs, the dismembered materials of culture.' (O'Sullivan, 2003, p. 67) Using the present tense of poetics, she comments, 'His work shows me to look away from, beyond the given.' (O'Sullivan, 2003, p. 67) Despite the slight conflict here between the found and the given, it is easy to see what O'Sullivan was admiring. Schwitters' was an art of odds and ends. His collages are indeed filled with the detritus of civilisation. This can be surprising for a viewer; from afar a collage such as 'Bild mit heller Mitte' (1919) looks like an expressionist canvas, but from close up one finds postage stamps and newspaper fragments in the image. In later works, he foregrounds the objects more openly: images are made of packaging, sweet and fruit wrappers ('Of South Africa'), bank receipts, torn American magazines ('Flashlight sonata on a service-club'), milk bottle tops, bus tickets, fairground rifle-range targets, ration coupons, envelopes. (Various images in Kurt Schwitters, 1985) The fragmentary presence of found language in the mix adds another dimension (and also alerts us to influences upon O'Sullivan's work who are not present in 'riverrunning (realisations', such as Bob Cobbing and Bill Griffiths). The influence is literal, of course, on O'Sullivan's visual work, but in the written works this becomes metaphorical, a facet of poetics, rather than a practice to directly assimilate. This is not to ignore the general influence of Schwitters as a sound poet of course; the tape of Joyce's *Anna Livia Plurabelle* that O'Sullivan played her audience was accompanied by a short burst of Schwitters' *Ur Sonate*. Schwitters' verbal fragments operate like discarded or atomised abandoned words, the supplement or remainder of communicative language. In some sense, and even in its title, which is quoted by O'Sullivan in 'riverrunning (realisations', *Excla*, the collaboration with Bruce Andrews, plays with this sense of language as material, in that the text is generated through an exchange of words and *parts* of words between the poets: 'EXCLA – SIASMS – BLED' (Andrews and O'Sullivan, 1993, n.p.)

O'Sullivan almost offers a definition of materiality that returns us to her revisions of Pound:

> Materiality of Language: its actual contractions &
> expansions, potentialities, prolongments, assemblages –
> the acoustic, visual, oral & sculptural qualities
> within the physical. (O'Sullivan, 2003, p. 64)

O'Sullivan (who was particularly inventive at one time with prefixes in her creative work) is drawn to repeat and elaborate on variations of the 'UN – the NON and the LESS' in 'riverrunning (realisations'. (O'Sullivan, 2003, p. 64) Her text contemplates the various 'unwisdoms' she can learn from these negations, so that the role of poesis, that of making, can involve its opposite, as found art reverts to its original matter: (p. 64)

> What 'Making' – 'Unmaking' is / a Mattering of
> Materials (motivations & practise) – Living to live in
> that Learning – Uncertain, Uncurtained Tonguescape
> (O'Sullivan, 2003, p. 65)

Instead of learning to live with this transformative activity, the process of continual learning becomes the *modus operandi*, of both poetics and praxis. This involves dwelling in the mysteries as Keats recommended, speaking of the unbounded negative capability in a voiced sound (that is also a scopic entity). O'Sullivan sees in this approach to her materials a subversive function.

> Engaging with the OUT, the UNDER – UN – the OTHER-THAN,
> The NON & the LESS – transgressions; trespass; disparity;
> subversion: Milton's 'UNTWISTING THE CHAINS THAT TIE'
> (O'Sullivan, 2003, p. 66)

Although this formulation does not quite rise to the overtly political – *un*-twisting might be the simplest example O'Sullivan could find – but it is significant it is a 'chain' that is being countered here. The 'Non' implies exclusion and the 'Less' that which is insufficiently regarded or continuously diminished. Turning the formal lesson of Schwitters' example to linguistic use, O'Sullivan envisages the kinds of material that might be accommodated by the literary context.

> In words, other rooming for what is at RISK inside out in language. Oppositional dialogues, realities, cartwheels, sway substances, Language, Undeniably, Ably drowsed, dowsed even.

The ambiguity on 'inside out' reads at first as another version of the 'other-than' but on closer inspection the text is suggesting that that which is at risk outside of the poem shall be given refuge within it; the poem is a repository for endangered linguistic practices. That includes all the neologisms she preserves in her work, dowsed out of etymology and history, as well as all the Schwitters-like supplementarity, the non-utile parts of language. In one passage she alludes to Bunting's condition of being 'earsick' and expands on the 'oppositional dialogues' she has in mind. She is not thinking of contrary arguments but of something altogether more elusive, unstable and contradictory: 'dither-sickings, Earsick tongue-spew – Displacement – Pluralities – Diversity – Convergence, Flux of Utterance, Mistakes'. (O'Sullivan, 2003, p. 64)

Reference to mistakes and – above – to 'sway substances', introduces a more contemporary figure, Joseph Beuys, although his 'concern for the retrieval of potentials within material' is compared to Schwitters'. (O'Sullivan, 2003, p. 67) But whereas a Schwitters assemblage is produced by an act of transformation, Beuys' art was so often the staging of an act of transformation. Indeed, 'in 1988,' O'Sullivan explains, 'after having been involved in the transformative experience of working on a television film on Beuys, I stepped out, away from the city to the moorland impress of tongue.' (O'Sullivan, 2003, p. 67) Passing over O'Sullivan's characteristic representation of landscape as 'tonguescape' (with its faint echo of Hopkins' theory of inscape), the work on Beuys preceded her resigning as a researcher on the BBC Arena programme. On arriving in the North (see her poem 'Narrative Charm for Ibbotroyd' in *In the House of the Shaman* for an anticipatory take on this move, (O'Sullivan, 1993, p. 44) she 'praised the trees & hugged & planted them – to make a wood', we are told. This reads at first sight as an embarrassing exhibition of hippie-dom, until it is recalled that one of Beuys' last works of art was indeed the planting of 7000 trees for the future of the world. Beuys' 'GuiDance', as she puts it, teaches a more kinetic sense of materiality. Beuys obsessively used certain materials, among them bees' wax, felt and fat, because they preserved energy. But in the case of fat it could also *transform* itself, as in his *Fat Chair*. Fineberg writes and quotes Beuys:

> The chair conforms to human anatomy and order. Fat signifies chaos because it undergoes radical metamorphosis with subtle shifts in temperature. For Beuys, 'everything is in a *state of change*' and the resulting 'chaos can have a healing character'. (Fineberg, 2000, p. 233)

O'Sullivan herself adapts some words of Beuys: 'FIRST I USED RUBBER, IT DID NOT SATISFY ME BECAUSE IT WAS TOO DIRECT, TOO DIDACTIC AND THEREFORE QUICKLY REDUNDANT'. (O'Sullivan, 2003, p. 61; on

p. 68 she quotes Beuys considering the texture of felt.) It may seem strange to think of the didacticism of unchanging (merely pliable) rubber, but Beuys' desire for the entropic and non-didactic translates directly into O'Sullivan's arguments about language. An obdurate thingness in language might become as didactic as didacticism itself: meaningless sound or unreadable ink. But in the movement that puns and neologisms provide, there is a kind of hypnotic sinking into the layers of language, semantic, associational, sonic, and even somatic: something the reader of both Joyce and O'Sullivan experiences in different ways (although Joyce additionally mimes the dissolving of dreams through the punning narratives). This is one reason why 'river-running (realisations' with all its Joycean 'HITHER AND THITHERING' (O'Sullivan, 2003, p. 62; Joyce, 1975, p. 216) edits in numerous quotations from O'Sullivan's poems, even weaves their textures into one passage which begins quite coherently (even didactically in its way) on the subject of her appropriations from Beuys, focussing on the title of her 1993 book:

> 'In the House of the Shaman' is borrowed from the title of one of Beuys' drawings. In naming my work after his I am tributing his work: fluid, changing, inviting new material, urging new responses. His urge to begin with mistakes, to show frailty . . . is at once starfish abdominal nuance its moorings unsuspected – rescued starlight. (O'Sullivan, 2003, p. 68)

The juxtaposition that produces the suggested sentence 'His urge . . . is . . . starfish', is beautiful and mysterious, an act of textual transformation that is also a tribute. Indeed – although she does not indicate this in 'riverrunning (realisations' – Beuys furnishes one of the epigraphs O'Sullivan uses in *In the House of the Shaman*, which praises the mutable materiality that both artists share with the practices of shamanism: 'To stress the idea of transformation and of substance. This is precisely what the shaman does in order to bring about change and development: his nature is therapeutic'. (O'Sullivan, 1993, p. 28)

Shamanism is present in a number of recent works, from J.H. Prynne, in a text like 'Aristeas, in Seven Years', which makes much of historical references (included at the end of the text), (Prynne 1982: 89–5) to the poetry of Tom Lowenstein, who has conducted ethnological fieldwork among the Inuit. When it appears in parodic form in the novels of Iain Sinclair and Angela Carter it can be used to telling literary effect. Even the sense in which Beuys – ventriloquised through O'Sullivan – uses it as an analogue for artistic practice, places it just within the realms of materialist ethics and poetics. Beuys figures shamanism as both conceptual and therapeutic. O'Sullivan eulogises 'the idea of transformation' throughout 'riverrunning (realisations', 'counter to the inert everydom that breathes the slave', as she beautifully puts it, again putting a political gloss on such imaginative transformations. (O'Sullivan, 2000, p. 54) But it is a shame that this passage has been removed from the final text. More positively, O'Sullivan has also removed from the book publication the politically negative remark, 'Beyond the materialist world', which undercuts her insistence upon materiality and suggests that some of the materials from ethnology and ethnopoetics that she will introduce, imply a metaphysical view of the world. (O'Sullivan, 2000, p. 54) Both deleted phrases might also have been regarded by O'Sullivan as didactic as Beuys' rubber, of course.

It is almost impossible to use the word 'ethnopoetics' without conjuring the name of the American poet and anthologist Jerome Rothenberg. Not that he has an exclusive interest in Native American poetry, or ancient texts, such as the numerology of the Gematria, since he is just as likely to be writing versions of Lorca, praising his Dada forebears (such as Schwitters) or excavating his own Eastern European Jewish heritage. In other words, his encompassing of the modernist and post modernist traditions and his considerations of shamanistic practices (in the past and in the present) perfectly mirrors the practice of O'Sullivan (or Beuys for that matter). One passage of 'riverrunning (realisations', a kind of verse paragraph, lists various arguments for the 'Materiality of Language' and then states emphatically, 'Also, the jubilant seep In So of Spirit' which praises shamanistic 'Articulations of the Earth of Language'. (O'Sullivan, 2003, p. 64) It is no wonder that O'Sullivan writes of her kindred spirit: 'Jerome Rothenberg and the exemplary work he makes wide is a key, too in my workings.' (O'Sullivan, 2003, p. 68) If at times he is too eager to collapse cultural distinctions (to see ancient texts as close to contemporary practice, to see 'coincidences between "primitive-archaic" & modern thought') (Rothenberg, 1981, p. 186), O'Sullivan's term 'a richness of difference' is a precise delineation of Rothenberg's work, particularly in performance. (O'Sullivan, 2003, p. 68) I am a veteran of hundreds of poetry readings, but one of the best was a Sub Voicive reading in London at which Rothenberg read a staggeringly varied programme. (His work as an anthologist is exemplary too, although I have similar reservations about his over-enthusiastic universalism which threatens to elide the 'difference' O'Sullivan justly celebrates. O'Sullivan herself is one of the few British-based writers to find her way into the second volume of the Rothenberg and Joris anthology, *Poems for the Millennium*.) Rothenberg's own writings on shamanism emphasise the equivalence between the Rimbaudian 'seer' and the traditional shaman, whose 'specialised technique' makes him (or her) 'a proto-poet, for almost always his technique hinges on the creation of special linguistic circumstances, i.e., of song & invocation'. (Rothenberg, 1981, p. 186) O'Sullivan quotes from her own 'Doubtless' again,

> THE SOILS OF
> SPELLING,
> SCRYED

to suggest the magic of language that is also 'A Blessing. A Curse' as well as 'A Spell' or even 'A Riddle winding Prayer'. (O'Sullivan, 2003, pp. 59–60) The shaman's trance and transformation (he or she may visit the land of the dead, enter into the spirit of a totemic animal or speak with the voice of an ancestor or god) seems to be hinted at in the lines

> Drifting, Shape-Shifting thinner stringed 8 leaning Loanded Ebb – like all dredger sepulchral – hold it/don't – (O'Sullivan, 2003, pp. 69).

The 2003 text breaks here where in earlier versions of 'riverrunning (realisations' it continued 'don't lose your expression', which again perhaps too explicitly tells the reader, rather than embodies the idea, of the precious expressiveness valorised here. But it is an expression suffused with the lexis of flow and transformation, although it also suggests that the sepulchral needs to be excavated. Could this be the sepulchre wherein St Patrick received the vision of god, although the shifting of shape more readily suggests Cuchullain in his battle frenzy? (See Flower, 1947, p. 8) 'Loanded' suggests the 'loan words' we receive from other languages, as indeed we have the word 'shaman' from Tungus, as Rothenberg and Eliade and others have pointed out. (Rothenberg, 1981, p. 186; Kershaw Chadwick, 1942, p. 15)

If, as Rothenberg claims, 'the new shaman experiences the breakdown of his familiar consciousness or world-view', then O'Sullivan seems to be presenting an analogue of this in a passage that piles her familiar negatives onto a dissolution of self (a process in the poetry which, as we have seen, Isobel Armstrong comments upon). (Rothenberg, 1981, p. 186) It stutteringly spells out an act through which one might un-identify with the self.

> Sounded by Un – I DENT / if /EYE / where, to, to, towards the far end – far away from: at fault: breach: in error: at a loss: outlying: rules out: caesarian: exiled: unknown: outCRY july i (O'Sullivan, 2003, p. 62)

This is also a gendered experience, marked by the rupture of childbirth. While for Rothenberg the shaman is representatively male, one of O'Sullivan's 'sources' used in her book, although somewhat dated, N. Kerhsaw Chadwick's *Poetry and Prophesy* of 1942, acknowledges the existence of shamanesses. As the book's title suggests, it emphasises the literary in the shamanistic experience, so that 'the gift of poetry is inseparable from divine inspiration'. (Kershaw Chadwick, 1942, p. 14) The shaman is often 'called'; in O'Sullivan's version of involuntary inspiration this becomes, as I have shown earlier, 'Poetry finds my life.' (O'Sullivan, 2003, p. 63) But *Poetry and Prophesy* also expresses scepticism about the claims of shamans to enter trance states, sees certain practices as, if not fraudulent, then as sleights of voice: talking in nonsense syllables (which are often a neighbouring district's dialect), for example. What is stressed, in the book, and what might well have appealed to O'Sullivan, is both the fact that the shaman 'holds a high status' (as opposed to the status of the Linguistically Innovative poet in contemporary Britain) *and* that knowledge and appropriate training were as important as inspiration. (Kershaw Chadwick, 1942, p. 14) 'The shamans are responsible for the preservation and transmission of all their aesthetic-poetical riches.' (Kershaw Chadwick, 1942, p. 44) Their archival function is often matched with an advanced performativity. 'Skill in the pedantic use of phrase and artificial language' was particularly prized amongst the ancient Irish. (Kershaw Chadwick, 1942, p. 48) O'Sullivan's increasing mining of her Irish heritage (which I deliberately have not hitherto dealt with) is tied to her shamanistic impulse, and is also reinforced by Kershaw Chadwick's statement that 'the cloak of the Irish poets and seers, largely composed of birds' feathers, recalls the costumes of the Siberian shamans'. (Birds' feathers are to be found often in O'Sullivan's assemblages; see the cover of O'Sullivan 1993 and compare to the photograph of a 'Buryat Shaman in ecstasy', Kershaw Chadwick, 1942, p. 65).

This Irish heritage is both cultural and personal. Elsewhere, in the poem '–that bread may be–', O'Sullivan notes both that 'Skibbereen was one of the most severely stricken areas of Ireland during the continuous famine,' and that 'half of my family' hail from there. (O'Sullivan, 1996, n.p.) In the 'Numerology' section of 'riverunning (realisations', which is prefaced with the characteristically negative words, 'It's easy to loss here', O'Sullivan notes that her skilled, but poor, grandfather was a mower, de-skilled by the development of mowing machines. However, this is counterpointed by the observation that 'Electricity didn't come to Skibbereen until 1962', which resists the romanticisation of rural labour, while reminding the modern reader of the comparatively recent development of remoter parts of Ireland. (O'Sullivan, 2003, p. 66) The Cromwellian genocide is invoked when O'Sullivan slightly adapts a startling quotation from Sean O'Faolain's *The Irish* (a book not designed to pander to Republican mythology, incidentally) which states that 'any man could earn £5 by producing the head of a wolf or a priest – it didn't matter which'. (O'Sullivan, 2003, p. 66; O'Faolain, 1947, p. 109) An offence against one of the poets is recorded in another of her liftings, this time from Robin Flower's book *The Irish Tradition*: 'One of the MacBrodins, poets of Clare, was cast over a cliff by a Cromwellian soldier who cried after him as he fell: "Sing now, little man".' (O'Sullivan, 2003, p. 66; Flower, 1947, p. 171) This is not just an act of cruelty but is used by Flower to indicate how 'at home the poets plunged deeper into destitution and despair . . . gradual degradation'. (Flower, 1947, pp. 170–1) Curiously O'Sullivan anglicises the quotation (which has the effect of making the soldier more English); in Flower, the soldier cries, 'Sing your rann now, little man!' (Flower, 1947, p. 171) The word 'rann' may be a contraction of the Irish *amhráin*, which O'Sullivan uses elsewhere. Once she has quoted Joyce – the single modernist Irish influence – concluding her opening meditation upon 'talk', O'Sullivan considers the nature of the relationship between saying and singing, which is little less than a consideration of the nature of poetry itself.

In Irish, AMHRAIN: CEOL:
A Song, A Song Said Otherwise, half-sung/half-said,
SINGS . . ..
The Irish again – ABAIR AMHRAIN – Say us a Song – (O'Sullivan, 2003, p. 59)

The passage liberally quotes from Séan Mac Réamoinn's introduction to his anthology *The Pleasures of Gaelic Poetry*, as well as from 'Doubtless' again (the 'half-sung/half-said' refers there to the scraps of traditional, probably Republican, ballads printed in that poem (O'Sullivan, 2003, p. 51–2).) The original Mac Réamoinn passage would clearly bolster O'Sullivan's oral poetic thinking and acts as a commentary on O'Sullivan's condensed poetics:

> I have referred to verse being either spoken or sung. This had had two lasting effects: the first being that poetry and music remained close allies to the point of some lexical ambiguity – *amhrán* can mean either a verse-form or a song; *ceol*, the usual word for music, may in Ulster be used of a spoken poem; and *abair amhrán!* ('say a song'!) is a common phrase of encouragement to the native *virtuoso*.' (Mac Réamoinn, 1982, p. 14)

In this passage one finds again an insistence upon poetic skill as a social function, and 'a long tradition of professionalism in Gaelic poetry', one that causes Mac Réamoinn to tell his own tale, part of which O'Sullivan quotes. (Mac Réamoinn, 1982, p. 14) He asked a 'farmer in a hayfield' about the poems of Raftery, which he could sing, along with anonymous folk songs. Asked how he could tell 'a great poet', the farmer replied, 'Better words . . . better placed . . . *the way you'd be building a wall and you'd know where to put the bricks*'. (Mac Réamoinn, 1982, pp. 14–5; O'Sullivan, 2003, p. 68; O'Sullivan quotes the words I have italicised.) This admission of skill, Mac Réamoinn comments, also acknowledges that 'poetic inheritance by blood is indeed part of the story', (Mac Réamoinn, 1982, p. 15) 'Live Blood' O'Sullivan calls it, perhaps thinking of her own Irish descent, and sensing, or hoping for, its connection with the shamanistic tradition, so that 'Then. Now. There. Here' exist in harmony. (O'Sullivan, 2003, p. 59)

O'Sullivan's poetry generally, and her work of poetics in particular, abound with linguistic transformations of the natural world (many more than I have quoted examples of here) and nature itself is presented as readable as a text:

TREMORING BUSTLE & MUTE
(– WRENS CROSS MY PATH –)
DO PLAY, DO SIGN (O'Sullivan, 2003, p. 61)

O'Sullivan celebrates vegetal and animal creation, as well as 'intervals between' species, which she traverses, like a shaman: (O'Sullivan, 2003, p. 64)

> interspeciel/interrrelamic Joy: stone of light water, flaxfield,
> scrub of juniper, shifting in the life of trees: SMALL PERPETUAL
> REDS OF HEAD & YELLOW SCARLETS / HURLING CLAW STUT

PIGMENT (BE IT FISH MAMMAL OR BIRD). (O'Sullivan, 2003, p. 68) Indeed, it is with a shamanistic bird that 'riverrunning (realisations' concludes. The words '& then maybe you go to another place' introduces the complete poem '2nd Lesson from the Cockerel' and suggests the model of shamanistic trance favoured by Rothenberg. (This ' 2nd lesson', and the first, originally appeared in *Unofficial Word* in 1988, but were written 1986–7.) The poem itself celebrates, and perhaps mourns, the 'RED STROUDERS DEW-BUCKLING WINTER', but the 'MUSEY TIGHT SADDED', the 'TONGUE-A-SAD-OF-ALL-BIRDS', their 'SHOT-OVER BELLIES READ WITH JASPER' result in the glorious 'JUTTING MULTIPLICATION' with which the poem of the eighties, and O'Sullivan's poetics of the nineties, triumphantly ends. (O'Sullivan, 2003, p. 70)

One result of the poetics developed here by O'Sullivan lies in the poetry it has provoked. 'Doubtless', which is quoted, often in altered (or earlier) versions, and – *that bread should be* – seem obvious candidates but *Red Shifts*, 'pre-text', 'Waterfall' and 'Winter Ceremony' also suggest themselves (although it is beyond the focus of this essay to examine these).[5] To suppose so is to point to one of the principal aims and uses of poetics as I have defined it. Despite its public oral and textural presentations, poetics is often aimed at the writer herself. As acts of reflective writing engage with previous acts of creative writing, they suggest, without dictating, the nature of the generation of further works of art. Poetics is less an argument than a working through. Those who read 'riverrunning (realisations' should not be too surprised to see the sources O'Sullivan uses fragmented and dispersed, unattributed and cut up. I have followed some of these trails in the production of this critical article to elucidate the process of thinking that went into the creation of a fascinating piece of poetics. In some ways this violates its teasing integrity. It risks taking the performative out of the writing, wherein lies the energising sense that here are hints and gists and names and piths to provoke further acts of creativity (or poetics), either O'Sullivan's or any of her auditors' and readers'. I have not, I hope, treated it simply as an essay. Its formal construction deliberately obviates this option; poetics will often *embody* the creative design decisions it suggests. Yet neither have I treated it as a poem, in that it announces at moments claims to provisional truths of an intellectual kind that belong to, or at least allude to, expository prose. These include authorial filiations to other artists who share her sense of linguistic materiality *and* transformation, and to those who share her belief in the apposite nature of the shamanistic metaphor, which she uses to express both her growing sense of (lost?) Irishness and the sense of her kinship with nature. Her sense of shamanism as a model for a developed and skilful social and cultural function for poetry today is paramount.

So why do we read poetics? It depends who we are. If we are the author, then we might use it to experiment with ideas for future work. We have no need of footnotes and citations, may indeed wish to develop the text (as O'Sullivan does) using the very techniques creative work employs. If we are other writers we read it, to some extent, against our own practice, either as a spur to creativity or to poetics itself, positively or negatively. If we are critics we can, if we choose, treat poetics as a secondary discourse that informs the author's writing, and the critic's reading, of the primary texts, though we would be wise to observe the mismatch there nearly always will be between poetics and creative writing. Much wiser (and I hope this has been my approach) is to read the poetics as an *act* of poetics, respecting its general nature, tracing not just the ideas contained in the piece, but the energy that runs through it, its provocation to creative writing and creative reading. There is little evidence that published work on poetics takes this critical approach.

One issue worries me. Can any of these readers *contest* a poetics? Crudely put, can we say a poetics is wrong? We may say Pound was wrong about the Chinese written character but wonderfully right in his development of the ideogrammic method, which he derived from it (although these are differing uses of *wrong* and *right*, one being factual, the other an aesthetic judgement). We are more concerned that Pound was wrong in his politics than his poetics (which is not to deny a connection between the two). What would it mean to challenge O'Sullivan's shamanistic borrowings as essentialist or partial? Would it matter that her 'sources' date from the 1940s? Or that her sense of Irishness might be thought by some to be selective and romantic? Put another way, if, as Charles Bernstein says, 'The test of a poetics is the poetry and the poetic thinking that results,' are these questions pertinent? (Bernstein, 1992, p. 166)

I suspect the answer lies in the fact that a useable *metapoetics* has yet to develop as a critical tool, to allow poetics its specificity as a discourse, while being able to make statements (other than creative writing itself or more poetics, which are the obvious writerly responses) about the appropriateness or efficacy of the discourse. Just as I suspect that poetics itself appears intermittently and surprisingly in other discourses, it may be that metapoetics appears in creative writing, poetics and even in critical writings (like this present essay). Perhaps 'riverrunning (realisations' carries its own self-critique, 'Challenging/ Transpiring / Provoking' itself, (O'Sullivan, 2003, p. 66) in its insistent and original 'urging' of 'new responses'. (O'Sullivan, 2003, p. 68.)

Robert Sheppard
Edge Hill University

This essay was written with the help of financial assistance from the Edge Hill University Research Development Fund, which is gratefully acknowledged. Thanks also too to Nate Dorward for answering a question so promptly.

Notes

1 To give one successful example of each: the 'Talks' series at Birkbeck College, curated by Robert Hampson, tellingly established by Perelman during a London exchange year, continues. SubVoicive colloquia, curated by Lawrence Upton, have been fruitful. There have been a number of large academic conferences, including 'Performing the Word' at Oxford Brookes University, May 2001, coordinated by Romana Huk, another American.

2 Bernstein's poem may be found in his 1992 *A Poetics*. Cambridge and London: Harvard University Press, pp. 9–89. Andrews' essay may be found in his 1996 *Paradise and Method: Poetics and Praxis*. Evanston: Northwestern University Press, pp. 227–31.

3 On Maggie O'Sullivan's work I have written 'Tune Me Gold: Notes on the Total Technique of Maggie O'Sullivan' in my 1999 *Far Language: poetics and linguistically innovative poetry 1978–1997*. Exeter: Stride Research Documents. pp. 51–53. See also chapter 10, 'Be come, Be spoke, Be eared: The Poetics of Transformation and Embodied Utterance in the work of Maggie O'Sullivan in the 1980s and 1990s', in my book *The Poetry of Saying: British Poetry and Its Discontents 1950–2000*. 2005. Liverpool: Liverpool University Press: 233–249. On poetics I have published a long essay collected as *The Necessity of Poetics*. 2002. Liverpool: Ship of Fools. This first

appeared as 'The Poetics of Writing: The Writing of Poetics', published in the proceedings of *the 1998 Conference on Creative Writing in Higher Education*, Sheffield Hallam University, and then as 'The Necessity of Poetics' on the PORES website, at www.bbk.ac.uk/pores/1/index.htm. See also 'The Poetics of Poetics: Charles Bernstein and Allen Fisher', in *Symbiosis*, 3:1, April 1999, for another account of writers' actual poetics.

[4] Writing about O'Sullivan in *The Poetry of Saying*, I quote Bakhtin: "'The movement that generates acoustical sound, and is most active in the articulatory organs, although it takes hold of the whole organism . . . is incommensurably more important than what is *heard*", not in a retreat from meaning, but because the poem has "taken possession of the whole active human being" (Bakhtin, 1990, p. 318). This literal incarnation, at the moment that poetic language comes into being, is what O'Sullivan achieves when she turns ideolect to a kind of dialect. Her "Earloads" are becoming *physical* burdens, for the performer-poet, as in Bakhtin's formulation of the lyric, "when the body, generating the sound from within itself and feeling the unity of its own productive exertion, is drawn into form." (Bakhtin, 1990, p. 314) This birth of language (a metaphor which unites nature and culture) is indeed a glorification of productive exertion in the body: the word made flesh.' (Sheppard 2005: 241–2.)

[5] 'Doubtless' appears in O'Sullivan 2003, pp. 31–56, and dominates the volume. The text – *that bread should be* – is the whole of O'Sullivan 1996. *Red Shifts* was published by Etruscan Books: Newcastle Under Lyme, in 2001, 'pre-text' appeared in Iain Sinclair's 1996 anthology *Conductors of Chaos* (London: Picador), pp. 307–14. 'Winter Ceremony' was included in the 1997 Etruscan Reader number three, pp. 1–15. 'Waterfall' appeared in *Pages 421–445*, pp. 422–428. *Pages 429–445* also features Lawrence Upton's long essay on O'Sullivan, 'Regarding Maggie O'Sullivan's Poetry'.

Bibliography

Andrews, B. and O'Sullivan, M. 1993. *Excla*. London: Writers Forum.

Bakhtin, M.M. 1990. *Art and Answerability*. Austin: The University of Texas Press.

Bernstein, C. 1998. ed. *Close Listening: Poetry and the Performed Word*. New York Oxford: Oxford University Press.

Bernstein, C. 1992. *A Poetics*, Cambridge. Mass: Harvard University Press.

DuPlessis, R.B. 1990. *The Pink Guitar, Writing as Feminist Practice*. New York and London: Routledge.

Fineberg, J. 2000 (second edition). *Art Since 1940*. London: Laurence King.

Mac S. Réamoinn. 1982. *The Pleasures of Gaelic Poetry*: London: Allen Lane.

Mark, A., and Rees-Jones, eds., 2000. *Contemporary Women's Poetry: Reading/Writing/Practice*. Basingstoke and London: Palgrave.

O'Faolain, S. 1947. *The Irish*. West Drayton: Pelican Books.

O'Sullivan, M. 1988. *Unofficial Word*. Newcastle upon Tyne: Galloping Dog Press.

O'Sullivan, M. 1993. *In the House of the Shaman*. London and Cambridge: Reality Street Editions.

O'Sullivan, M. 1996. *– that bread should be –*. Sutton: RWC.

O'Sullivan, M. 2000. 'riverrunning (realisations For Charles Bernstein' in Mark, A., and Rees-Jones, eds., 2000. *Contemporary Women's Poetry: Reading/Writing/Practice*. Basingstoke and London: Palgrave, pp. 47–57.

O'Sullivan, M. 2003. *Palace of Reptiles*. Willowdale: The Gig.

Perelman, B. 1998. 'Speech Effects: The Talk as Genre', in Bernstein 1998, pp. 200–216.

Perloff, M. 2002. *21st-Century Modernism*. Oxford and Malden: Blackwells.

Prynne, J.H. 1982. *Poems*. Lewes: Agneau 2.

Pound, E. 'How to Read', in ed. Eliot, T.S. 1954. *Literary Essays of Ezra Pound*. London: Faber and Faber. pp. 15–40.

Rothenberg, J. 1981. *Pre-Faces & Other Writings*. New York: New Directions.

Schultz, S. 1997.'Poetics at Buffalo', in *Boxkite: A journal of poetry and poetics*, number 1, pp. 137–9.

Sheppard, R. 2002 *The Necessity of Poetics*. Liverpool: Ship of Fools.

Sheppard. R. 2005. *The Poetry of Saying: British Poetry and its Discontents 1950–2000*. Liverpool: Liverpool University Press.

The Tate Gallery. 1985. *Kurt Schwitters*. Tate Gallery: London.

States of Transformation: Maggie O'Sullivan's 'Busk, Pierce' and Excla

Scott Thurston

Maggie O'Sullivan's 'Busk, Pierce' from *States of Emergency* (1987) is a remarkable poem which is exemplary of the sheer energy and exuberance of her output. It is also especially interesting by virtue of its inclusion of a diagram taken from Claude Lévi-Strauss' book *Structural Anthropology* (1968). In this essay I offer a detailed reading of the poem, and explore it through the link with Lévi-Strauss, developing an awareness of the metaphor of shamanism in relation to O'Sullivan's poetics. I then trace this poetics in the different context of O'Sullivan's collaboration with the North American Language Poet Bruce Andrews, entitled *Excla* (1993), drawing comparisons between their approaches and recognising how the shared technique of the book enables both Andrews' socio-linguistic critique and O'Sullivan's 'shamanic' approach.

O'Sullivan's poetry strikes the eye and ear first before specific meanings begin to establish themselves. Short lines, often reminiscent of Anglo Saxon alliterative verse: 'gutteral gardenias | screed | sneak', 'leaden | belenders | lie & blister', and multiple margins skew across the page instilling the poem's figure with kinetic energy. Instead of syntactically normative sentences, the main unit is the phrase, poised and juxtaposed in space and given extra energy by the high frequency of neologisms. Constructing a meaning-paraphrase of the poem necessitates a focus on local intensities – as the poem is structured in an accretive, musical way, rather than by narrative or lyric argument.

The poem opens with the italicised phrase *'Injure Tinglit'* which acts almost as a sub-title. *'Tinglit'* contains within it an unavoidable echo of the Tlingit: the Native American tribe of peoples who inhabit parts of Alaska. To *'Injure Tinglit'* might be an imperative from another voice being confronted in the poem – as if to announce the concerns of the poem as a possible protest against the persecution of indigenous peoples.

The second line 'fusen deam stroboscope deam skidder' appears linked to the first in that both are separated from the main body of the text by a long dash. The line illustrates O'Sullivan's juxtaposing approach to syntax and can be read as enacting an exchange of semantic energy from one end to the other. This arises from the two end words 'fusen' and 'skidder': 'fusen' suggesting a state of fusedness, perhaps coherency or burnt-outness, and 'skidder' suggesting one who habitually skids, careers, perhaps out of control. Between these two words and the central word 'stroboscope' – an instrument for determining speeds of rotation by flashing intermittently – the repetition of the neologism 'deam' is suggestive. One can imagine the line as a small machine with the stroboscope in the centre sending out light flashes (or 'd-r-eams') which illuminate the words 'fusen' and 'skidder' at the ends, both of which may be outcomes of some kind of process – 'fusen' denoting the receipt of the charge and 'skidder' the physical use of that energy. Placed near the beginning of the poem, and in proximity to '*Injure Tinglit*' this line may be read as enacting the means by which this issue will be explored – through an exploration of the materiality of language, rather than through didactic, rhetorical means.

The neologism 'TLOKETS' stands at the opening of the poem proper: a suggestive agglomerate of tokens, lockets, tickets. If these are what the reader needs to gain entry to the poem then it seems we are immediately within a register of mourning and death:

> TLOKETS
> mourn, leaden
>
> belenders
> lie & blister——
> fetched silvers, these
> *NECRO*
> gutteral gardenias————

                    (O'Sullivan, 1987: unp.)

Nevertheless, it is difficult to read these lines with anything like a stable paraphrase-able content. That the 'TLOKETS' 'mourn, leaden' suggests a possible echo of lead figurines used in ancient mourning practices – whilst 'belenders', also a possible object of 'leaden', evokes both the notion of 'blending', which seems an apt term for how neologisms are formed in this poem, and a new noun evoking something borrowed or lent. 'Belenders' can also be the subject of 'lie & blister' where 'lie' is suggestively ambiguous. The theme of death becomes writ large in the word '*NECRO*', whilst the 'fetched silvers' suggests some kind of salver, as if something is being presented to someone in authority. The 'gutteral gardenias' conflate orality with the conventionally mute, in a way which seems in tune with other evocations of death, objects and nature in this poem, underscored by alliteration.

The verbs and potential verbs here: 'mourn', 'belenders', 'lie', 'blister', 'fetched' seem to sketch out an impression of a funerary rite vitiated with exchanges, deceit and injury in the absence of the power of the dead: as if a vacuum has been created which is releasing old hostilities. The subsequent lines 'screed | sneak tintering || Grief Entry' can be read as extending this argument: the screed – an unduly long harangue that takes the form of a list of grievances – seems an appropriate artefact in this provisional semantic context. That it is linked with 'sneak tintering' suggests a divisive cunning taking the form of tinting or tinkering with that list which evokes the 'Grief Entry' of the funeral itself, or tomb.

The 'screed' joins up with other intensities in the poem which seem to figure the position of the maker of the poem within the possible context being described: a 'Jagged Pebble Song' is evoked, as is an 'inadequate coal'; suggestive of the Shelleyan 'fading coal' of the mind in creation. What links these evocations of text together are the different forms of rock: pebble and coal, alongside a possible pun on 'scree' – as a pile of loose rocks on a mountainside. Another sustained section also seems to enact statements about the nature of textuality:

        O
how the filthy
        Keepsakes
Truckle Back Tripling
        Ash.
Ink, launjer, red on leash,
        BLOOD.
Crooked Swatch (ish. yellow) ———
    Fling Flaunden
        Sheenies

Quick Poppy Tie of Axe ————
Drumcut strip strung twists
       brooch
          &
pen Funerary tabletter, armistice,
        Drown!
                  (O'Sullivan, 1987)

In this section more conventional lyric markers such as 'O' and the concluding exclamation give firmer indicators of tone. It is possible that the *tlokets* of earlier are refigured as 'filthy | Keepsakes' – their possible function as grave objects reversed to what one might carry to remember the dead. The attitude towards these objects as 'filthy' suggests rejection and anger and, as the section builds, it becomes possible to place the death that is hinted of as taking place in the context of war. The keepsakes 'Truckle Back Tripling | Ash', where 'Truckle' – with its possible meanings of submitting to authority as well as a pun on 'trickle' (as in to 'trickle back') – results in the 'Tripling' (i.e. a multiplication) of 'Ash', which could bring the crematoria of Auschwitz into the poem's frame. At this point the *tlokets* and the filthy keepsakes might be seen as the plunder extracted by the Nazis from their victims. The next line appears to be refiguring the writer's place in this situation in a complex way – perhaps one informed by an Adornian poetics: 'Ink, launjer, red on leash, | BLOOD'. The mention of 'Ink' suggests the writer's activity, although the proximity of *blood* suggests an identification between the two substances. Whilst 'launjer' is hard to resolve semantically, it can be heard as a pun on 'lounger' – almost as if the writer is being taken to task for a relaxed complicity in the face of horror. Like the word *necro* earlier – the word *blood* emphasises the concerns here – that 'red' is 'on leash' suggests that it is controlled but can also be *un-leash*ed at any point.

'Crooked Swatch (ish. yellow)' evokes the criminality of the situation, its crookedness, with 'Swatch', read as a sample of cloth qualified in an unusual way as '(ish. yellow)', might suggest a Star of David. The imperative to 'Fling Flaunden | Sheenies' evokes uncomfortably the disposal of corpses – reading 'Sheenies' as a derogatory term for Jew, and 'Flaunden' as a corrupted flaunt. The next line 'Quick Poppy Tie of Axe' also seems to stage a scene of execution, although the word 'Poppy' might be recuperated more straightwardly in a frame connected to the First World War, as does 'armistice' a few lines later. The 'Drumcut strips strung twists | brooch', with its virtuoso sound play, seems to turn back towards a possible figure of an artist/musician, but the 'pen Funerary tabletter' seems more strongly to evoke a writer who bears witness to events by pen, on the tablet of a gravestone or monument and possibly even by the 'tab' and 'letter' keys of a typewriter. That an armistice is mentioned shortly before the exclamation 'Drown!' creates a pessimistic tone to the close of this section – although one which seems vitiated by a righteous anger that is evoked as much by the sheer energy of sound and rhythm as by its connotative possibilities.

This anger can be felt elsewhere in the poem in lines like 'Dolly Puke, Doily flak, Pinnie Gullet' where, although the intensity of sound play almost boils over into pathos, there seems to be an argument of association implicating a feminist critique of female domestic experience. This is suggested by the metonymic chain of *dolly-doily-pinnie* linked with violent symptoms of rebellious reaction: *puke, flak* and *gullet* – where the gullet functions as the medium for vomit and invective. This line is immediately followed by 'KISS MY ARSE | | rebellion | backwards', where the rebellion so strongly evoked seems rather condemned to failure. The poem ends with a forceful conclusion enacting the 'states of emergency' of the book's title:

> *zigzag, plateau, zigzag*
> GRIEVED, GROUND,
>
> knarls move/Expulsions Deal/Galliards
> Brung,
> *FLAME & WILDERNESS.*
>
> (O'Sullivan, 1987)

The '*zigzag, plateau, figure*' suggests a graph of intensities where a line is measuring some kind of process or activity with peaks and levels. The 'GRIEVED, GROUND' echoes the 'Grief Entry' of the earlier part of the poem, and yet *ground*'s association with land appears to historicize the phenomenon of death as, potentially, a consequence of colonial conquest. O'Sullivan's awareness of the history of Ireland (see my 1999 interview with O'Sullivan) may be relevant here as the word 'Expulsions' – alongside the actions of moving, dealing and bringing – suggests processes associated with colonial projects. 'Knarls' functions as a possible reference to wood, whilst 'Galliards' – a Celtic word meaning a dance in triple time (which looks back to the 'tripling' encountered earlier and the threefold processes described here) – is more difficult to resolve. It can also mean 'valiant strength' which could be positive or ironic in this context. At any rate, the poem refuses to resolve any semantic tension and closes with the bleak invocation of '*FLAME & WILDERNESS*' – evoking a past, present or future disaster.

Such paraphrases may or may not convince a reader tackling the interpretive difficulties of this poem. Indeed, it may be inappropriate to attempt to force such a poem to *mean* when it invests so much energy in avoiding easily recuperable patterns of sense. What one experiences instead is an overwhelming sense of immersion in language – in the very interstices of meaning and history. Robert Sheppard has described this poetry as 'the very creation of meaning' (Sheppard, 1999: p. 52), which gets close to explaining why it is hard to paraphrase it. Despite this, one certainly registers strong meaning-impressions on reading the work, due at least in part to its powerful and relentless sound symbolism. As many commentators have pointed out, these impressions are particularly rich when hearing the work read by the author.

There is indeed reason to suggest that O'Sullivan regards her writing as primarily an aural experience which is then notated on the secondary medium of the page. In his essay 'The Contemporary Poetry Reading' (1998), Peter Middleton provides a valuable summary of various commentators' responses to O'Sullivan's work, whilst speculating on the relationship between speech and writing. Pointing to the 'indeterminacy of writing's representation of sound' Middleton suggests that poets may be 'trying to utilize an imperfect set of written signs to indicate aural complexities that then compel new forms of recognition of links between thought and language' (Middleton, 1998: p. 288). This almost suggests that the performance of a poem could be considered as primary, whilst the text exists only as a notation of it, a score for re-performance. O'Sullivan herself has discussed this relationship in a statement she produced in *Word Score Utterance Choreography* (1998):

> spoken or performed aloud – a text dances its
> sonic selves in depths different from written or
> marked – different weights vernaculars gestures
> colourings & magnetisms – different mobilities

different errrings birth & shimmer
(O'Sullivan, 1998: unp.)

Similarly, she characterises the process of writing as one in which

> i allow the musics and airs of the verbal word/sound
> patterns in the ear my work is gestured or danced around
> to suggest their visual & sonic locations within the
> page's ground
(O'Sullivan, 1998)

The latter remark suggests that for O'Sullivan the act of writing is itself a kind of performance. She refers to the 'constructional | performative dynamics & magnetisms of a text's | emerging' and yet when it comes to live performance part of the intention is 'to enact | &/or further improvise/discourse upon the | marks/signs of a text by bodying forth fresh | aural oral torsional terrains' (O'Sullivan, 1998).

There is, however, a part of 'Busk, Pierce' which remains relatively silent on the page, transmitting as it does a primarily visual impression. Whilst suggestive of a scored sound pattern, to sound this figure with the voice would be a challenge:

```
1    2        4            7
     2   3    4        6        8
1             4    5        7    8
1    2             5        7
         3    4        6        8
```
(O'Sullivan, 1987)

An identical pattern of numbers is also to be found in Claude Lévi-Strauss' book *Structural Anthropology* (1968), suggesting that O'Sullivan is in some way 'quoting' it in her poem. In order to consider what this might mean in the context of the poem so far read, it is necessary to look at this design in its original context.

In Lévi-Strauss' book the pattern functions as a diagram illustrating his thinking about the structure of myths. Using Saussure's distinction between *langue* and *parole*, Lévi-Strauss approaches myths as particular recombinations (parole) of a finite number of elements (langue). Each element in itself contains a link between a certain function and a given subject (e.g. 'Oedipus kills his father'), which Lévi-Strauss calls a 'relation'. However, the meaning of the myth is generated by the way in which these relations are combined rather than the relations themselves. He calls these recombinations of elements or relations, *bundles*:

> The true constituent units of a myth are not the isolated relations but *bundles of such relations*, and it is only as bundles that these relations can be put to use and combined so as to produce a meaning.
>
> (Lévi-Strauss, 1968: p. 211)

Thus behind any individual telling, or *parole*, of the myth one senses the *langue* behind it, and, behind that, a *'super-langue'* which holds the fundamental meaning. As Terence Hawkes notes:

> a 'bundle' can best be defined as all the versions of a particular 'relation' that have ever existed, being simultaneously perceived [. . .] through whichever particular version is being used at any particular time.
>
> (Hawkes, 1992: p. 44)

Lévi-Strauss is therefore seeking to describe the interaction between the synchronic and diachronic, between *langue* and *parole*, that the telling of a myth like the myth of Oedipus will always generate. Thus myth acts on both axes at once like a score which must be read diachronically left to right, page by page and synchronically up and down – the verticality creating a bundle of relations. In a performance we encounter the score only diachronically and infer the significance of each bundle. The diagram that O'Sullivan quotes in 'Busk, Pierce' is used by Lévi-Strauss to illustrate his decoding of the Oedipus myth. He introduces it in the following way:

> The myth will be treated as an orchestra score would be if it were unwittingly considered as a unilinear series; our task is to re-establish the correct rearrangement. Say for instance we were confronted with the sequence of the type 1, 2, 4, 7, (8), 2, 3, 4, 6, 8 [. . .], the assignment being to put all the 1's together, all the 2's, the 3's, etc.; the result is a chart.
>
> (Lévi-Strauss, 1968: p. 213)

After attempting such an arrangement with the elements of the Oedipus myth, Lévi-Strauss asserts:

> Were we to *tell* the myth, we would disregard the columns and read the rows from left to right and from top to bottom. But if we want to

understand the myth, then we will have to disregard one half of the diachronic dimension (top to bottom) and read from left to right, column after column, each column being considered as a unit.

(Lévi-Strauss, 1968: p. 214)

Thus generating the *langue* of the myth, Lévi-Strauss is able to offer a fundamental meaning of it in structural terms. This method also allows him to shift from one variant of the myth to another.

O'Sullivan's use of the diagram in her poem invites several interpretive possibilities. Firstly, she may be using it to represent the processes she sees as extant in her own work. Since the poem might be said to break down into a succession of small clusters or intensities, demarcated by space, sound and punctuation, O'Sullivan may be proposing that these may be read vertically as well as horizontally and treated as bundles that form part of a larger structure. As a poet who is concerned very much with performance and treating the page as a score (indeed Lévi-Strauss uses this metaphor to describe his diagram) this may be a gesture to remind the reader to examine the text in this synchronic way rather than purely diachronically. Having suggested this, all sorts of problems emerge about how distinct these units really are and whether a synchronic combination into a pattern would yield any new readings.

Alternatively, it is possible that O'Sullivan offers the figure as a model of structure to be criticised for its oversimplification and subordination of the materiality of language to larger themes. Furthermore, O'Sullivan might also be placing the diagram in her text as an act of appropriation: removing it from structural anthropology to poetry, using the technique of collage. We might ask if it is still possible to read this table as if it *were* Lévi-Strauss's diagram. Arguably it has simply become an abstract complex which suggests both horizontal and vertical reading, and a possible sound score.

Yet another possibility is that O'Sullivan is expressing an identification with the function of myth, the diagram as a kind of utilitarian, even 'magic', figure that could be applied in a certain situation. It is at this point that I wish to turn to the chapter in Lévi-Strauss' book that precedes the chapter containing his diagram. This chapter is concerned with shamanism, to which Lévi-Strauss also applies a structural analysis and interpretation, and considers the role of myth in shamanic healing.

Shamanism is a loaded term in considering O'Sullivan's work as it has become an oft-used metaphor by her critics. The shamanic

metaphor has to be handled with care as it has accrued so many associations and meanings in Western culture that its usefulness in
discussing O'Sullivan's poetics may be obscured. Part of the reason for
the use of this metaphor is O'Sullivan's titling of her 1993 book *In the
House of the Shaman* after a drawing by Joseph Beuys. Beuys' relationship
to the idea of shamanism is well-documented, and O'Sullivan herself
underwent a 'transformative' experience in working on a documentary on Beuys in 1988. O'Sullivan's affinities with Beuys are openly
declared in her poetics piece 'riverrunning (realisations' (1995), dedicated to Language Poet Charles Bernstein. In this text, O'Sullivan links
Beuys' influence to that of Kurt Schwitters in encouraging her to 'look
away from, beyond the given' at 'THE UNREGARDED, the found, the
cast offs, the dismembered materials of culture' (O'Sullivan, 1995:
p. 68). She further describes her relationship with Beuys as: 'I am trib-
uting his work: fluid, changing, inviting new material, urging new
responses. His urge to begin with mistakes, to show frailty' (O'Sullivan,
1995: p. 69). O'Sullivan has explored this influence not only as a writer
but also as a painter – some of her assemblage works are described
in/as poems in *Palace of Reptiles* (2003), and she has presented several
book works as amalgams of the textual and the visual – most strikingly
in *Red Shifts* (2001).

The second book of *In the House of the Shaman*, 'Kinship with animals',
has an epigraph from Beuys:

> To stress the idea of transformation and of substance. This is precisely
> what the shaman does in order to bring about change and development;
> his nature is therapeutic.
>
> (O'Sullivan, 1993: p. 28)

In an interview I conducted with O'Sullivan in 1999 (reprinted in this
volume) she stressed her view of the transformative nature of language
as linked to the materiality of language: analogous to Beuys' terms of
transformation and substance. I want to consider what transformation
in particular might mean within the context of the metaphor of
shamanism, and what implications it has for understanding
O'Sullivan's poetics.

Lévi-Strauss in *Structural Anthropology* describes shamanic healing as
follows:

> That the mythology of the shaman does not correspond to an objective
> reality does not matter. The sick woman believes in the myth and

belongs to a society that believes in it. The tutelary spirits and malevolent spirits, the supernatural monsters and magical animals, are all part of a coherent system on which the native conception of the universe is founded. The sick woman accepts these mythical beings or, more accurately, she has never questioned their existence. What she does not accept are the incoherent and arbitrary pains, which are an alien element in her system but which the shaman, calling upon myth, will re-integrate within a whole where everything is meaningful. Once the sick woman understands, however, she does more than resign herself; she gets well.

(Lévi-Strauss, 1968: p. 197)

He analyses this healing in the following way:

The shaman provides the sick woman with a *language*, by means of which unexpressed, and otherwise inexpressible, psychic states can be immediately expressed. And it is the transition to this verbal expression – at the same time making it possible to undergo in an ordered and intelligible form a real experience that would otherwise be chaotic and inexpressible – which induces the release of the physiological process, that is, the reorganisation, in a favourable direction, of the process to which the sick woman is subjected.

(Lévi-Strauss, 1968: p. 198)

This description seems analogous to the kind of metaphorically shamanic activity that Beuys believed himself to be engaged in, although Beuys in fact redirects the healing process from order to chaos when he describes the transformation process in his art as an attempt

to break off all the residues present in the subconscious and to transfer a chaotically detached orderly procedure into turbulence, the beginning of the new always taking place in chaos

(cited in Kuspit, 1995: p. 38)

Beuys' healing therefore takes place in the context of breaking out of old ordered patterns into a therapeutically 'healthy chaos' (Kuspit, 1995: p. 38). He attempts this in his art by constructing performances which represent psychic states by refiguring various symbols: the cross, the hare, the piano. This seems analogous to the process in O'Sullivan's writing whereby the lack of any framing narrator or orderly described setting faces us with an apparent chaos of language where words are transformed and re-ordered into new patterns.

Most criticisms of the use of the shamanic metaphor in Western art attack the Western idealisation of the shaman as an entranced, wise and benevolent figure as a distraction from recognising his historical implication in societal power structures. Ironically, it was precisely this more historicized view of shamanism that Beuys was criticised for when he was accused of being a showman rather than a shaman. It seems possible, however, to collapse these distinctions one into the other – that shamanism only gains its power by the force of its illusions, its showmanship, the power of its stories. Whilst O'Sullivan disavows any straightforward understanding of her work as therapeutic, it seems possible to read her work as 'shamanic' to the extent that its transformations of normative language amount to the appearance of an urgent re-ordering of marginalized psychological states into something approaching a healthy chaos. In 'riverrunning (realisations' O'Sullivan makes the statement that her works are

> Engaging with the OUT, the UNDER – the UN – the OTHER-THAN, the NON & the LESS – transgression; trepass; disparity; subversion: Milton's 'UNTWISTING THE CHAINS THAT TIE'
>
> (O'Sullivan, 1995: p. 68)

Therefore she seems to be engaging in a poetics which seeks to articulate areas of experience that are not normally recognised in mainstream culture. Thus O'Sullivan's use of Lévi-Strauss's diagram might ultimately be intended to evoke something of the power of myth as a structure for 'overcoming contradiction' (Lévi Strauss, 1968: p. 229). 'Busk Pierce' atomises meaning whilst, at the same time, appearing to negotiate a history of struggle: of the Tlingit, of European wars, of feminism, of the colonisation of Ireland. Lévi-Strauss's 'contradiction' enters the poem as historical conflict, but the form of poem itself is also vitiated by contradictory impulses. Written in an idiom which looks deeply into the history of words whilst operating associative arguments through sound play, the poem suggests a poetics that seeks to re-enact the struggles it describes – or to register the damage done to language, and people, by such struggles – holding the referential (meaningful) and non-referential (expressive) elements of language in tension. When the poem almost breaks down in the intensity of its anger: 'Dolly puke, Doily flak, Pinnie Gullet', its patterning achieves virtually concrete status; forming a structure that appears to 'capture' the feeling of anger and take power over it. Potentially the Lévi-Strauss diagram acts as a kind of charm for the similar purpose of capturing strong 'contradictory' (conflict-riven) impulses and ordering them in a way which is empowering.

O'Sullivan's remarkable collaboration with Bruce Andrews, *Excla* (1993), continues to develop this 'shamanic', transformative and politicised poetics through a technique invented by Andrews. Andrews' technique itself emerges from a structural analysis of language and society, which bears comparison to Lévi-Strauss' work on myth, but which goes further in determining the political applications of such a theory in the formation of poems. This view is clearly presented in Andrews' essay 'Total Equals What: Poetics & Praxis' (1985).

Andrews' structuring metaphor for society and language consists of three levels that exist as a series of concentric circles. Concerning society, Andrews argues:

> You can talk about this surface level or this first level as a social order as a kind of decentred constellation of different practices, of differences, of heterogeneity, of pluralism, a micro-politics of fragments on this inner circle. Second, beyond that, you can talk about those multiple interests or points of activity being organised into a dominant hegemony and a variety of counter-hegemonies trying to challenge that hegemony [. . .] And then third [. . .] you can talk about the outer limits of something like a totality, an overall horizon of restriction and constitution [. . .] A dominant paradigm.
>
> (Andrews, 1985: p. 48–49)

By arguing that language is socially constructed, Andrews frames it within the same system:

> If you talk about language in terms of these same levels [. . .] first, on the surface, you would talk about it as a set of differences, the production of meaning (as signification). Outside that you can talk about the structure of discourses: the way in which those differences get organised into a polyphony – of different voices, different literary traditions – [. . .] Finally [. . .] there's this final concentric circle for language in which polyphony is embedded. The polyphony inside [. . .][is] limited in certain ways by [. . .] this outer horizon [. . .] this overall body of sense that makes language into an archive of social effects.
>
> (Andrews, 1985: p. 49)

By characterising both language and society in this structural way; as sites of plurality which are nevertheless ultimately structured by specific, then general, paradigms of classification and/or possibility, Andrews develops a base on which to found a concept of a 'totalizing' poetics – one which seeks to comprehend the entire social whole and then work inwards: exposing the ultimate framing of social reality constituted by the outermost circle. This is opposed to a practice which might be simply restricted to a oppositional role within the second circle or a private insularity within the first circle. As Andrews elaborates:

> To imagine the limits of language [. . .] is also to imagine the limits of a whole form of social life – in this case of a predatory social order [. . .] that desperately needs to be changed. [. . .] Often the horizon goes unrecognised – and unchallenged – so that those limits, and the social world as a whole, are seen as natural, or they're not seen at all. [. . .] The political dimension of writing isn't just based on the idea of challenging specific problems [. . .] it's based on the notion of a systemic grasp – not of language described as a fixed system but of language as a kind of agenda or as a system of capabilities and uses.
>
> (Andrews, 1985: p. 53–60)

Andrews advocates a writing practice of a broadly-conceived defamiliarization – enacted within a totalising conception of what is the 'familiar': laying bare not just the device but the rules that constitute socio-linguistic reality. For Andrews, writing is a means of running up and down the scale of language from fragments to a totality, and in this way measuring the social dimension of the relationship between *parole* and *langue*. His ambitions for this are nothing short of Utopian:

> You're raising the possibility of something entirely new taking shape: constructing a set of common meanings, some common network into which people can move, a way of exchanging different kinds of awarenesses. This would allow desire to register as a kind of community-building and put writing at the forefront of envisioning what a positive social freedom and participation might look like.
>
> (Andrews, 1985: p. 59)

Andrews' evocation of a 'set of common meanings' or a 'common network' within which different awarenesses can be exchanged suggests the way in which myths function interpersonally and historically in order to progress, as Lévi-Strauss puts it, from 'the awareness of oppositions towards their resolution' (Lévi-Strauss, 1968: p. 224). The connection with O'Sullivan's poetics as established in relation to 'Busk, Pierce' is partly enabled by the comparison with Lévi-Strauss, but

O'Sullivan's poetics of a re-ordering of states of conflict in the powerful vortex of her poetry seems close to the political agenda evinced by Andrews, which itself goes beyond Lévi-Strauss' work. However, it is also the shared technique used to produce *Excla* that unites O'Sullivan's and Andrews' poetics.

Andrews has developed a poetic technique that enables the desired exchange between the outer totality of *langue* and inner fragments of *parole*. In an interview he described how this technique developed from initially facing a particular problem for his writing:

> If I want larger constructions, then getting the kind of shifting and open availability of juxtaposition that allows me to explore rhythmic possibilities, those things haven't been made available to me by a process of sitting down and writing a poem. Often, for me, when I did that – too much reliance on brands of continuity given to me without thinking them through, seamlessness, a more static or regularized rhythmic possibility, a range of references that were often very restrictive, you know – the range of references I might be in the midst of in a given hour would often seem narrow, not by choice but by imposition.
>
> (Andrews, 1996: pp. 103–104)

Andrews' solution to this problem was as follows:

> Being able to have a wider range of materials written in different points in time, wildly disparate points in time, out of different contexts, seemed to open up possibilities for composition, for the editing, and I began to work in more and more discrete, modular units to accommodate that. [. . .] Lately the time gap between the writing of words on small sheets of paper and the editing or final composition process are now far more separated in time, [. . .] plenty of people do this with notebooks. I found that trying to work off of things I'd written in notebook form just didn't allow the range of editing opportunities I wanted, whether it was just a physical fact of there being writing on the backs of pages that were in one single volume, or whether it was something about the context of the original composition of those words still clinging to them in the notebook, that I couldn't ignore, couldn't get around [. . .] So it's similar to the way people operate with notebooks, but more discrete, more modular, opening up.
>
> (Andrews, 1996: p. 104)

Although Andrews does not link this technique explicitly to his totalising poetics, the little pieces of paper with words on them are analogous to the 'fragments' on the inner circle of language/society. In his account of the composition of his poem *Lip Service*, Andrews describes a

procedure in which very large structures are built on the basis of literally thousands of these little pieces of paper or cards (Andrews, 1996:
p. 251). In this way he can effectively avoid being co-opted into the pre-
established discourses of the middle-ground between fragments and
totality (the 'brands of continuity'), wherein most writing takes place.
Andrews' technique is a unique way of working with *parole* in as raw
and unmediated a form as possible, and in this way constructing a
platform on which to build a larger structure of analysis and social
critique.

Both Andrews and O'Sullivan used this technique in *Excla*. As
O'Sullivan described in the interview I conducted with her in 1999:

> MO: [Bruce Andrews and I] had corresponded for some time, I'm a
> great fan of his work, and he came to London to read at Sub-Voicive
> and we met and it just emerged in the conversation, how about doing
> a collaborative piece. What we thought we'd do was to read each
> other's work as a starting point and respond to the thematic, lexical
> and sonic tints in the language until we each came up with about 3000
> handwritten words on tiny pieces of paper. Then each held back half
> these words and sent the remaining half to the other person. So we
> each had 3000 words to work with – this number being composed of
> 1500 of one's own input plus 1500 from the other person – divided into
> fifteen sections each. We organised the work into thirty sections, in
> three parts A, B and C, with five texts from each person for each
> section. A1 was me, which is two pages and then the next A1 is from
> Bruce and it follows on in sequence. I had the final responsibility for
> the first A1 and Bruce had final responsibility for the second A1, and
> so on.
>
> ST: Why the small pieces of paper?
>
> MO: The suggestion of using the small pieces of paper was Bruce's,
> because that's his methodology. I'd never worked in that manner before
> and I found it immensely liberating, because I think it encourages a
> greater freedom with the language. You have little bits of paper with
> one word or two words or phrases and the great beauty is that you can
> have them with you in your pocket and collect words from everywhere.
> (O'Sullivan and Thurston, 2004: pp. 10–11)

O'Sullivan here, in a slightly different way, also aligns herself with
Andrews' poetics in terms of finding a 'greater freedom with the
language' to 'collect words from everywhere'. These points seem to
echo Andrews' desire to avoid entering into any pre-determined

discourses and to keep open to encountering *parole* in its rawest, most fugitive state.

Excla is an extraordinary book because of the harmony exhibited by the work of its two authors. Although there is no system in place to indicate the author of a given text, in addition to O'Sullivan's explanation I found that I recognised the writers' respective photo-copied typefaces from appearances in little magazines where their work had also simply been photocopied as CRC (camera ready copy), rather than typeset. Both use distinctive electric typewriter faces with equal spacing – creating a visual harmony on the page. As well as this detail, any reader familiar with either poet's work will detect traces of gestural repertoires, in spite of the shared vocabularies; although there are passages where the writers seem to be by turns consciously adopting or resisting the other's words. Andrews' work retains the hard-edged urban wit that characterises works such as his *I Don't Have Any Paper So Shut Up, or Social Romanticism* (1992), whilst O'Sullivan favours a more rural set of references. Both poets pun vigorously throughout, appearing also to deform given words to create extra variety.

As with 'Busk, Pierce', there are no managing frames of lyric argu-ment or narrative to organise these poems for the reader. Many lines, phrases and individual words operate as near-autonomous structures, giving the texts a fragmented appearance. Nevertheless, patterns of connection resonate and reverberate throughout the whole and it is these continuities that animate the book. Both poets' work seems to be predicated on direct statements about the world as if behind every line or fragment stands the meaning: 'this is happening'. One of the most striking recurring features in this book is when words are positioned in a line in such a way as they assume almost equal weight in terms of stress patterns as they interact with meaning; perhaps a direct product of the technique of composing with words on small pieces of paper. The effect of this is not unlike the impact of a newspaper headline. As Adrian Clarke has pointed out of Andrews' and O'Sullivan's work, William Empson's quotation of the headline 'ITALIAN ASSASSIN BOMB PLOT DISASTER' in *Seven Types of Ambiguity* (1947), as an example of a form of statement which might 'give back something of the Elizabethan energy to what is at present a rather exhausted language', seems an apt descrip-tion of the effect of this strategy (cited in Clarke, 1998: unp.). I want to examine some examples of this kind of writing as a way of getting closer to the impact of the work as a whole in enacting aspects of both O'Sullivan's and Andrews' poetics. The book is unpaginated although it is organised into sections. I will add the additional symbol 'MO' (Maggie O'Sullivan) or 'BA' (Bruce Andrews) to indicate the author concerned. The first poem in the book 'A1: MO', begins:

Auriferous
crim ribbering m'd minjo quarty
Somes Tremor / Song & pal part ate part RAINBOW
part LIP
EXCLA – SIASMS – BLED –

(Andrews & O'Sullivan, 1993: unp.)

The opening word 'Auriferous' ('yielding gold') evokes a metaphor of alchemy for the creative process – an apt one given the complexity of the procedures of mixing many different elements together in this book. The line 'crim ribbering m'd minjo quarty' however, begins to have the impact of Empson's headline and demands a form of close reading where the dictionary is involved for every word almost as a process of translation. A host of possible associations converge here in these neologisms, although they read like corruptions of standard words, as if O'Sullivan is resisting the given vocabularies that form the book. Thus the line enacts (like the second line of 'Busk, Pierce') a semantic *movement* rather than being 'about' something. Whilst it is possible to hazard approximate associations for most of the words: 'crim' for criminal, 'Ribbering' read as *ribbing* – to poke someone in the ribs to draw their attention good-naturedly, 'Minjo' read as a pun on *mangy* – an amalgam of mean and stingy, and 'Quarty' as punning on *quartation* – a process of combining three parts of silver with one part of gold as a preliminary in purifying gold (linking back to 'Auriferous' as well as punning on qwerty); the word 'm'd' rather resists any such reading, unless taken as a elided form of 'made', which might impart a small degree of grammatical order to the line. One could then read the line as suggesting a situation in which boisterous criminal cama- raderie is juxtaposed with a mean practice of alchemy. This could be interpreted as an amusing reflection on the process of collaboration being undertaken by the two writers – as if they are partners in crime good-naturedly ribbing each other about their contributions to the project. But such paraphrase again feels inappropriate when faced with the sheer energy of this work and its resistance to following clear patterns of meaning. To attempt to read the entire book in this way would require almost superhuman interpretive energy and yet, one suspects, would get one no closer to an authoritative reading of the text's meaning. In short, the text is designed to release meaning in only partially reconstituted fragments: 'part ate part RAINBOW | part LIP'. Even the title as presented here in the sequence 'EXCLA – SIASMS – BLED –' reads as a fragment of the word 'exclamation' juxtaposed with the fragments 'siasms' and 'bled', (although the latter is also readable as the past of 'to bleed'). This affects a reconfiguration of language into a new tripartite word, or a new kind of sentence, where the reader must supply missing contexts to imagine a potential deformation of '*excla*mation enthu*siasms* tum*bled*', which, whilst more approachable as regularised vocabulary, still poses problems of interpretation.

However, it is possible to make provisional readings that seek to explore the way in which the text's patternings evoke a defamiliarization of a total socio-linguistic horizon. Later in 'A1: MO' we are presented with the boxed line:

| True Rampant Allege Repeatedly Arbitage |

(Andrews & O'Sullivan, 1993)

This is one of the many occasions in the text where both writers draw lines onto the pages of their typescript. Although the use of lines to box-in text or to make small diagrams on the page is more characteristic of Andrews' work, O'Sullivan is no stranger to combining text and visual elements: indeed her collages, formed from treated fragments of the text, mark the intervals between the parts of the book and are used on the cover. The force of the above line is perhaps even stronger than the earlier example, due to its enclosure and the use of capitalisation – bringing it closer to the format of the newspaper headline. It can be argued that the force of the line in fact derives from its resemblance to the syntax and presentation of a headline in tension with its obscure yet suggestive semantic import. One could suggest a paraphrase along the lines of the 'True Rampant' as an upright and powerful citizen who accuses someone or something of repeated arbitration and/or arbitrariness. Whether one finds this convincing or not, the point is that it is only by recourse to some sort of framing discourse that any interpretation can be attempted at all. Indeed each word in itself may be considered to be a frame. In this way, although the statement could be referring ironically to an imagined critical reception of the book, the word 'arbitage' with its overtones of arbitrage, arbiter and arbitrary, might evoke, for a particular reader, the frame of Saussure's arbitrariness hypothesis – a cornerstone of the poetics of the Language Poetry project and crucial to Lévi-Strauss's work. This illustrates how such writing provokes a reconnection between defamiliarised fragments of language and the totality of the social horizon from which they derive. One is obliged to confront the fact that these fragments exist in contesting relationships with one another – the verbs 'ribbering' and 'allege' are suggestive of power relationships that are elsewhere present in the fundamental structure of socio-linguistic reality. We are reminded that making sense of poetry is to confront the everyday violence, coercion and property that defines social existence. The power of this poetry lies in its attempt to evoke this socio-linguistic critique from the smallest units up rather than making statements that would otherwise be easily absorbed into hegemonic discourses and neutralised. In accordance with the shamanic metaphor, the conflicts are being transformed into new configurations, to expose them and to make them visible in such a way that they may be resisted.

Other examples of the headline-style of writing are deployed to varying effects: 'CARRION ADMITTED TO THE SHELVES' ('A5: MO') almost reads as a conventional headline – exposing poor food standards – were it not for the slightly quaint tone of *carrion* and *admitted*. However, 'ROAST ORPHAN BRAIN MONSTROUS FOREVER' ('C4: MO') feels parodic in its unlikely monstrosity. Alternatively, 'SENSATIONS – PSYCHIC HOTLINE' ('B3: BA') reads like a direct quotation of an advertisement, whether from a newspaper or hoarding signage. Other examples such as: 'gagged peddle grief | denominating homing delirium' ('A2: BA'), 'Apricot's Rescind Spat Vocal Astro Drizzle' ('B4: MO'), and 'gland Syllabary Animal Sticker Picture Habitat' ('B1: BA'), all share similar characteristics with the 'True Rampant Allege Repeatedly Arbitage' example analysed above, in that they evoke complex series of referential contexts without settling for any dominant pattern of sense.

Elsewhere in the book one is offered experiences of vertiginous movement up and down the scales of language. As 'A2: BA' opens:

> Ida kinder LISTEN-UP mashie stress light
> unleashing riddle ruby homes you
>   zig zag doing the act
>   Odes | Anthems | O –
>   LOBELITHIC rosette surprise
>   vomiting objectlike threat process
>   jag cliché violet ransom
> gyp taunt – tinsel rupt
>   milton opportunity glob

(Andrews & O'Sullivan, 1993)

The effect of these lines is at once of an exuberant flow of confrontational street-speech, 'LISTEN-UP', and the sense that this speech is multiple in its cutting across registers. It presents itself, in other words, as constructed. There are references to high cultural artefacts 'Odes / Anthems' and persons 'milton'; pseudo-scientific terminology 'LOBELITHIC' and an awareness of violence and aggression: 'vomiting objectlike threat process', 'violet ransom', 'gyp taunt'. There even seems to be an oblique reference to Dorothy's ruby red slippers in *The Wizard of Oz* in the line 'unleashing riddle ruby homes you'. The conjunction of 'milton', if read as the poet John Milton, with 'opportunity glob' is typical of the irreverence of this technique. In this way the reader is faced with a constructed voice that appears to be absorbing any materials in its path and putting them to poetic use.

Thematically-speaking, however, it is possible to distinguish a thread of argument in the book which self-consciously reflects on the relationships between language, writing and politics that the book otherwise enacts and critiques by its form. There are many meta-linguistic tags throughout these poems: 'Metonymical UtterANceD' ('A1: MO'), looks forward to 'Lexical Sirens' ('A2: MO') and 'SYNTAX a con matters' ('A3: BA') as well as "'desyntaxed'" ('C3: BA'). The metonymic movement of the poems is therefore linkable with a view of language as a potential seduction or con to be resisted, but also one that is under deconstruction. As O'Sullivan casts it later: 'UNASSAIL-ABLE SIRENS | DISHEVELLED SYNTAX UNCHARTABLE SHEEN' ('C5: MO'). The 'unfinished' question 'How do sentences?' ('A3: BA') gives another example of the linguistic critique on offer – refiguring the question-fragment as the speech act 'how do you do?'

Within this awareness of language as material is an awareness of what it means for anyone to speak: 'HE-PLAY / SHE-PLAY | *they speak us*' ('A4: BA') locates the role of hegemonic discourses speaking for others, whilst 'Outside of the little hammers, we speak' ('B4: MO') suggests a division between the writer's expression on the typewriter's 'little hammers', and what the writer says elsewhere. This division may lead to 'what is really meant – || is as yourself | in little narratives' ('B4: MO'), where the identification of meaning and the subject is linked with the idea of little narratives, perhaps those opposed to the hegemonic meta-narratives of modernity. However, to evoke meaning and subjectivity is itself also an appeal to the grand narratives' dictations about the status of the subject and meaning, which complicates this statement. In a similar way, other seemingly direct remarks emerging in the text become ambivalent. The statement: 'THERE IS NO NIGHT | WE ARE ALL EQUAL' ('B2: BA'), could be read as a politically hopeful disavowing of evil and an evocation of unity, but, because of its suspension out of the frames of discourse, it also offers itself as a problematically absolute statement to be resisted – who is 'we'? The poems constantly undercut such statements in ways which relativise their meanings within the socio-linguistic field. 'LEARNING FROM || belligerent margins' ('C1: MO'), whilst suggestive of a progressive politics oriented against a central position, is rendered ambivalent by the uncertain tone of 'belligerent', and recasts itself as a critique of maintaining minority political positions against the possibilities of total unity: a unity in turn tainted with absolutism. As Andrews writes: 'stifle raw democracy | cried & tried to' ('C2: BA').

The parenthetical lines: '(how it was as if the writing, yet to be | written | as we pen & pen again | not that that makes)' ('C1: MO') evoke again the predicament of the writer in the contemporary world – the phrase 'yet to be written' recalls Lyotard's definition of post-modern art as that which is seeking the rules of 'what will have been done' – yet the syntactical conjunction of 'how it was' and 'as if' places the writing 'yet to be written' in a complex relationship to the past and to the future. The reiteration of 'pen & pen again' and the abruptness of 'not that that makes' cast writing as an endless activity that has at best inconclusive outcomes: one might complete the latter phrase with 'a difference', but one can also hear a possible 'open' behind the pens here, which might balance the elided pessimism.

Other stagings of the problems of the writer's position appear present in 'clot up fiction stratify candy best of | frozen their language' ('A5: BA'), where the clotted fiction candy amounts to an immobile language as in 'an entrailment of words incurably to darkness' ('C2: MO'). The energetic phrase 'wordsmoke crescendo' ('B4: BA') gets refigured in 'smokescreen [the verb] tract | elope permissible OUTSIDE' ('C2: BA'), where, again, the awareness of what is outside the text, here possibly a freedom one can escape to, is contrasted with the text's own potential word-smoke-screen tract – whether this is the poem itself, or other abuses of language: 'magnifying deVICEs OPPOSITIONALITY you're poison oak to' ('B4: BA').

The concluding poems in the book attempt gestures of open closure to this argument. O'Sullivan's 'C5' poem points to 'the totality of disadvantage', refiguring absolutism once again as a resounding negative, situated '"under a system called"' where it doesn't matter what the system is called, just the fact that it is a system that one is 'under' – the hidden metaphor of oppression exposed. This analysis leads the poem to attend to 'A SUBTRACTIVE PROCESS' that causes 'hunger zones'. Andrews' 'C5' poem offers the hopeful 'repeace out of scrap world HONING' which seems evocative of the processes of composition of the book, whilst the deleted phrase 'complete resiStance', both resists and evokes its double meaning.

The poetry's commitment to a totalising approach towards socio-linguistic reality is tensed against the powerful effects of a relentless immersion in language. Voices within voices suddenly emerge, both funny and frightening, and one feels momently addressed before being reabsorbed into the flux and chaos. In this way, the text tries to evoke a sense of a metaphorically 'schizophrenic' encounter with reality as if 'this is happening'. The text allows all the repressed minutiae of every-day language to speak – and evokes the flux of a potentially healthy chaos within which marginalized psychic states might begin to be heard and to discover their own forms, contents and extents in transformation.

Bibliography

Andrews, B. 1986. 'Total Equals What: Poetics & Praxis' in *Poetics Journal* 6, 48–61.

Andrews, B. and O'Sullivan, M. 1993. *Excla*. London: Writers Forum.

Andrews, B. 1996. *Paradise & Method: Poetics & Praxis*. Evanston, Illinois: Northwestern University Press.

Clarke, A. 1998. *Millennial Shades & Three Papers*. London: Writers Forum.

Hawkes, T. (1977), 1992. *Structuralism and Semiotics*. London: Routledge.

Kuspit, D. 1995. 'Joseph Beuys: Between Showman and Shaman' in *Joseph Beuys: Diverging Critiques*, ed. by David Thistlewood. Liverpool: Liverpool University Press and Tate Gallery Liverpool, pp. 27–49.

Lévi-Strauss, C. 1968. *Structural Anthropology*, trans. by Jacobsen, C. and Grundfest Schoepf, B. London: Allen Lane The Penguin Press.

Middleton, p. 1998. 'The Contemporary Poetry Reading' in *Close Listening: Poetry and the Performed Word*, ed. by Bernstein, C. New York and Oxford: Oxford University Press, pp. 262–299.

O'Sullivan, M. 1987. *States Of Emergency*. Oxford: ICPA.

O'Sullivan, M. 1993. *In the House of the Shaman*. London: Reality Street.

O'Sullivan, M. 1995. 'riverrunning (realisations' in *West Coast Line* no. 2 vol. 29, 62–71.

O'Sullivan, M. 1998. Untitled statement in *Word Score Utterance Choreography in Verbal and Visual Poetry*, ed. by Cobbing, B. and Upton, L. London: Writers Forum.

O'Sullivan, M. and Thurston, S. 2004. 'Emerging States' in *Poetry Salzburg Review* 6 (Summer 2004), 6–20. Reprinted in the current volume.

Sheppard, R. 1998. *Far Language: Poetics and Linguistically Innovative Poetry 1978–1997*. Exeter: Stride.

Writing / Conversation with
Maggie O'Sullivan

Redell Olsen

This interview was conducted by email between November and December 2003. It was first published in the Spring issue of How2 in 2004[1]

D.O: For the past decade or so you have been living away from London in Hebden Bridge in Yorkshire, how has this shift from the urban to the rural environment affected your poetics?

M.O'S: Living in a place that is in close relation beside other-than-human sentience has deepened my trust in the provisional, the precarious, in the precisions of the transient – of "what is not yet known, thought, seen, touched but really what is not. And that is"[2]

. . . having a feeling of being part of an intimate, boundless, round-me turning of "Non, nothing, everything"[3] – aware of the sky as an infinite environment of ephemeral vice versa imperatives and winged pathings – particularly at transitional times of great energy such as spring and autumn. . . and the blizzards, the driving, horizontal rains and the battering winds. And the sonic plunging of water to the earth, into the becks, springs and falls. . .

. . .such breaking up and breaking apart within utterances and hearings, de-constructing/re-constituting-as-(being)-heard is embodied in my poetics . . .

I seem to have moved away from making the large colourful expressionistic assemblages/paintings I did in London (when I was in my thirties) and right up to about the mid-nineties, (when I was in my forties) when I was first here – side by side with my making poetry – towards my work now – where potencies, energy fields, traces of actions/activities move in an open, ongoing dissolving/deformance of the verbal/visual/ sculptural into one practice of many heuristic pathings.

D.O.: When I read or hear you talk about your work I am struck by the rich terminology which you employ to reference your poetics. Words and phrases such as "deformance" and "re-constituting-as-(being)-heard" imply a sense of violence and destruction as well as an assembling of raw materials and energies. A "re-constituting-as- (being)-heard" suggests that writing, for you, is bound up with recapturing the fleeting sense of an overheard, or chance encounter which one is never fully able to be part of, or reassemble. It seems to me that the place of the page for you is a place of transformation but also of struggle, dissolution and loss. Would you agree with that?

M.O.S: Yes. A place of damage, savagery, pain, silence: also a place of salvage, retrieval and recovery. A place of existence, journeying. A sacred space of undiminishment. Of dream. Of ritual. Of magic. Also a "re-constituting-as-(being)-heard" in the sense that as we hear, we also are heard in an intertwining of potential exchange of hearing-(being)-heard of other-than-(as well as human)-sentience.

D.O.: You have mentioned your need for "other-than-human sentience" in your environment. Animals feature in many of your poems, especially *An Incomplete Natural History* (1984), *From the Handbook of That & Furriery* (1986), *Unofficial Word* (1988), how does this understanding of the "other-than-human" find its way into your poems?

M.O.S: I spend a lot of time in the hearing of birds/hearing birds, and indeed all manner of animals. I feel part of a particular kind of multi-sonic/trans-somatic environment that is filled with other-than-human voicings/breathings /existences – that is always in flux, in-process, unhushed.

I have always felt tremendous empathy with animals. As a child, I was appalled at the casual cruelties and unquestioning hatred and abuse of animals in the world at large. Exploitation and violation of other-than-human beings underpins our society and is embedded at every level in our h/arming hierarchies. I always felt I was no different from other animals. Having lived beside/shared life with animals, I feel this more passionately than ever now. The celebration of the transformative, merciful intelligences and energies of animals is in all my work.

D.O.: I was wondering how this understanding of the "other-than-human sentience" might have impacted in a formal way on your poetics? I was thinking of the way in which it might go hand-in-hand with an opening up of the usual structures of language and communication. A movement towards a feeling for the other that also entails an *other* form of writing; one that draws on and engages with cycles and energies not defined as human?

M.O.S: New/ancient forms of imaginings without limits that engage with evolving multi and meta-physical breathing/soundings and fluidities - 'human' or 'page' or 'dog' or 'keyboard' or 'waterfall' – where does one threading run out to begin another?

D.O.: Artists such as Ana Mendieta, and writers such as Cecilia Vicuna would seem to have much in common with your approach to landscape, ritual and indeed performance. How do you see yourself in relation to this tradition of female artists who are working directly with the landscape in relation to their own bodies?

M.O.S.: Much of what I've already said above could be said again here – particularly, the drawing upon the earth and the other-than-human – voicing my body/bodying my voicings – Cecilia Vicuna's powerful practice has been particularly meaningful for me: particularly her commitment to what I call an eco/ethico politics of the earth.

> To feel the earth as one's own skin
> (Cecilia Vicuna)[4]

> embraced
> one single feather
> to thatch
> a house
> is
> in many
> Irish stories
> (Maggie O'Sullivan)[5]

D.O.: "Voicing my body/bodying my voicings" is a very powerful idea, how do you see it in relation to the possibility of an eco/ethical politics?

M.O.S.: What 'Making' – 'Unmaking' is / a Mattering of
    Materials (motivations & practise) – Living to live in

that Learning – Uncertain, Uncurtained Tonguescape
SUNG. SHUNTS. ARM WE. Living Earth Kinships on the
vast-lunged shores of the Multiple Body imbued with
wide-awake slumberings & cavortings. Constructions.
Intuitions. Transmissions. Radiations. Thinking.
ATTENDING.

(RIVERRUNNING (REALISATIONS
                                          (Maggie O'Sullivan)[6]

and,
And If I devoted my life
to one of its feathers
to living its nature
being it understanding it
until the end
Reaching a time
in which my acts
are the thousand
tiny ribs of the feather
and my silence
the humming the whispering
of wind in the feather
and my thoughts
quick sharp precise
as the non-thoughts
of the feather.
                                          (Cecilia Vicuna)[7]

D.O.: There also seems to be some very interesting connections between Vicuna's weaving and shaping of natural objects detritus and your own practice of weaving and assemblage on the page, and indeed in performance. I was thinking of your description of the performance of *From The Handbook of that & the Furriery* in 1983 in which you wove a red net down the central aisle between the seated people and your voice was accompanied by your taped voice, as well as slides. I understand that you wove yourself around the edges of the room, and in effect around all of the audience. Is this weaving in of the audience something that you see as being like Vicuna's weaving of spaces and territories? Vicuna seems to me to be weaving across spaces in an attempt to problematise and disrupt the comfortable space of the detached spectator? Was this true of your performance?

M.O.S.: Yes. IMPLICATION was at the core of that performance. I mentioned the page as a place. Also, profoundly, its PLACELESSNESS.

And what's going on away from the page – moving through space and time to DISPLACEMENT of the page.

D.O.: There is clearly a strong relationship between live performance and writing in your work which is clearly evident in your readings. I wonder if you could tell me a little about how this relationship shapes your working processes?

M.O.S.: My work has always been body-intensive – writing by hand, redrafting the words by hand – bending, sticking, cutting, shaping marks, shaping sounds into the recorder, pain(t)ing and building – all inscriptions of my body's breathing. This heuristic trans-forming has become paramount in *murmur* where I am using the sight/site of the ear/page as a foundational textu(r)al, sonic, visual bodily dimension to move out from.

D.O.: You seem to be describing a kind of synaesthesic practice that is moving towards an interchange of senses: hearing seems to become sight and vice-versa. Do you feel that the relationship between language and each of the senses is also something that you are working to interrogate and transform?

M.O.S: Yes, very much so.

D.O.: I know that the artist Joseph Beuys has been an important influence for you. How do you relate to his concept of the artist as a kind of shamanic figure who is capable of transformation and healing through the process of art making? Is this idea something which has political resonance for you now?

M.O.S: For me, his widened/wide-open concept of total human compassionate creative living – his "social sculpture" – his processual trust in the mysteries and soul imbued in material is transFORMative – melting across all apartheids of genre and specialism.

Yes, it does have resonance for me at ALL possible levels – PER/forming/TRANS/forming within a poetic intuitive process as a first step in opening up possibilities for radical changes in and between consciousnesses.

D.O.: Clearly the late Bob Cobbing was also important to you both in terms of publishing and in encouraging your early work? Could you say a little about how he specifically influenced you?

M.O.S.: A good deal of what I feel about Beuys could also, apply to Bob Cobbing – for Bob too, there was simply no division between the engagements of living life and the imaginative processes of working. Bob embraced and celebrated the multi-form with energy and ease.

I met him I think when I was 20 or 21 when I found my way to his Writers Forum Experimental Workshop, then held at the Poetry Society. I knew immediately I'd met a kindred spirit. When I lived in London we worked a lot together on books, and to a lesser extent, in performances. His radically inventive creative spirit, generosity and openness was staggering. He was without limits.

I made a small IMPROVIsation as tribute for him which Bill Griffiths put up on his own website at Bob's death:

in my casting some summoning of Bob's utterly besotted aviating moment in moment making/doing language's VISIBLE PHYSICAL Exuberance this practise this life by which we breathe scream by always new all ways surprising always way way ahead – fluctuate? hold down the grass—

title it – VEER

D.O.: You are responsible for editing one of the most important anthologies of innovative writing by women (*Out of Everywhere: Linguistically Innovative Poetry by Women.* London: Reality Street Editions, 1996) that has emerged in recent years. How did you go about gathering and deciding on this material? What kind of correspondences did you find between the British and the American writers?

M.O.S.: I did a reading tour in the US and Canada in autumn 1993 which exposed me to a lot that was going on there and I went about gathering and deciding the material using the input from that trip as well as drawing upon the work of poets who had inspired my own practice. I drew up initial lists with Ken/Wendy (Ken Edwards, Wendy Mulford of *Reality Street Editions*). We pretty much agreed on core contributors. I was keen for a large US representation, for younger Canadian poets, whose work I'd encountered in Canada as well as a preference for poets working in multimedia off-the-page performance work. Originally, the book was planned to have twenty contributors with about five pages each, but it was soon obvious that it would have to be upped to thirty to have meaning. Even within the scope of thirty, I had to omit poets whose work was important.

Obviously, I found correspondences between the engagement with formally progressive language practices, the range of visual and linguistic attentions, the engagement with cultural, social and philosophical perspectives, as well as the engagement with long poetic sequences and project-orientated work, embracing inter and multi-media work and performance practises. And also, the fact that a good many of them found themselves excluded from canonical anthologies of women's poetry.

D.O.: Writing about *Out of Everywhere* a number of commentators, including Ann Vickery, Marjorie Perloff and Kathleen Fraser, have commented on the visual nature of many of the pages. Ann Vickery in particular observes that the anthology "maps work that visually challenges reading habits" in its emphasis on "the politics of the page" (*Leaving Lines of Gender*, Wesleyan UP, 2000, 144). She points out that this is very much in contrast to the predominately left margined poetry of, for example, Silliman's anthology, *In The American Tree* (Orono: National Poetry Foundation, 1986). Was this a feature, or a tension, which you were particularly wanting to foreground when you were putting the anthology together? Do you feel that this attention to the visual potential and possibilities of the page is something that has led to the exclusion of some women writers from canonical anthologies?

M.O.S.: By today's standards I was late in learning to 'read'. Before this, I used to paint and draw and copy out writing – using whatever materials were at hand, entranced. I've always been intoxicated with writing/drawing/painting – in essence, it all boils down to mark making, exploding the visual, somatic potentials of the page. There has never been a separation for me. So, obviously, I wanted to draw attention to the multivalent physiques of poetic practices by women when editing *Out of Everywhere*. The general blindness towards actualising the potentials and possibilities within poetic language - of the page as a poetic site, as part of poetic language – has always baffled me. Any poet, irrespective of gender, who visually expands the possibilities of the page is excluded from canonical anthologies – because fabricators of canons don't want awkwardnesses.
     That's why the work of Jerry Rothenberg and his visionary assemblings have been such a sustaining force in my life.

D.O.: I have been looking over your 1993 collaboration with Bruce Andrews which is extraordinary in its scope. Could you tell me how this collaboration came about and how the process of writing the book worked? Did you exchange pages by mail? Did you work on specific themes or ideas? Procedures?

M.O.S.: I think the idea about doing a collaborative piece was raised when Bruce did a *Sub-Voicive* reading in London. What we thought we'd do was to read each other's work and respond to the thematic, lexical and sonic, textural tints in the languages until we each came up with about 3000 handwritten words on tiny pieces of paper. The small pieces of paper was Bruce's suggestion. We each held back half of these words and sent the remaining half to the other person. So overall we each had 3000 words to work with (this number being composed of 1500 of one's own input plus 1500 from the other person) – divided these into 15 sections each. So, we organised the work into 30 sections, in three parts A, B and C, with five texts (of 2 pages) from each person for each section. We did it all by mail.

D.O.: Your recent work seems to have exploded the confines of the line and the page in colourful and energetic new directions. How do you account for this shift in your relationship to the shape of the line, the word – and indeed the book? Is this fraught relationship between the verbal and the visual something that emerged suddenly (for example in the rich textual surfaces of *red shifts* (2001), or do you consider it to always have been an issue in your work?

M.O.S.: *murmur* has extended my searchings within the sculptural, painterly, textural, sonic and aural in an immersioning of multi-level verbal visual languages.

In *"all origins are lonely"* I am continuing my multi-level dances and speculations within the sensual, bodily architectural MATTER of poetry/poetics

> "Perception
> Has Got to
>
> Have a Body!"
> (Madeline Gins)[8]

> and,
> "Not truth but apportionment"
> (Arakawa)[9]

D.O.: This "immersioning of multi-level verbal visual languages" that you describe implies a process of absorption for the reader as much as the writer in the space of the work?

M.O.S.: Since the beginning of *red shifts*, I have been constructing my work on the wall. So far, the A4 sized pages of *murmur* fills one and a half walls of my workroom. When I walk through the doorway of my workroom its energies enfold me. I'd like it to be encountered in such a way, so that the viewer/perceiver/reader could walk up to it and walk along beside it, stretching their body to its uppermost height or stooping to its lowest edge, threading in and out/unravelling its fields of languages, touching it with their eyes and ears and body entering and leaving at any point.

My preoccupation with the poetic work as a multidimensional, kinaesthetic, sentient terrain or environment for the body to enter and move through, is a thread that runs through all my work over the past twenty years – the seeds of these concerns were sown/sewn in my work of the 1980's – particularly in multi-coloured works such as *A Natural History in 3 Incomplete Parts*, which I brought out from my own Magenta press in 1985 when I lived in London and which Bob Cobbing and I made together at his place – (we constructed the entire book going from xeroxing my original pages, collating, binding, glueing, trimming the A5 pages, etc. and it took us a 5-day working week – Monday – Friday – to do this – working intensively from 10 til 5 every day and getting to grips with the brand-new binding. machine Bob had just bought!). We'd planned to launch it on the Saturday, so it simply had to be done that week!

D.O.: You recently performed the first section of *murmur* at Birkbeck College in London and many of the people who saw that performance commented on the way in which you moved among people, quite deliberately laying out pieces of the text all around the room. You seemed to draw them into the poem itself . . .

M.O.S.: The reading on the 6th November 2003 was the first public presentation of *murmur* in its fullest form, to date.
I cradled the seventy-page stack of specially enlarged A3pages on my left arm. I stood and performed each page and then stooped to place it, face-up, on the floor. I stepped forward and did the same again and again for all the seventy pages. I weaved *murmur*/*murmur* weaved me over the floor space created by the circle of seated people (many were sitting on the floor) until there were no pages left on my cradling arm. For the 'purpled madder' section I used a keening by Kittie Gallagher made in Gweedore, County Donegal, 1952 – her lament, muffling out from the

tiny cassette/recorder in my jacket pocket as I moved among the pages around the floor.

This was one verbal installation of the work, specific to that particular physical location, that situation.

D.O.: Which implies that there might be other possibilities for its performance and inhabition in other spaces? Might these places be back in the landscape, or in other site-specific places-beyond the usual confines of what where we expect to find poetry readings and performances?

M.O.S.: Yes, I hope so.

Notes

¹ "Writing / Conversation: An Interview with Maggie O'Sullivan". *How2*, Vol 2: 2, 2004. http://www.asu.edu/pipercwcenter/how2journal//archive/online_archive/v2_2_2004/current/index.htm

² "how to achieve by not achieving? how to make by not making? / it's all in that. /it's not the new. it is what is yet not known, /thought, seen, touched but really what is not. /and that is." Eva Hesse. Lucy Lippard, *Eva Hesse* (New York: New York UP, 1976) 165.

³ "I wanted to get to non art, non connotive, / non anthropomorphic, non geometric, non, nothing, / everything, but of another kind, vision, sort. / from a total other reference point. is it possible?" Eva Hesse. Lucy Lippard, *Eva Hesse* (New York: New York UP, 1976) 165.

⁴ Cecilia Vicuna, "Entering", *Unravelling Words & the Weaving of Water*, trans. By Eliot Weinberger and Suzanne Jill Levine (Saint Paul, Minnesota: Graywolf Press, 1992) 5.

⁵ Maggie O'Sullivan, *red shifts* (Buckfastleigh, Devon: etruscan Books, 2001) np.

⁶ Maggie O'Sullivan *Palace of Reptiles,* (Willowdale, Ontario: The Gig, 2003) 65.

⁷ Cecilia Vicuna, "Precarious", *Unravelling Words & the Weaving of Water*, trans. By Eliot Weinberger and Suzanne Jill Levine (Saint Paul, Minnesota: Graywolf Press, 1992). p. ?

⁸ Madeline Gins, *Helen Keller or Arakawa* (Santa Fe and New York: Burning Books with East-West Cultural Studies, 1994) 9.

⁹ Madeline Gins, *Helen Keller or Arakawa* (Santa Fe and New York: Burning Books with East-West Cultural Studies, 1994) 37.

"My tend sees errant, Vulnerable Chanceways": Maggie O'Sullivan's House of Reptiles *and recent American Poetics*

Nerys Williams

I

In rehearsing the performance of a poem, or the recital of a song, Welsh speakers frequently gesture to a process of *'lliwio'r darn.'* Translated literally as the 'colouring of the text' – this idiomatic saying has little to do with 'filling in' the blankness of an outline. Instead it emphasises the tonal structure of the poem or lyric; how certain resonances can be accentuated through the modalities of voice. Fortuitously perhaps *lliwio* is also phonetically identical to *'llywio'* – to steer, to give direction. Pivotal to the 'colouring' of any text is the process of interpretation, the translation of words on the page or score into an empathetic and emotive performance. This act of interpretation hinges upon the willingness of the performer to somehow *inhabit* the work.

Though my reference to this practice of colouring the text has its currency in recent Welsh culture, we can trace this fascination with the performance of poetry through an extensive bardic literary tradition with its emphasis on the lyric as oral transmission. Within current Welsh language poetic performance there is a resolute insistence that the poem must not only be rehearsed extensively beforehand but also learnt by rote.[1] Here mnemonics comes into a creative play with the

---

[1] Here I am referring to the particular tradition of the 'Eisteddfods' a festival which includes competitions for reciting poetry.

modalities of voice; highlighting specific resonances which may have remained concealed in the original text. But the audience of this performance is faced with a certain paradox and one which I hope may allow us a way 'into' investigating Maggie O'Sullivan's poetry. The colouring of the text in a Welsh language performance emphasises the immediacy of expression. Yet as an audience we are also made aware that the 'spontaneity' of the performance is also heavily mediated, rehearsed, if not instructed.

In pondering over some of these ideas on poetic performance I came across by chance an obsolete Welsh language manual entitled *Ysgol Yr Adroddwr* (The Reciter's School, 1908) by Reverend J. Gwrhyd Lewis.[2] This volume's aim is towards the perfectibility of the recitation of the poem through attention to the craft or artistry of performance. Turning to the contents page one wonders at the meticulous subdivisions and clauses that Lewis directs us to. Not only are there lessons in the physiology, emotive utterance, breath and timing but the volume also grapples with problems of stammering and physical postures on stage. One section focusing on the dramatisation of the poem even illustrates fifteen different physical gestures which convey various emotions ranging from fear, hatred, and nationalism to ardour, nostalgia and an interesting pose entitled 'Taraniad' (Thundering).

The Reciter's School, as the title itself implies, is navigated by an intense formalism or ambition for the poetic performance as a definitive reading. While it might be unfair or simply misplaced to compare the ideals of this booklet now almost a century old with more recent poetic practice, Lewis's valiant attempt to somehow rid the performance of the text of inconsistencies and flaws seems a useful base to start from. Indeed what I will eventually propose in broaching O'Sullivan's poetry is that it is precisely these so called 'errors' of articulation which the poems themselves are grappling with and attempting to incorporate. A visual stammering or stuttering on the page coupled with the inclusion of unfamiliar neologisms and portmanteau words are central strategies in many of her poems. And frequently the emerging and shape-shifting formulations of a key phrase provide an unexpected rhythmic incantation.

---

[2] *Ysgol Yr Adroddwr: Gwersi ar Adrodd* (Briton Ferry: DL Jones Publishers, 1908)

Undoubtedly approaching O'Sullivan's work presents complexities since she is visual artist, performance artist and poet. These subdivisions sometimes can often appear too constricting since there is a fluid interplay between these different media in her work. On reflection the Welsh idiom provides a further initial point of reference for considering her work. The 'colouring' of the text implies not only an awareness to the interpretative performance of a poem but also gestures to words themselves as a painter's palette, the swathes of brushstrokes in the text heightened in performance.

There is also an instructive and informing context of important predecessors which can inform a reading of O'Sullivan's poetry, such as her acknowledged debt or inspiration from English sound poet Bob Cobbing and German installation artist Joseph Beuys. But my investigation in this essay will be based on her written texts- primarily focused in her most recent volume *Palace of Reptiles* (2003) but drawing reference at the close to *In the House of the Shaman* (1996) and *Red Shifts* (2002).[3] Though known within an experimental English poetry context my intention is to read her work somewhat 'aslant' within an American context of poetry and poetics. While I do not propose that O'Sullivan's own poetics can be sourced exclusively from this American 'vein', one certainly senses in her later work that there is an important interplay between her ideas and an extensive lineage of American poetic practice. Indeed, even from a cursory reading of O'Sullivan's volumes one is alerted to citations from modernist precursors such as William Carlos Williams, Gertrude Stein and Ezra Pound. These explicit literary references exert a historical 'framing' of the poetry within an earlier investigative American poetic tradition. This tentative transatlantic relationship comes to the fore in her co-editing with Wendy Mulford of the anthology *Out of Everywhere: Linguistically Innovative Poetry by Women in North America and the UK.*[4] The volume's loaded subtitle suggests that there are continuities and correspondences to be addressed between recent poetry in the UK and American poets associated with language writing such as Lyn

[3] *In the House of the Shaman* (Cambridge: Reality Street Editions, 1996); *Palace of Reptiles* (Willowdale, Ontario: The Gig, 2003); *Red Shifts* (Etruscan Books, 2002).
[4] Eds. Maggie O'Sullivan and Wendy Mulford *Out of Everywhere: Linguistically innovative poetry by women in North America and the UK.* Cambridge: Reality Street Editions 1996.

Hejinian, Rae Armantrout and Susan Howe. O'Sullivan's poetry and language writing attempt to establish a provocative dialogue with a particular vein of American Modernism. Indeed in the editorial for this work O'Sullivan gestures towards a shared interest in female poetic precursors whose work perhaps only in the last couple of decades has been given significant attention. O'Sullivan directly points us towards a distinct modernist lineage:

> Historically such pioneering poets as Gertrude Stein, Mina Loy HD and Lorine Niedecker have done much to shape an energetic and influential though marginalised tradition of innovative writing practices. (10)

In the same editorial O'Sullivan hints that there is a shared preoccupation with form and a historical lineage of experimental investigation which tentatively links the writers in the anthology:

> Many of these poets are involved in long poetic sequences or in project-orientated work, the textual, aesthetic and political perspectives of which can only be glimpsed here. This engagement with larger poetic discourses and practices embraces inter and multi media work and performative directions and celebrates poetry as event. (10)

Since I will be focusing on *Palace of Reptiles* this investigation will be limited to the textual reading on the page of O'Sullivan's work. But this excerpt raises crucial questions for the ambitions for the long poetic work. For instance How can a poetry that challenges conventional ideas of narrative sustain its momentum and investigation over the course of a volume? Can a written text enact the celebration of 'poetry as event'? Indeed one might want to suggest at this early stage that the freighted term itself 'event' implies a certain spontaneous performance. But how can this be navigated by a written text?

Providing a reading of error in O'Sullivan's poetry will offer an alternative mapping of the ambitions of her work. Her most recent volume *Palace of Reptiles* closes with an essay /talk 'Riverrunning (realisations' dedicated to the American poet Charles Bernstein. Considering O'Sullivan's work briefly in tandem with Bernstein's poetics may allow us to configure a further understanding of an 'erring' reading of O'Sullivan's work. Eventually we will tease from the poetry a configuration of error not only as a typographical stammering in the text but as a form of investigation which in the poet's own words is '*errant. vulnerable chanceways.*'⁵ An interpretation of the erring momentum of O'Sullivan's work promises to offer an insight into her gesture to poetry as event and the ambitions of the longer poetic work. But before this mapping, it is worth introducing O'Sullivan's poetry and the immediate demands that her work places upon the reader.

II

Turning to O'Sullivan's *Palace of Reptiles*, a companion volume to her earlier *In the House of the Shaman*, offers the reader a way into the extensive range of her poetry. Divided into three sections – the final a concluding statement of poetics 'riverrunning (realisations', this volume serves as a sustained development of various occasions of poetry which are rethreaded, redeveloped during the course of the book. The initial overwhelming inflexion of sound in the opening poem 'Birth Palette' is accompanied by the inclusion of a visual score at the second section's close. One sense at various points a proglema for poetry in the opening section's titles which such as 'Narcotic Properties' and 'Theoretical Economies' which play with an instructive principle of composition.

The poem 'Orphée' which features in this opening section, is more immediately lyrical in its ambitions. The title returns us to familiar inter-textual territory- with its referencing of the Orpheus and Eurydice myth and the figure of the musician in the underworld attempting to reclaim his love. O'Sullivan's subtitle quotation from Jean Cocteau also draws us more recently to Cocteau's film *Orphée* (1950), placing the myth into a context of poetic jealousy and retribution. These available intertexts and contexts for O'Sullivan's poem suggest that one can read the poem as a meditation of the practice of poetry. The aural performance of the poem works against the immediate seduction of narrative. One senses that the sonic inflexions of this poems work both to disrupt and enhance the texture of the text. Finding a critical vocabulary to broach this tension in O'Sullivan's work will hopefully inform our eventual reading of error and erring in her poetics.

---

⁵ *Palace of Reptiles* (Willowdale, Ontario: The Gig, 2003), p. 64

'Orphée' opens with a visually arresting mirror scene which serves as a cue to the poem's fascination with surfaces, reflections and transformations:

> The mirror is open. Overturning
> pencils of water.
>
> Twenty-two hundred and ninety-four dreams
> Embroidered on the black white wind –
>
> Orphée, the Singer
> sung mirrors from the mask of noon.
>
> One glass of water illumines the tongue –
> fable. Death comes
> & goes &
> becomes
> water
> & the dreams
> drum as
> the Bird sings its fingers-ladders to
> exist. The mirrors are pearled liquid
> again – the pages blank. Anonymous.
>
> Auric,
> Assuredly
> Coded. (13)

Immediately one might sense the running of cinematic frames in this opening stanza, how surprising juxtapositions succeed in suturing the thread of a narrative. Drawing directly from Cocteau's film we have a point of entry which is a mirror. This sense of the mirror as a point of entry is an important one since it abandons the idea of self-circumspection as narcissism. Abstract properties are given concrete resonance or imagistic density; dreams become 'embroidered', Death is initially a figure which transforms into water. There is also a sense of magical incantation associated with these moments of shape shifting. The dreams 'drum' is associated with the surreal impression of 'Bird sings its fingers'. Could the fingers be a reference to a musical chord, or some sense of notes in tandem, a climactic rise or crescendo associated with 'ladders'? There is certainly some reference to a heightened performance which is cut short. The initial point of entry disappears as the mirror's surface resumes to 'pearled liquid'.[6] A poem which initially started with a premise of a story, or an oral story in the form of a 'tongue-fable' ends in this stanza as a withholding the pages are 'blank' and 'anonymous'. One wonders over the reference to 'Auric'. There appears to be a fascination for what is sonically transmitted, or what cannot be decoded or unscrambled. An emergent tension exits between the sonic performance of words and how they may be transcribed upon the page.

Certainly one perceives reading on into the poem that this is a work fascinated with the properties of interpretation and readerly reception. The poem as a whole gestures to this in its emphasis upon the language of media and its hardware; 'broadcasts' 'transmitting' 'satellites' and 'headphones'. Although I am somewhat wary of reducing 'Orphée' to a self-reflexive examination of poetic inspiration, there is evidence that O'Sullivan poem like Cocteau's film, is fascinated by a menacing forcefield of desire:

> Chained to the ear, Death comes
> & broadcasts & waits
> behind the mirror.
> The gloves too, shadow &
> flag & roar the trees
> around, but cannot.
>
> One glass of water
> Transmitting
> episodic
> articulations.
>
> A glazier walks through the earth calling the ruins strapped
> on his back an angel.
>
> One glass of water spells a fabled syncopation of keylit
> memories.
>
> Death falls in love with Orphée. Her black
> whispering road is not usual and the gloves are dreams.
> Cockerel silt – both nicotines – both nerves – both
> satellites backwards.

---

[6] As an additional intertext to the poem it is perhaps noteworthy that one of the trick mirrors that features in Cocteau's film was actually a thousand-pound tub of mercury.

Rubbles of security distress the mirror twice as fast.
Silence.
Lake Touch.

The zone haunts all thickness, all privilege
Each night, poetry beats its fish.
Each night, Death watches over.
Headphones and windswept tenors twin at the gate,
veil and fracture.

A squiggle of hyacinths swing their sleeves.

Invisible. (14–15)

The premise of an oral story or 'tongue fable' which opens the poem is asserted in the digressive patterning of sound. I earlier drew attention to the shape-shifting properties of this poem. Looking closer there is also a focus on the transformative shifting of nouns and their associations. Menace is possibly associated with the anonymous 'gloves' that frame a distinctly unsettling landscape. Provocatively O'Sullivan's 'Orphée' dismantles divisions between interior and exterior and later we are faced with the statement that the 'gloves' are dreams. As readers we remain uncertain of whether we are reading a psychic landscape of impressions or an instructive fable. Undoubtedly there is a fascination with the uncanny and the fantastical in these stanzas. One has only to consider the glass of water 'transmitting episodic articulations' and spelling 'a fabled syncopation of keylit memories'. Initially perhaps a Ouja board springs to mind, but one might wonder at what 'keylit memories' might suggest. Undoubtedly the poems reference to a text that is 'coded' alerts one to a fascination with a transmission which cannot be unlocked or unscrambled.

Inflections of apocalypse haunt the text as well as images from the *Inferno*. Yet O'Sullivan's humour should not be overlooked. While there is an apocalyptic resonance in the image of a glazier walking 'calling the ruins strapped on his back an angel', it also retains a sense of absurdity too. Similarly the zone that frames the close of the poem might draw one to speculate on Dante's *Inferno* with its indication of gates as well. And comically in the midst of this there is the penitent impression of poetry beating a fish. Overall we might ponder whether death is the muse which propels the poem. Paradoxically the prevalence of surfaces whether they are bodies of water or mirrors which engulf the poet, refuse to grant us a human reflection. This noted absence is echoed in the closing word 'Invisible'. On hindsight there is an asserted mistrust of the act of seeing in 'Orphée' There is a sense in which Death's voice which is described as a 'black whispering road' blinds the poet. Far from being a siren song the sound which seduces Orphée is described as a kind of glottal fur in the startling word combinations of 'Cockerel silt' and 'both nicotines'. As we will see these surprising word combinations which question their availability as nouns or adjectives are a characteristic of O'Sullivan's poetry.

This brief discussion of 'Orphée' alerts us the more evident features of Sullivan's work: its fascination with word association and sonic incantation in preference to the linear chronology of a narrative. In this vein we could possibly link O'Sullivan's technique of defamiliarising nouns and a reliance upon a sense of accretion of sound, rather than a direct presentation of narrative to Stein's poetics. Famously Stein gestures to composition rather than writing, as she maintains in her essay 'Composition as Explanation':

> The time of the composition is the time of the composition. It has been at times a present thing it has been at times a past thing it has been at times a future thing it has been at times an endeavour at parts of all of these things. In my beginning it was a continuous present a beginning again and again and again.[7]

This form of temporal folding in Stein's work suggests an accretive measure. The insistence on the 'time of the composition', allows us to consider the text as an ongoing method of description which is not harnessed to immobilising or objectifying the world. Equally O'Sullivan is interested in how words assert their meanings and the valences of interpretation. Furthermore one might want to tentatively consider that the accumulative patterning of O'Sullivan's work mark an insistence of that earlier freighted phrase 'poetry as event'. This sense of sonic accumulation functions especially in a work such as 'Birth Palette'. Her work requires that the reader immerses herself in the immediacy of deciphering sound shifting neologisms which can be retraced to an earlier associational matrix in the text. This in turn complicates the idea of the poetic event as a solely a spontaneous expression.

---

[7] Gertrude Stein, *Look at Me Now and Here I am*, ed. Patricia Meyerowitz (London: Penguin, 1984), p. 29.

This associative patterning in O'Sullivan's work as an erring momentum deriving from Latin *errāre* – to stray, wander or rove. Yet we need to consider in greater detail how sound associations establish and investigate meaning in O'Sullivan's poetry. One way possibly is to consider the sound structures of her work as music. Pound suggests that music in poetry or what he configures as *melopœia* can be viewed as having an epistemological function. Furthermore he indicates that *melopœia* works as an access to the unconscious, describing it as:

> a force tending often to lull, or distract the reader from the exact sense of the language. It is poetry on the borders of music and music is perhaps the bridge between consciousness and the unthinking sentient or even insentient universe.[8](26)

In this light *melopœia* would appear to work in tension with *logopœia* – the intellectual or emotive association of the words themselves. This simultaneous gesture to accuracy and 'distraction' begins to indicate a useful connection with our consideration of erring even as a friction between the sonorous ambitions of the 'tongue-fable' and an awareness of the written text in O'Sullivan's 'Orphée'.

Roland Barthes essay 'The Grain of the Voice,'[9] provides a further approach to the sonic density of O'Sullivan's work. In his essay Barthes adopts Julia Kristeva's terms *phenotext* and *genotext* to an application of understanding music and its performance. The genotext in Kristeva's account lends itself to melodic devices, a form of ecstatic drive closely allied to the semiotic, while the phenotext suggests the communicative level of language, that is the structures which underpin grammatical rules and conventions. Kristeva states the phenotext 'obeys rules of communication and presupposes a subject of enunciation and an addressee.'[10] In 'The Grain of the Voice,' Barthes transposes Kristeva's configuration to *pheno-song* and the *geno-song*. In the context of music the pheno-song is the impulse towards articulation, expression and performance. By contrast the geno-song works at the level of signification, delighting in the *jouissance* of the production of sound, drawing attention to the materiality of language. As Barthes

[8] Ezra Pound, *ABC of Reading* (New York: New Directions, 1987), p. 26.
[9] Roland Barthes, 'The Grain of the Voice', in *Music Image Text*, trans. Stephen Heath (New York: The Noonday Press, 1977), pp. 179–189.
[10] Julia Kristeva, *Revolution in Poetic Language* (New York: Columbia University Press, 1984), p. 87.

elucidates the geno-song has 'nothing to do with communication' instead it is:

> that apex (or that depth) of production where the melody really works at the language – not at what it says, but the voluptuousness of its sound-signifiers, of its letters- where melody explores how the language works and identifies with that work. It is, in a very simple word but which must be taken seriously, the *diction* of the language. (182–3)

It seems significant that 'The Grain of the Voice' places a particular emphasis on the display of the geno-song in the recital, as a form of writing. That is the recital through its heightened performance of the geno-song becomes in turn a text. Barthes is categorical since he states 'The song must speak, must *write* – for what is produced at the level of the geno-song is finally writing' (185). This emphasis on the 'grain' forces us to reconsider how one applies the analogy of music to poetry; as an element of resistance or aberration in the recital the grain raises a challenge to the idealisation of closure and perfection.

Immediately one might add that at points it might be difficult to ascertain the nature of the pheno-song since O'Sullivan's work resists an easy reduction into formal categorisation such as lyric or sonnet, elegy or narrative which serves to loosely provide governing rules of articulation and expression. Yet evidently given the dialectical nature of Barthes's discussion, one cannot exist without the other. Marjorie Perloff in an insightful discussion of recent poetry, which includes O'Sullivan's work, urges us to consider the visual mapping of the page as a form of score. Perloff suggests that above performance activates the text:

> We have in any case a poetics of non linearity or postlinearity that masks not a return to 'old forms', because there is never a complete return, no matter how strongly one period style looks back to another, but a kind of 'afterimage' of earlier soundings, whether Anglo-Saxon keenings, formally balanced eighteenth-century prose, Wittgensteinian aphoristic fragment. The new poems are, in most cases, as visual as they are verbal; they must be seen as well as heard which means that at poetry readings, their scores must be performed, activated. Poetry, in this scheme of things, becomes what McCaffrey has called "an experience in language rather than a representation by it"[11]

---

[11] Marjorie Perloff, After Free Verse: The New Non Linear Poetries' in *Poetry On &Off the Page: Essays for Emergent Occasions* (Evanston, Northwestern University Press, 1998) p. 166. All further references are embedded in the text.

O'Sullivan's densely sonorous 'Birth Palette' offers an understanding of this interaction between score as a form of measure and the more explosive eruptions of sound which permeate the piece. The title in itself appears to straddle two conflicting impressions, a violent entry and contrastingly an ordering or even a taxonomy. Here one may also want to draw again on the idiom of 'colouring the text', how certain resonances are accentuated through the sonorous performance of the poem. Indeed the opening section of 'Birth Palette' bears a striking resemblance to the performance of an operatic aria and seems to have more than a passing resonance with the tenor of Barthes's essay:

> Lizard air lichens ivy driven urchin's pry to pounce.
> Scribbled terrestrial traor, the paw actions tainy blee
> scoa, blue scog. In eat, gashed harmonica stresses to
> skull icon, jigged but shower, Crushtative bundles,
> Doe, Owl, the Hare mantled in a planetary pivot.
> Vulture-Jar, dragonfly & waterbeetle are we,
> each veil of a glide species. (11)

On an immediate reading of this opening one is struck by a sense of excess, or a delighting in the *jouissance* of sound which draws constant attention to the materiality of language. But what emergent process is being delineated here? On one level there is a sense of a primordial violence, consider for example the verbs 'pounce' and 'gashed' coupled with the neologism 'crushtative'. This word in acting as an adjective points us towards 'crush' and possibly even a word such as 'emotive'. As a portmanteau word it dramatically sutures or even slams together two words creating in turn a lexical violence of its own.

One way of interpreting this opening is section is as gesturing to an evolutionary process; the poem in effect enacts its own archaeological dig investigating the history of plant life, molluscs and an animal food chain. There are suggestions of archaeology inherent in the text, take for example the 'scribbled terrestrial traor'. These words in combination suggest a lexicography on the strata of rocks, which the archaeologist or palaeontologist is required to decipher. The neologism 'traor' at its most immediate evokes the word 'terror'. In consulting the dictionary where the word 'traor' might comfortably sit we are given the word 'tanter' meaning 'hawker' or 'carrier', an interpretative context which might not seem so far removed from the atavistic violence explicit in this section. A further interpretation

could be 'traor' as 'tracer' which refers us once more to the movement of retreading, reviewing and unearthing which this section
builds upon.

Can Barthes' pinpointing of inflexions of geno-song and pheno-
song in a text actually aid us in approaching the sonic density or
performance of 'Birth Palette'? Possibly if we begin to read the movement of O'Sullivan's poetry as an accretive patterning, a volition
which is not predetermined in advance. O'Sullivan builds upon and
redeploys sound measures which establish a friction with the 'evolutionary' overview of the poem. Overall the poem builds towards a
taxonomy, a structuring of an evolution but a form of *erring* momentum is created by the interaction between this aim (or pheno-song)
and the associative if not explosive sound patterns generated within
'Birth Palette'. Looking closely one might want to identify an ecstatic
drive with such lines as 'the paw actions tainy blee scoa, blue scog.'
While at first these words appear nonsensical, within the resonance
of these sounds there is an evolutionary process to be traced. A 'paw'
suggests a crude rough gesture which is then possibly linked to Scots
dialect or even and Anglo-Saxon evocation 'tainy blue', which then
asserts itself as 'blue scog'. We can suggest that 'Birth-Palette' is as
much about the evolutionary matrix of language as of animal
species. The poem displays a fascination with how one dissects, analyses and organises through poetic language. Final lines from this
section enforce this reading providing us with the tensions between
this analytic impulse and an erratic movement. A 'Vulture-Jar' could
suggest an observation case or a specimen container for the study of
organs. In opposition we have the fleeting momentum associated
with 'dragonfly & waterbeetle' as the 'glide species.' Similarly
perhaps we could again connect with Pound's referencing of a simultaneous gesture to accuracy and 'distraction' inherent in poetic
composition.

Considering erring then as a momentum generated by the associative sound patterings of language, one might wonder what sense
of evolution can be gleaned from O'Sullivan's 'Birth Palette'
Although there is no immediate linear trajectory, a traceable
chronology does appear to emerge. Within the sonic evolution of the
poem there are veiled references also to a 'birth' of a primitive
industry, or at its most basic a navigating and exploitation of
natural resources:

Sheer Shoe-Show darks, Weem Cyclicity,
Threads &Wisps.
Yesterday's loaf soaks on the spindle,
sky blue large the sea's purple Octopi bickerings
re-in-indigo dozens indignant.
Options Falter.
Rodent, Bat Swing Mare-O-Crow-O Crane
Midscales cache,
untilled kestrels carded,
ancestrous to a Song

Earth scalded, wired lame.
Yew Hung Abbatoir Voltages.   (11)

Traces of a historical narrative emerge here, even a detailing of primi-tive communities can be found in 'Yesterday's loaf soaks on the spindle' and the referencing to 'Yew Hung Abbatoir'. These interpreta-tions are of course open ended but there is a sense in which one is reminded of the survival of a basic human community within a force-field of nature. What is apparent is how the sound patterning of this section almost pre-empt these historical shards in the text. Take for example the combination of words as 'Weem Cyclicity Threads &Wisps'. Here we have the action, measure and momentum of the spindle. What is also distinctive in this section is how the poet succeeds in characterising a visual sensation through aural resonance. We could read this as a form of synaesthesia. Remarkably O'Sullivan sets the colour of the sky as 'purple Octopi bickerings/ re-in-indigo's indignant', indicating at once not only colour but momentum evok-ing the patterning of the sky as a chromatogram of watermarked dyes. Above all the reader is given the sense that there are valiant attempts to somehow control the environment but that these 'Options falter' since the kestrels are 'untilled' and the 'Earth scalded'. A communal history is also glimpsed at here with the reference to kestrels as being 'ancestrous to song'. The overall impression is that we remain far from the cycle of 'tongue-fables' recalled in 'Orphée', that forms a historical testimony to a struggle for survival.

Viewing 'Birth Palette' as an erring momentum generated between an evolutionary overview and the eruption of sound encourages us to read the poem as an investigation of how history may be recuperated or reimagined. The closing stanza draws again on fragments of a histor-ical testimony but we are also made aware of meaning that is gener-ated by the sound associations within the text:

Ricochet, straw cauldrons, water sickle
rooting turbid Rails.
Pig gathers in the lemon.
Cow, later of wood.
Lioness, 'twas all moon down in the brainstem,
tally-sticks –
Jackal woke fresh, key made from Butterfly depths,
the Chrysalis,
the Spider.
Treasury Futures.
Asterisms liced from the Skull.
Nerve Surge.
Expulsions to a Rope. (12)

The language of warfare, commerce, punishment and even legal credo make their appearance in this closing section. In startling combinations we move from the shot of a shell 'Ricochet' to a naive 'straw cauldron', from the fiscal implications of 'tally sticks' and 'Treasury Futures' to Jackals and stars or 'asterisms'. The indications of punishment as a ritualised killing is indicated in the final line 'Expulsions to a Rope'. Within these fragments or indications of historical testimony is the momentum of animal and insect life. Overall the momentum of the poem invites us to read these remnants of human cycles in opposition with the patterning of the natural world. It would be reductive to pronounce 'Birth Palette' as a critique of a sanitised view of historical evolution; but the erring momentum of this work reimagines and embraces the folds and pleats within history which are often erased into a convenient chronology. In effect the digressive momentum of an errant trajectory allows O'Sullivan to enfold an evolutionary process which refutes not only resolution, but a hectoring judgement.

III

In my introduction I suggested that O'Sullivan's recent poetry establishes a productive correspondence with recent American poetics. Her introduction to the anthology *Out of Everywhere* gestures that there are continuities and correspondences between recent poetry from the UK and North America. Providing a context for some of these shared preoccupations enables a further way of considering *Palace of Reptiles*. Moreover understanding O'Sullivan's work through a considered American perspective will provide a further mapping of the errant trajectory which we have contemplated thus far.

Perloff argues that although *Out of Everywhere* is an anthology of female poetry, the volume's general fascination with deconstructing language and an exploration of form if not the epistemological role of poetry itself, is also reflected in the work of male poets of the same generation. Perloff is not discounting here the validity of remarks such as Susan Howe's that typographical experimentation may function as 'abstractions' from 'masculine linguistic formations' (166). But in attempting to evaluate a general tendency of what Perloff loosely calls 'a poetics of non-linearity or post-linearity' she comments that the poems in *Out of Everywhere* have 'many counterparts in the work of Clark Coolidge and Steve McCaffrey, Charles Bernstein and Bob Perelman, Bruce Andrews and Christian Bok'. In an important statement she adds that 'my own sense is that the transformation that has taken place in verse may well be more generational than gendered' (166).

Certainly the emergence of 'language writing',[12] in the States during the mid seventies upped the ante in debates over the role and function of poetry as a vehicle for political examination. Historically, language writing can be characterised as a poetry which frequently works in terms of diminished reference, questioning the 'transparency' of language, or language's unequivocal claim as a finite medium of representation. The disruption of syntax, narrative and the foregrounding of language's generative properties through its slippages, puns and word play serve to create a poetry of intense linguistic opacity. This writing was predicated on the belief that the divergence of poetic language from customary discourse does marked out the ground for political agency.

While these well-rehearsed, historical 'characterisations' of language writing are familiar territory for most readers, mapping out a claim for this tendency's transformative impact will help us to establish a linkage between O'Sullivan's work and American contemporary poetics. One could state language writing's notorious resistance to a pedagogical summation of its poetics was indicative not only of the multiplicity of its poetics, but of a strategic indeterminacy at the core of the writing. In surveying the compendium of early poetics in *The*

---

[12] Here I am following Lyn Hejinian's sketch of the 'emergence' of language writing in her collection of essays *The Language of Inquiry* (Berkeley: University of California Press, 2000.). Hejinian suggests that as a 'specific social moment' it could be situated 'around 1976', p. 320.

L=A=N=G=U=A=G=E Book and *In The American Tree*,[13] Jed Rasula asserts that the only consensus that may be said to have been attained through the diverse writings was 'the restoration of the reader as coproducer of the text, and an emphasis on the materiality of the signifier.'[14] Rasula's observation on language writing's overall focus upon the reader as a 'coproducer', appears to align the tenor of their poetics neatly with Roland Barthes's identification of the 'writerly text.'[15] Barthes as one recalls suggests that the writerly text can be understood as *'ourselves writing'* (5), and characterises its goal as a desire 'to make the reader no longer a consumer, but a producer of the text' (4).

Although language writing by its detractors has been characterised as merely ventriloquising the investigations of post-structuralist theory, it is worth noting the *transformative* aspect of the imbrication of theory and poetry. Michael Greer astutely notes in examining Lyn Hejinian's pivotal essay 'The Rejection of Closure',[16] that the particular value of this writing is the way in which 'many of the familiar-sounding terms are transformed, rewritten in a largely post-structural mode and context'.[17] Greer adds importantly that 'at the same time, a common vocabulary, an already existing discourse for talking about poets and poetry, is reactivated and, quietly politicized' (350). Interestingly, Hejinian herself notes more recently that the distinctions between theory and poetry in her own work are indeed negligible:

> Theory asks what practice does and in asking, it sees the connections that practice makes. Poetic language, then, insofar as it is a language of linkage, is a practice. It is practical. But poetry insofar as it comments on itself . . . is also theoretical.[18]

---

[13] *The L=A=N=G=U=A=G=E Book* eds. Bruce Andrews and Charles Bernstein (Carbondale: Southern Illinois University Press, 1984); *In the American Tree: Language, Realism, Poetry*, ed. Ron Silliman (Orno Maine: National Poetry Foundation, 1986).

[14] Jed Rasula, *The American Poetry Wax Museum: Reality Effects 1940–1990* (Urbana: National Council of Teachers of English, 1996), p. 397.

[15] Barthes, *S/Z*, trans. Richard Miller (Oxford: Blackwell, 2000). Further references are embedded in the text.

[16] Lyn Hejinian, *The Language of Inquiry*, pp. 40–58. Originally published in 1985.

[17] Michael Greer, 'Ideology and Theory in Recent Experimental Writing or, The Naming of "Language Poetry"', *Boundary 2*, 16.2/3 (1989) 335–55 (p. 350).

[18] Hejinian, *The Language of Inquiry*, p. 356.

The intervention of theoretical concerns, particularly in early language writing, are not discursive accounts of propositions themselves, but were attempts to motivate some of the tenets of these discussions into a certain 'textuality' of writing.

Palace of Reptiles includes in its final section a poetics talk 'riverrunning (realisations' dedicated to Charles Bernstein. The talk was originally given for the Poetics Program at Buffalo University in 1993 and in the bibliography of sources for the work O'Sullivan includes Bernstein's volume of writings *A Poetics*. While the overarching poetic ambitions for both these poets may be markedly different, there are certain correspondences between 'riverrunning (realisations' and Bernstein's celebrated essay in verse 'Artifice of Absorption'[19] which provide a useful context for reading O'Sullivan's poetry as indicative of what Perloff points to as a 'generational' tranformation in poetics. Bernstein's designation of his key terms 'artifice' and 'absorption' allow us to draw a reflective connection between our earlier discussion of pheno-song and geno-song in Barthes's 'The Grain of the Text'.

Provocatively, Bernstein's celebrated essay in verse draws attention to what he calls 'official verse culture' and its privileging of authenticity and sincerity. Bernstein associates the workshop lyric with a certain directness or 'transparency', which can be understood as the conceptualisation of language as an unproblematic vehicle for communicating thought and perception. By now it has become somewhat axiomatic to attend to the contrasting 'opacity', of the poetry associated with language writing, understanding this 'density' in the text as the foregrounding of the generative properties of language itself. But what is most compelling about this essay, is how its key terms 'artifice' and 'absorption', are given provisional interpretations, since both these terms 'shift' notably during the course of the discussion. While one would intuitively associate the 'transparency' of the workshop aesthetic with a certain 'absorption', and the 'opacity' of more innovative poetry with a certain 'artifice', Bernstein problematises these categories by suggesting that a poetry of 'impermeability' can also be 'absorbing':

> In my poems, I
> frequently use opaque & nonabsorbable

---

[19] Bernstein, 'Artifice of Absorption', in *A Poetics* (Harvard: Harvard University Press, 1991), pp. 9–89.

```
elements, digressions &
interruptions, as part of a technological
arsenal to create a more powerful
("souped-up")
absorption than possible with traditional
& blander, absorptive techniques. This is a
precarious road because insofar
as the poem seems
overtly self-conscious
as opposed to internally
incantatory or psychically
actual, it may produce
self-consciousness in the reader
destroying his or her absorption by theatricalizating
or conceptualizing the text, removing
it from the
realm of an experience engendered
to that of technique
exhibited.
This is the subject of much of my
work.                    (53)
```

Candidly Bernstein here gestures to a problematic in his own technique of applying 'nonabsorbable' elements in his poetry. While he suggests that his overall intention is to engage the reader, such tactics can also generate a self-consciousness or even anxiety in reading too. To his gesturing to the incantatory texture of an absorbed reading as 'an experience engendered', echoes O'Sullivan's own gesture to 'poetry as event'. Earlier on in 'Artifice of Absorption' Bernstein also gestures to error as providing a digressive element in the grain of the poem, working against a conclusive pattern:

```
Indeed, part of the meaning of a poem may
be its fight for accumulation; nonetheless, its
text will contain destabilizing elements- errors,
unconscious elements, contexts of (re)publication
& the like- that will erode any proposed
accumulation that does not allow for them. (16)
```

Returning to our initial dilemma over the terms 'artifice' and absorption', it is apparent that Bernstein associates the foregrounding of language's generative properties with a certain engagement from his reader. This is made apparent when he gestures in an earlier essay to a 'writing that incorporates the issue of interpretation and interaction.'[20] Approached from this perspective of 'readerly' engage-ment, it is not surprising that Bernstein suggests in 'Artifice of Absorption' that the term absorption could be read as 'engrossing, engulfing completely, engaging . . . enthralling: belief, conviction.' (29). Indeed, Bernstein links the 'artifice' of poetry, or what he calls, 'writing centered on its wordness',[21] with an overall ambitious polit-ical and social claim:

> Language is commonness in being, through which we see & make sense of & value. Its exploration is the exploration of the human common ground. The move from a purely descriptive, outward directive, writing toward writing centered on its wordness, its physicality, its haecceity (thisness) is, in its impulse, an investigation of human self-sameness, of the place of our connection: in the world, in the word, in ourselves. (32)

While O'Sullivan's own 'riverrunning (realisations' does not be making the same explicit social and political claims as Bernstein's poetics, her essay broaches the density or opacity of poetry as an enabling device for her own 'tongue-fables':

> The words I make Celebrate ORigns/ ENtrances- the
> Materiality of Language: its actual contractions &
> expansions, potentionalities, prolongments, assemblages-
> the acoustic, visual, oral & sculptural qualities
> within the physical: intervals between; in & beside.
> Also, the jubilant seep In So of Spirit – Entanglement
> with vegetations, thronged weathers, puppy-web we agreed
> animals. Articulations of the Earth of Language that is
> Minglement, Caesura, Illumination.
> Heart.   (64)

In gesturing to both a celebration of 'origins' and 'entrances' O'Sullivan's points us towards a fascination with etymologies and neol-ogisms in her poetry. Similar to Bernstein's poetics her essay also focuses on the 'haeccity' of language itself. Most pertinently O'Sullivan's 'Riverrunning realisations)' appears to share a similar preoccupation with the text as a multiplicity of contradictory impulses moving from 'contractions & expansions, potentionalities and prolong-ments'. Although this section initally focuses on a temporal impulse in

---

[20] Bernstein, 'Writing and Method', in Content's Dream, Essays 1975–1984 (Los Angeles: Sun & Moon Press, 1996) pp. 217–36 (p. 233).
[21] Bernstein, 'Three or four things I know about him', Content's Dream pp. 13–33 (p. 32).

the writing, as it proceeds the proposal of her poetics moves attention
to a spatial awareness. One might wonder at the shift to the proposition
of 'articulations of the Earth of Language.' The concluding statements
suggest an incantatory power of language to provide a shamanaistic
translation of the natural world in the text.

Bernstein's discussion of the terms song melos and charm melos
recalls our earlier discussion of Barthes's geno and pheno song. Here
Bernstein is discussing the potency of incantation in the poetic text:

> This is related to
> the *spellweaving*
> & spellbinding functions of
> nonoccidental,
> nonoriental poetries, such as those collected in
> Jerome Rothenberg's *Technicians of the*
> *Sacred,*
> especially if considered in the light
> of Andrew Welsh's distinction, in *The Roots*
> *of the Lyric*:
> *Primitive Poetry & Modern*
> *Poetics,*
> between "song melos" (externally imposed
> meter) &
> "charm melos" (internally derived from sound &
> rhythm patterns).
> Charm melos depends on
> "artificial", jaggedly rhythmic
> prosodic elements to create a centripetal
> (or vortical)
> energy in the poem that is able to capture (not
> just conscious attention, but the imagination
> or
> psyche). The power of charm melos is *technical*
> in the precise sense of Rothenberg's title:
> the superficially antiabsorptive elements
> (disjunction,
> repetition, accentuated stresses, nonlexical "scat
> sounds) are the basis for this
> souped-up poetic engine.   (47–48)

Understanding this impact between 'song melos' and 'charm melos'
as establishing a contradictory momentum in the poem, Bernstein
draws us once more to our consideration of the poetic work as
enacting an errant trajectory. While initially we are focused on the

development of the overarching structure of the phenosong or song melos, the internal and deliberate intersection of 'antiabsorptive elements' draw attention to a further synchronous dynamic. Earlier on in his essay Bernstein understands this process of reception as a mutual dependency between the tale told and its process of telling as a form of unfolding:

> texts are written to be read or heard,
> that is, exhibited; but the degree the "teller"
> or "way it's told" are allowed to come
> into focus affects the experience of "what"
> is being told or 'what' is
> unfolding.   (31)

Comparatively O'Sullivan in 'riverunning realisations)' draws us into considering her work as the tracing the passage of a pleated textual body and its enfolding of infinite interpretative variations: 'THE FOLD INTRODUCES ANOTHER MOVEMENT, IN CONTRAST TO THE STRAIGHT-FORWARD PILING OF FELT' (68). Like Bernstein she also draws attention to the opacity of her work as emanating from a dense musicality. Interestingly she links this element to a tradition of Irish language oral story telling:

> In Irish, AMHRAIN: CEOL:
> A Song, A Song Said Otherwise, half-sung/ half-said,
> SINGS- Speaking the Self/ whom sang/ Singing over/-
> The Irish again- ABAIR AMHRAN- Say us a Song –
> Say, Speak/ Words Spoken/ Give US Your
> Tongue It to See. (59)

While evidently this evocation to a historical nexus of song and music draws our attention to the storytelling tradition of the spoken word, this extract alerts us to the passage of subjectivity as a constant becoming an insistent 'speaking' of the self. Not only is there an indication of an 'absorbed' attention by the audience but a corresponding alertness to the mechanics or as Bernstein would phrase it 'artifice' of the telling as in 'Tongue it to See'. Yet a somewhat problematic question remains to be answered. In both Bernstein and O'Sullivan's poetics there is an evident appeal to an early practice of poetry as chant, initiation and incantation. But somehow we need to contextualise this evocation within an understanding of recent poetics. Turning to the following passage from 'Riverrunning Realisations)' will allow us to see how an erring momentum could be read in tandem with initiation or incantation in a postmodern poetic context:

> Words, Breath,
> Divergence & Multiplicity, my tend sees errant, Vulnerable
> Chanceways –
> BECOMING
> Strains of Lament & Desire
> & Perpetual Strong SONG –
> physical fictions, vertiginous & angular swole divulgements,
> resistances, unwisdoms, dither-sickings, Earsick tongue –
> spew- Displacement- Pluralities – Diversity- Convergence,
> Flux of Utterance, Mistakes, Da-mage, Duncan's 'MISUSE,
> MISUNDERSTANDING, THE WHOLE SPIRITUALISED UNIVERSE'
>   activated
> closely, broadly, introspectively – Charting ambiguity,
> tending the possibilities in language. In Saying this I am
> Telescoping/ have you witness I am Sing Lingered, Indeterminate:
>   (64)

O'Sullivan's 'errant' tend here could well be read as an associational patterning of words, and the plurality of meanings, leading us to metaphorical forks in the journey, crossroads and junctions. But in addition to this more general reading of linguistic indeterminacy this passage also builds up its own textual world, a mapping which appears to built paradoxically upon errors, mistakes, a misunderstandings. These resistances, aberrations or obstructions in the text O'Sullivan suggests generate a movement which cannot be predetermined in advance, but hold us hostage to the 'flux of utterance'. An intense speculation on the spatial organisation in this passage moves the reader from displacements, to pluralities, and from diversity to convergence. But does this emphasis on charm melos within the passage enact an incantatory initiation? If so what form of initiation is O'Sullivan drawing our attention to? Is it paradoxically as she states a 'charting' of 'ambiguity' and the tending of 'the possibilities of language'?

Ihab Hassan's general observations on the aesthetics of postmodernism provides a further reading of the errant momentum of O'Sullivan's poetics. In focusing an attention upon the term 'immanences' Hassan gestures to a capability of an artwork to generate its own self-referential symbolic structure:

I call the second major tendency of postmodernism *immancences*, a term which I employ without religious echo to designate the capacity of mind to generalize itself in symbols, intervene more and more into nature, act upon itself through its own abstractions and so become increasingly, immediately its own environment. This noetic tendency may be evoked further by such sundry concepts as diffusion, interdependence, which all derive from the emergence of human beings as language animals. Homo pictor or Homo significans, gnostic creatures constituting themselves, and determinedly their universe, by symbols of their own making.[22]

This impetus on creating a textual world, a labyrinth of linguistic trajectories comes to the fore in O'Sullivan's poetics:

> What 'Making'- 'Unmaking' is/ a Mattering of
> Materials (motivations & practice) – Living to live in
> that Learning- Uncertain, Uncurtained Tonguescape
> SUNG. SHUNTS. ARM WE. Living Earth Kinships on the
> vast-lunged Shores of the Multiple Body imbued with
> wide-awake slumberings & cavortings. Constructions.
> Intuitions. Transmissions. Radiations. Thinking.
> ATTENDING. Feeling. Will –
> Digressions.
> Pauses.   (65)

O'Sullivan performs her poetics as epistemology, a poetics enquirying after linkages generated by its own linguistic landscape. The danger inherent perhaps of 'learning to live in that Learning' and one that Hassan points us towards is that one is held in an incessant self-referential circuitry. This 'making' and 'unmaking' taken at its most extreme threatens to become textual self-cannibalisation. Turning finally to sections from the earlier volume *The House of the Shaman* and the more recent *Red Shifts* might not serve to thoroughly exacerbate this underlying problematic gestured to in Hassan's account. I want to close on gesturing how the errant trajectory of O'Sullivan's work invites our participation and attempts, not unlike Bernstein's poetics, to situate 'the place of our connection: in the world, in the word, in ourselves.'

> *when your animal is brought back*
> *you*
> *too*
> *water & ice & leaves & snow become*
> *you*

---

[22] Ihab Hassan, 'Towards a Concept of Postmodernism', *Postmodernism: A Reader* ed. Thomas Docherty (New York: Columbia University Press, 1993) pp. 146–56 (p.153)

too
Day Door Sky & Sing
you
too
scald & crow down ink
you
too
stiffen swoop on ridge
you
too
topple turn hills many more turns
you
too
the Beasts do the rain not the Birds do another
you
too
call the Pulsing home   (17)

In its unfolding and incantatory movement this section from *The House of the Shaman* certainly reels in the reader. At its most basic O'Sullivan succeeds in narrativising a landscape without immobilising it into a series of static images. Furthermore the relationship between the subject and object forms an interdependency as the passage moves. On one level the lines gesture to a shared understanding if not a pervasive sense of animism. Possibly this is a narration of bird flight or weather cycles- as readers we are situated in this landscape not as impassive observers but as participants. Turning to Bernstein's analysis of the performative ambitions of poetry helps to clarify the overall impression of participation which is created in the passage:

> In sounding language, we sound the width and breadth and depth of human consciousness – we find our bottom and our top, we find the scope of our ken. In sounding language we ground ourselves as sentient, material beings obtruding into the world with the same obdurate thingness as rocks or soil or flesh. We sing the body of language, relishing the vowels and consonants in every possible sequence. We stutter tunes with no melodies only words.[23]

Whether one agrees with Bernstein's ambitions for poetry's place in the world through it's 'haeccity', or Hassan's more sceptical pronouncement of a postmodern aesthetic as content to exist in its own self referential symbolic structure; an errant trajectory allows

---

[23] Bernstein *Close Listenings: Poetry and the Performed Word* (Oxford: O. U. P, 1998) p. 21.

O'Sullivan to enfold an evolutionary process not easily accommodated by conventional historical accounts. Turning to O'Sullivan's *Red Shifts* grants a final opportunity to chart an associational matrix which gestures to histories which have previously been displaced, overwritten, made unutterable or even unnavigable:

> i have found this red
> is breathed
> or reply
> water's edge, ~~DECOMPOSITIONS~~
> **drawing breath's**
> broken fanging-
> Nion, the Ash, this 3rd
> letter of salvages
> bridle & gut
> aquacity staltic-
>
> pearlful
> shoreline paler pelt
> amber peep in step in in draping-
> the fourth son-over six foot & large square shoulders
> & no way heavy & the long light legs &-
> pennant flut of a red
> kin speckled- raw
> pulse/ raw/ child/ raw/ trout/ raw
> singing
> half to self
> shut erred
> with erred
> cant ———
> cant eat it cant eat it ——
> **cant hold my breath/ my breath**
> sobbing ——
> —— sea's water (sea-ah)
> hard gutteral
> ~~threadened~~ ~~threatened~~ to kill
> reddened
> sorrel reaches ——

Though we are unsure whether 'this red' could possibly be a book or manuscript, the passage reveals an unfolding preoccupation with a buried or semi-legible text or 'a 3rd letter of salvages'. Following through with this reading there is an ambitious aim of reanimating history into an oral story from the gestures to 'breathed' 'reply' and 'drawing breath's'. The landscape created in *Red Shifts* is an atavistic one, one that also points to properties of divination. 'Nion' is the Gaelic word for Ash which was often used for the making shafts of spears and in folklore even magical wands. Etymologically 'Nion' draws from the root meaning an object produced. There are intimations here also of ritual killings which are developed through O'Sullivan's emphatic colouring of the text through the linkages and references to the red 'sorrel' coat of a horse; a cryptic embedding of red with violence in 'threadened' and the gesture to a lifeblood or measure in 'red kin speckled – raw pulse/ raw/ child/ raw/ trout/ raw singing'. Yet in this tracing of sound and visual sensations our overall impression is of a movement which cannot be predetermined in advance into a narrative or retelling.

O'Sullivan's poetry creates a form of 'raw singing' particularly if we understand its rawness as sensations which are prior to their formulation into a system of knowledge. Paradoxically *Red Shifts* strives towards a way of evoking these physical 'resonances' into a resolution, but the tactic of 'shut erred/ with erred' points towards this overall impossibility. While it is tempting to reduce this passage from *Red Shifts* as merely extolling the impossibility of closure, this errant impulse in her work can be understood as a form of poetic investigation. O'Sullivan's poetry challenges the fixing of a chronology; the cry **'cant hold my breath/ my breath'** resists completion. Most importantly an errant reading of O'Sullivan's work emphasises an understanding of poetic investigation itself as a transitional locus. Taken from this perspective we may eventually find some correspondence between our own enquiry, and Martin Heidegger's alluring proposal that '[e]rror is the space where history unfolds . . . Without errancy there would be no history.'[24]

Bibliography

Barthes, Roland. *Music Image Text.* Trans. Stephen Heath. New York: The Noonday Press, 1977.

_____. *S/Z.* Trans. Richard Miller. Oxford: Blackwell, 2000.

Baker, Peter *Obdurate Brilliance: Exteriority and the Modern Long Poem.* Gainesville: University of Florida Press, 1991.

---

[24] cited in Peter Baker, *Obdurate Brilliance: Exteriority and the Modern Long Poem* (Gainesville: University of Florida Press, 1991), p. 45.

Bernstein, Charles *A Poetics*. Harvard: Harvard University Press, 1991.

_____ *Content's Dream Essays 1975–1984*. Los Angeles: Sun & Moon Press, 1986.

_____ *Close Listenings: Poetry and the Performed Word*. Oxford: O. U. P, 1998.

Greer, Michael. 'Ideology and Theory in Recent Experimental Writing or, The Naming of "Language Poetry."' *Boundary 2*, 16.2/3 (Spring 1989): 335–55.

Hassan, Ihab 'Towards a Concept of Postmodernism.' *Postmodernism: A Reader*. Ed. Thomas Docherty. New York: Columbia University Press, 1993 pp. 146–56.

Hejinian, Lyn. *The Language of Inquiry*. Berkeley: University of California Press, 2000.

Kristeva, Julia *Revolution in Poetic Language*. New York: Columbia University Press, 1984.

Lewis, J. Gwrhyd. *Ysgol Yr Adroddwr: Gwersi ar Adrodd*. Briton Ferry: DL Jones Publishers, 1908.

O'Sullivan Maggie. *In the House of the Shaman*. Cambridge: Reality Street Editions, 1996.

_____ . *Palace of Reptiles*. Willowdale, Ontario: The Gig, 2003.

_____ . *Red Shifts* Etruscan Books, 2002.

_____ . (Eds.) with Wendy Mulford *Out of Everywhere: Linguistically innovative poetry by women in North America and the UK*. Cambridge: Reality Street Editions 1996.

Perloff, Marjorie. *Poetry on and Off the Page: Essays for Emergent Occasions*. Evanston, Northwestern University Press, 1998.

Pound, Ezra. *ABC of Reading*. New York: New Directions, 1987.

Rasula, Jed. *The American Poetry Wax Museum: Reality Effects 1940–1990*. Urbana: National Council of Teachers of English, 1996.

Stein, Gertrude, *Look at Me Now and Here I am*. Ed. Patricia Meyerowitz. London: Penguin, 1984.

Maggie O'Sullivan and Scott Thurston:
An interview

This interview was conducted at Edge Hill University, Ormskirk, Lancashire on 15 July 1999 shortly before O'Sullivan gave a reading accompanied by Bill Griffiths and Ken Edwards[1] as part of the Unpacking the Anthology *conference which began the following day. It was first published in* Poetry Salzburg Review 6 *(Summer 2004). Thanks are due to the editor Wolfgang Görtschacher and for his permission to reproduce it here.*

Scott Thurston

ST: To begin with, I'm interested in whether your approach to composition is spontaneous or whether you're more interested in applying particular procedures to materials that either you've previously written or that come from other sources?

MO: Well, I think I do both in my work. Just to give you an example, *UNASSUMING PERSONAS* [1985] came out of using existing texts as source material, rather as Tom Phillips, the painter, did when he went out and chose the first book he could find for threepence, which he treated visually in order to arrive at his own text.[2] I found three secondhand books: *Windsor Castle*, an historical romance by William Harrison Ainsworth published in the late 1800s, *The Story of the Heavens* by Sir Robert S. Ball, published in 1910 and *The Private Life of Helen of Troy* by John Erskine, published 1926, in my local War on Want shop in Acton one Saturday morning and used these – as well as my own diary and journal – as the foundation for *Unassuming Personas*, an elegy for my mother who died in 1981. I collaged 'my own' language, with other vocabularies/languages.

ST: Can you give me an example of the other approach?

MO: The improvisatory approach? *States of Emergency* [1987] is an example of that, where it collages languages from all kinds of sources, visually and orally.

ST: How much do you revise texts that you've produced by either approach? With *States of Emergency*, for example, does that stand much as your very first draft of those poems or did you go through a process of revising?

MO: I went through an intensive process; the entire work (visuals and text) was made in five months, which seems to me now to be quite a feat, considering I had a demanding full-time day job as well. I don't think revising is an appropriate term for what I do, which is not so much a going over, a revisiting of the ground of the draft, but more a building away from, a going out from the initial material/s.

ST: Lawrence Upton was comparing versions of 'Giant Yellow'[3] that had appeared at different times and noting the revisions, but they were also developments.

MO: Developments, yes. Does this tie in with drafts?

ST: I suppose so, although I think – like revision – they both imply that there's a very fixed idea of what it is you want to achieve.

MO: And it's taking the work along a preordained course, which really isn't what I do. Hopefully, I think with all the works, even where I'm working with found languages as in *UNASSUMING PERSONAS*, the hope is always to move with the language, to move in a course that the language might present.

ST: So it's not the case that you often have a very specific idea of what the finished poem will look like?

MO: Oh absolutely not, I haven't got a clue. It's always tremendously exciting when I think the work has declared itself, for it to move away from me to such a point that it's finished because it's always so unexpected. I guess it's just a muddling through! For example with 'winter ceremony',[4] one of my recent pieces, it started off as one text of about six or seven pages, but the more I developed it, it broke itself into islands of text, utterances, and then I went with that, as it seemed appropriate – thematically and linguistically – for that work.

ST: Do you plan a sequence or a book, or do they find their own form and you think OK I want to present those pieces together as a book?

MO: I've never really thought about it. Each book has followed on consecutively from the previous one; I'll finish one piece, it'll come to the natural end of its cycle, and then some new work will emerge. I'll keep on working until I feel that's finished and then that becomes its own reality. However, at the moment, I think I'm engaged in something much longer, and I hope it'll be multi-dimensional, this is *her/story:eye*, which I hope eventually to be presented in various book forms. One of them Nicholas Johnson's publishing, *red shifts* [2001], which is a tiny little book, six by six square, and will be part of a longer overall project. So it's the first time I'm envisaging a work that's going to take me years and across presentations in its making.

ST: But it's not necessarily something you envisage as presenting just in one form, the bits will come out as they are written?

MO: The bits will come out as they are made, and it may not just be written, there could be visual work or sound.

ST: Is there any relation between such a project and particular materials you get interested in, in other words, is there any sense that you could say this is exploring specific territory or does it tend to come more out of a moment of being that you happen to be in when you're writing?

MO: The current project, *her/story:eye* very much explores an ancestral self and particularly my political and linguistic heritage. Both my parents are from Southern Ireland and my father was brought up against a republican background and as a child I was strongly influenced by his side of that struggle – and more so, now – because he was a singer and so I was brought up on songs of exile and rebellion. So *her/story:eye* comes out of my awareness of Irish work really, Irish history and politics and literature.

ST: How much is that true of earlier books? Can you think back to a book and say that was negotiating that particular area or are there always books which are just about what you were thinking and feeling, living at the time? Do you make a separation in any way?

MO: No, it's all part of the web of input. *A Natural History in Three Incomplete Parts* [1985], for instance, was very much to do with the current political situation at that time in Britain plus my own concerns and preoccupations with natural history, the natural world. With *Unofficial Word* [1988], I was very much influenced by the poetry of Lorca, because I worked on a film about his work and life and I spent time in Granada. I love the sounds that he achieves. Although I only have a smattering of Spanish I can haltingly read it, and I've heard it read in Spanish and particularly there is one elegy, 'Llanto Por Ignacio Sanchez Mejias' which is powerful in its use of sounds.

ST: You were talking about your interest in this large project in exploring your Irish roots and identity and those issues of language. Do you make a direct connection in terms of your politics with what's going on now in Ireland?

MO: Well, there have always been conflicts but they've become even more complex, and too complex really for me to come to terms with.

ST: That's interesting, because I wonder how many writers feel that they can contribute to that debate and whether you feel that you do?

MO: For me I couldn't possibly do it in a linguistically transparent way. One of my texts which is part of *her/story:eye*, which was printed in *Pages*, 'Waterfalls',[5] two things really contributed to the birthing of that text. Both my mother and Bobby Sands were dying at the same time – she in Lincoln and he in Belfast - and both were buried on the 7th of May 1981. I remember each day visiting hospital to be beside my mother's bedside amidst a flood of news coverage on Bobby Sands and his hunger strike.[6] So, I was drawing in material about the situation of the hunger strikers and going back to the Brehon Laws – the Anglo-Irish chronicles which were themselves overlaid on the old Irish vernacular law tracts in use until the break-up of the Gaelic order in the period following the Elizabethan reconquest of Ireland at the turn of the 16th century – and back to pre-Christian Ireland – where fasting, as in many cultures, was an acceptable weapon as a means for trying to achieve justice, where a person who was seeking justice would be able to go and fast on the threshold of the one, say a king or queen, or chieftain, who had the power to dispense justice. Yeats refers to it in 'The King's Threshold'.[7]

ST: Do you feel that your writing in some way has a political import by nature of its approach to language?

MO: Absolutely, we're coming to the crux of the matter now, why didn't you come out with it earlier?! I think anybody who's working in Britain who isn't working within the referential, transparent language axis, is ostracised, invisible, shut out, unheard. I suppose in that way, what all of us are doing in using radically imaginative language practices and procedures is very political and subversive.

ST: Many people who have written on your work have stressed the importance of performance for you and I wonder if you could say something about how you anticipate an audience's experience of your work – possibly that's also political in that it's about interacting with people. What kind of considerations do you make in a performance?

MO: I'm not sure that I make any considerations; I just hope that an audience would listen with open ears. Again I feel that the actual making, the constructing of a work continues into its performance. Often I've performed pieces and have gone back to the texts after my performance, developing them as a result of the audiences' response. I just hope that in the listening, seeing, and inhabiting, the audience are taking part in the construction of a work.

ST: Do you feel that you get a non-verbal response that's quite strong when you're reading?

MO: Absolutely, yes. I've had very strong palpably physical feelings from an audience, when I feel there's been a great degree of openness and they've inhabited a work with me. But at the other end of the spectrum I've had terrible experiences when I felt the audience hadn't heard me or refused to hear.

ST: Do you feel that you're taking a risk by entering those different spaces, is it quite important for you to feel that you take risks as a writer?

MO: Yes, I think it's important, because I have to go into what I don't know. I never think of anything I do as risk-taking, it never enters into what I do; I think I just do what I do because I have to. I think the need of the work dictates as its own necessity really.

ST: I think the term risk-taking implies that it's slightly more calculated than what you're talking about.

MO: Yes.

ST: I want to ask you something much more specific now about *EXCLA* [1993], the collaboration you did with Bruce Andrews. I wonder if you could tell me how that came about and how it was organised?

MO: We'd corresponded for some time, I'm a great fan of his work, and he came to London to read at Sub-Voicive and we met and it just emerged in the conversation, how about doing a collaborative piece. What we thought we'd do was to read each other's work as a starting point and respond to the thematic, lexical and sonic tints in the language until we each came up with about 3000 handwritten words on tiny pieces of paper. Then each held back half these words and sent the remaining half to the other person. So we each had 3000 words to work with – this number being composed of 1500 of one's own input plus 1500 from the other person – divided into fifteen sections each. We organised the work into thirty sections, in three parts A, B and C, with five texts from each person for each section. A1 was me, which is two pages and then the next A1 is from Bruce and it follows on in sequence. I had the final responsibility for the first A1 and Bruce had final responsibility for the second A1, and so on.

ST: Why the small pieces of paper?

MO: The suggestion of using the small pieces of paper was Bruce's, because that's his methodology. I'd never worked in that manner before and I found it immensely liberating, because I think it encourages a greater freedom with the language. You have little bits of paper with one word or two words or phrases and the great beauty is that you can have them with you in your pocket and collect words from everywhere. It was also very useful to know that somebody else was dependent on you to engage in a text; the degree of urgency was important.

ST: I find it a very exciting book and what struck me straightaway was that I wouldn't always think of Maggie O'Sullivan and Bruce Andrews in the same sentence – in that you are very different writers – yet here you're making a really strong identification with each other's poetics. It's like an essay on the relationship between British and American poetics just by presenting the work.

MO: Temperamentally we're akin in that respect. I find there are immense similarities between mine and Bruce's attitudes to language. I feel we're coming from a similar core and I think our attentiveness to language is coming from the same source.

ST: I think it would be interesting to talk about the concept of transformation, and how that is linked through your interest in Beuys to ideas of shamanism. Do you feel that transformation in poetry is about mimicking nature or is language itself always in some state of transformation?

MO: I think language is essentially transformative. Transformative power, ability, essence is inherent in language, all languages. I think by working with language one can tap into this and use it, by making it more visible, more of an active physical presence in the world. I was very influenced by Beuys, *In the House of the Shaman* [1993] is a tribute to him, it's entitled after one of his drawings. About the shamanism, it's very difficult to talk about it, because it seems so new age.

ST: Do you feel that part of the impulse in your work is miming the experiences around you, so transformative in that sense?

MO: I don't think they're miming, no, definitely not. It's using different energy sources to create new structures. The language is becoming itself, or more than itself, more importantly. Not mimicking or emulating.

ST: Some critics are sceptical to a poetry that does mimic, because it can then fall into these traps of shamanism and new ageism. I think you don't necessarily need to read your work like that.

MO: No, definitely not. I suppose my own philosophy of how I am in the world, how I see and react and live, is very much attuned to other ways, means of perceiving, if you like, but I hate to put it into stronger terms. So that is there at the core I suppose, that's foundational. Coming back to language, I planted eight hundred and fifty trees, which to me is an act of poetics, just as my language work is an act of poetics. And I would say the two have equal presence for me as a practice of poetics: of making meaning.

ST: So transformation in that sense is something that's just lived and that's the normal state?

MO: Fundamentally it's language – the materiality of language – that I'm concerned with and not whether it's the Irish political situation or the natural world or whatever. I've never felt the language or languages around me in any way to be enough, so I've had to make a way, and, even more importantly, to make in language/s a way that I don't know. The language work to me is where it's all happening, the mining and the shaking language up and the looking for new languages.

ST: That fascinates me, for example the word 'TLOKETS' in 'Busk, Pierce',[8] which seems to have so many different potential meanings: tickets, tokens, lockets etc. Is that something you compose that just comes to you and you put it down or do you combine a number of words together?

MO: With that work particularly, *States of Emergency* [1987], so many of those words came as you see them in that book. I heard – and I still do often hear – whole pieces of language. Coming back to something I said earlier, I said that I don't revise or redraft, that it's a development of the work. Just narrowing that down, huge sections of my work often come to me in clusters of words and sounds. They seem to come together by some magnetic force and they often stay as they are from the original, right through to the end of the work. It's not those that I change in any way, it's the choreography and the actual shaping of a text, bringing it to a body.

ST: The feeling of the poems in that book particularly is certainly of very strong momentum and flow but there's also a precision of placement in it. I think people are tempted to say it is just pure flow but at the same time there's a weight and measure going on.

MO: Yes, absolutely. I think it's a combination of both. I think in that work there's great flow, great energy, languages in the ear, but also I collect languages from visual sources everywhere and a great deal of my raw material is from misheard and mispronounced words. However, that's one element of the compositional process, but another is the developing and extending, constructing of that, through the close, scrupulous attention to the textual reality, by tuning, working with the page's reality, the spacial reality of the page and the sonic terrain of the language or languages, that tends to be very much how my texts emerge.

Notes

[1] To celebrate the launch of OTHER: *British and Irish Poetry since 1970*, ed. by Richard Caddel and Peter Quartermain, (Hanover, New England and London: Wesleyan University Press, 1999).

[2] Phillips found a copy of *A Human Document*, a Victorian novel by W.H. Mallock, which he transformed into the successive versions of *A Humument*, published in sections between 1967 and 1977 following which there have been three 'complete' editions, each progressively revised, in 1980, 1987 and 1997. The work itself continues.

[3] In Upton's 'Regarding Maggie O'Sullivan's Poetry' in *Pages* 421–445 (1998), 429–445. 'Giant Yellow' was published in O' Sullivan, *In the House of the Shaman* (London: Reality Street Editions, 1993) and first appeared in *Responses 6: Maggie O'Sullivan* (1991).

[4] See O'Sullivan et al, *Etruscan Reader III* (Buckfastleigh: Etruscan Books, 1997), pp. 8–21.

[5] *Pages* 421–445 (1998), 422–428.

[6] Bobby Sands, aged 27 died after 66 days on hunger strike on 5th May inside Long Kesh and was buried on 7th May 1981. He had been imprisoned for 8 years. During his hunger strike he was elected as MP to the British Parliament for Fermanagh/South Tyrone. Through the summer of 1981 another 9 IRA prisoners died on hunger strike for demands which included improved conditions, fair trial and political status for Irish Nationalist prisoners.

[7] KING . . . He has chosen death:
Refusing to eat or drink, that he may bring
Disgrace upon me; for there is a custom,
An old and foolish custom, that if a man
Be wronged, or think that he is wronged, and starve
Upon another's threshold till he die,
The Common People, for all time to come,
Will raise a heavy cry against that threshold,
Even though it be the King's.
– *The King's Threshold*, (1904) W. B. Yeats

[8] See *States Of Emergency* (Oxford: ICPA, 1987), unpaginated.

Lightning Source UK Ltd.
Milton Keynes UK
171211UK00001B/44/P